Ancient Chiefdoms of the Tombigbee

Ancient Chiefdoms
of the
TOMBIGBEE

JOHN H. BLITZ

A Dan Josselyn Memorial Publication

The University of Alabama Press
Tuscaloosa & London

Library of Congress Cataloging-in-Publication Data

Blitz, John Howard.
    Ancient chiefdoms of the Tombigbee / John H. Blitz.
        p.   cm.
    Includes bibliographical references and index.
    ISBN 0-8173-0672-2
    1. Lubbub Creek Mound (Ala.)   2. Mississippian culture—
Tombigbee River Valley (Miss. and Ala.)   3. Chiefdoms—Tombigbee
River Valley (Miss. and Ala.)   4. Tombigbee River Valley (Miss.
and Ala.)—Antiquities.   I. Title.
E99.M6815B55   1993
976.1'2—dc20   92-28876

British Library Cataloguing-in-Publication Data available

Contents

Tables and Figures

Tables

Figures

Acknowledgments

I
T HAS BEEN SAID that many who are attracted to archaeology are driven by a deep-seated desire to satisfy some unconscious feeling of loss. Whether this is often so, I cannot say. My own experience with archaeology has been marked not by loss but by gain, and the greatest gain has been the acquaintance of many people who have enthusiastically aided and motivated me in my personal exploration of the past. I take this opportunity to express my deepest gratitude to all of them.

This book is a revised version of a dissertation completed at the Graduate School and University Center of the City University of New York in 1991. I wish to thank the members of my dissertation committee for the knowledge they have so generously shared with me: Warren R. DeBoer; Bruce Byland; Gregory A. Johnson; and Vincas P. Steponaitis. Each contributed his own unique scholarly counsel and personal encouragement, for which I am truly grateful. I thank Frank Spencer, Sara Stinson, James Moore, and Paul Welch at the Laboratory of Anthropology, Queens College, for their aid and friendship. Sandee Kotler and Pamela Ferdinand assisted in the preparation of the final manuscript.

I have drawn upon a wealth of archaeological data generated as a result of the Tennessee-Tombigbee Waterway Project in the 1970s and early 1980s. Good archaeology is teamwork, and many people with whom I participated in these excavations helped me form some of the perspectives expressed in this study. Their contributions are cited throughout this work. I wish to sincerely thank some of those at The University of Alabama who first showed me what archaeology is all about, both in the classroom and in the field: the late David L. De-Jarnette; Eugene M. Futato; J. B. Graham; Charles M. Hubbert; Ned J. Jenkins; Richard A. Krause; Carey B. Oakley; and John A. Walthall.

The University of Michigan investigation of the Lubbub Creek site is central to this study. These excavations were liberally sponsored by the U.S. Army Corps of Engineers, Mobile District; Christopher S. Peebles was the principal investigator. Dr. Peebles provided me with the opportunity to participate in the Lubbub Creek project and encouraged me to pursue this research. The quality of the information recovered by the project was due in part to the outstanding staff that Dr. Peebles assembled: Caroline Albright; Jeanie Allan; Gloria Caddell; Ben Coblentz; Gloria Cole; C. B. "Sonny" Curren; Baxter Mann; Mary Powell; and Susan Scott. I learned so much from each of you, and I thank you, everyone.

Because the Summerville Mound excavation under my supervision is emphasized in the following pages, I wish to thank the skilled crew members who rescued this information from oblivion: John Brandon; Mark Branstner; Pat Bridges; Mary Ellen Fogarty; Charlie Prose; Ken Russell; and Michael Wilson.

Earnest Seckinger of the U.S. Army Corps of Engineers, Mobile District; Eugene M. Futato and the Office of Archaeological Research staff, Alabama State Museum of Natural History, University of Alabama; and John W. O'Hear, Cobb Institute of Archaeology, Mississippi State University, kindly permitted me to examine several of the "Tenn-Tom" archaeological collections. Analysis of archaeological materials in Alabama and Mississippi was made possible by a Sigma Xi Grant-in-Aid of Research. I gratefully acknowledge this support.

I count myself very fortunate because three special people stood by me through many difficulties and frustrations. The devotion of my loving wife, Pat, and my mother and father served to break down all barriers. Without their unwavering support and boundless love, I would never have completed this book.

Ancient Chiefdoms of the Tombigbee

Introduction

W E ARE CONCERNED here with an interpretation of the material remains of prehistoric farmers who once inhabited the central Tombigbee River valley in what is now Alabama and Mississippi. For much of the 1970s a dedicated team of archaeologists and students, supported by universities and federal agencies, labored to retrieve information about these ancient societies before their dwelling places were destroyed by a lock-and-dam system. The product of these efforts was an enormous data base with which to generate a rich, elaborate cultural history of 10,000 years of Native American life.

In the following pages I focus on one part of this time span, from around A.D. 900 until the early sixteenth century, an interval during which the Tombigbee societies reached their zenith of cultural complexity. In doing so, I hope to reveal something of what life for members of these societies was like, their material conditions, their social circumstances, and some of the problems they confronted and solved. From this perspective the Tombigbee societies can be related to a broad cultural development that accompanied the advent of intensive maize cultivation in the Eastern Woodlands, a development collectively referred to by archaeologists as the Mississippian. I have attempted to isolate some of those factors that operated within Tombigbee societies that promoted the unfolding of the Mississippian way of life and to illustrate how similar or different these factors were in relation to other Mississippian societies in the Southeast.

At another analytical level, Mississippian societies can be placed within general categories of sociocultural complexity in the evolution of human societies. With this orientation, understanding the rise and de-

cline of Mississippian societies along the Tombigbee River may provide
insights into processes of cultural change, and specifically the development and maintenance of chiefdoms and social hierarchies. Over the
last twenty years Mississippian societies have come to be regarded as
chiefdoms, or ranked societies. The former label refers to a type of
sociopolitical organization characterized by "an autonomous political
unit comprising a number of villages or communities under the permanent control of a paramount chief" (Carneiro 1981:45), while the latter
term pertains more to the structure of social relations. As Fried
(1967:109–110) puts it, a ranked society has "fewer positions of valued
status than individuals capable of handling them."

My objective here is not to fit the prehistoric Tombigbee communities into an evolutionary pigeonhole or to propound lawlike principles. Because evolutionary categories, such as chiefdom, encompass
a wide range of human societies, I have tried to identify a number of
variables that would reveal, however incompletely, the basis for leadership, the degree of social ranking, and aspects of resource control that
characterized the Tombigbee communities. Archaeologists must above
all document the actual course of human prehistory, and it is from case
studies firmly rooted within specific cultural-historical contexts, such as
I hope to present here, that the broader mechanisms and regularities of
cultural evolution may be placed in proper perspective.

Southeastern historical and archaeological research reveals that Mississippian societies varied considerably in size and social complexity.
However, current archaeological interpretations of Mississippian social
and economic systems are most developed for settlement systems with
large, multiple-mound centers, such as Moundville, Alabama. These
systems are considered complex chiefdoms; and archaeological correlates of ranked social organization, craft specialization, and differential
access to resources have been proposed. In contrast, less attention has
been devoted to the widespread settlement systems that consist of a
single-mound local center and surrounding farmsteads. One such system is found at Lubbub Creek, 53 km west of Moundville. Lubbub Creek
does not represent a microcosm of the social order claimed for Moundville, and its location on Moundville's periphery raises interesting questions about the developmental relationships between small-scale and
large-scale Mississippian polities.

In Chapter 2 I discuss organizational variability in native southeastern societies as revealed by historical and archaeological research. A
positive correlation between polity size, degree of social ranking, and
resource control can be tied to cycles of development and fragmentation

of chiefdoms. Models of Mississippian social organization and political economy, developed from research at Moundville, are examined.

In Chapter 3 the late prehistory of the study area is discussed. Chronological, economic, social, and developmental factors are interpreted. Excavations at Lubbub Creek and four farmstead sites are summarized.

The excavation of the earthen platform mound at Lubbub Creek is presented in Chapter 4, and evidence for a developmental relationship among feasting, group ritual, and the emergence of sanctified authority is evaluated.

In Chapter 5 social and economic conditions that led to the establishment of the local-center–farmstead settlement system—and how these conditions shaped the emergence of formal positions of leadership at Lubbub Creek—are investigated. Aspects of site seasonality, site permanence, and subsistence activities are examined with data from the Tombigbee farmsteads, and evidence of farmstead–local-center interdependence is evaluated. I focus my interpretations on how the logistics of maize production, defense, and storage created two potential sources of political influence: (1) management of pooled food surpluses through appeals to sanctified authority; and (2) leadership in war.

The question of preferential access to valued craft items is addressed in Chapter 6 through the examination of fineware ceramic distributions in the Lubbub Creek community.

In Chapter 7, expectations about access and control of resources derived from studies of Moundville and other large-scale Mississippian societies are explored through a comparison of farmstead–local-center distributions of prestige goods, evidence of craft production, and other artifact categories. The effect of regional exchange/alliance networks on the development of small-scale Mississippian societies is explored through the comparison of nonlocal artifact frequencies in Tombigbee and Moundville burials.

I conclude Chapter 8 with a summary of social, economic, and political characteristics of the farmstead–local-center unit and place this interpretation within a specific regional as well as general theoretical context.

There is general agreement that late Mississippian populations in the southeastern United States were organized as ranked societies, or chiefdoms. Chiefdoms are of great anthropological importance because it is in this kind of society that social hierarchies were first institutionalized. Yet much remains to be learned about how chiefdoms form and about the basis of social ranking. Worldwide, pristine chiefdom societies can no longer be observed directly by social scientists, and while short-term historical accounts are available, only archaeological studies have the necessary chronological perspective to fully illuminate these questions.

Archaeologists are increasingly aware that Mississippian societies were characterized by considerable organizational variability. Both large and small population clusters existed, but there has been little comparative study to determine how sociopolitical and economic organization varies with polity size. Understanding the relationship among polity size, degree of social ranking, and resource control is necessary for an interpretion of the developmental cycle of chiefdom formation and fragmentation.

CHAPTER 2

Organizational Variability in Mississippian Societies

W HEN THE EARLY Euro-American pioneers first encountered earthworks in the interior river valleys of eastern North America, their discoveries sparked a tradition of inquiry that has escalated and evolved with each passing generation. An initial question centered on the origins of the mound builders: Who were these people? Popular speculation favored ancient vanished races or earlier Old World colonizers—in short, almost any group except ancestors of the Indian nations then being driven from the surrounding lands. Sixteenth- and early eighteenth-century observers' accounts of mound construction and use by native North Americans were largely forgotten. Traditional native claims to the sites were mostly ignored. An intellectual climate limited by ethnocentrism and the social circumstances of "manifest destiny" slowed the widespread acknowledgment of a native origin for the monuments. But by the latter nineteenth century, with the growth of the infant science of archaeology, the initial steps were taken to answer a second question: What manner of society did the ancient Americans possess? Perhaps those first explorers of the past did not anticipate that so reasonable a question would generate a multitude of hard-won answers in our present century.

Within the last 50 years archaeologists have discovered that around the tenth century A.D., native southeastern people began a process of cultural development far more complex than anything that had occurred previously. These late prehistoric peoples and the era in which they lived are known as Mississippian. Mississippian societies are characterized by intensive maize cultivation, sedentary communities with earthen platform-mound-and-plaza arrangements, extensive exchange networks of raw materials, shared symbolism, and hierarchical social organization (Griffin 1985; Steponaitis 1986).

Typically, Mississippian societies described as chiefdoms or ranked societies are recognized by a number of organizational characteristics: ranked social structure with ascribed status categories; hierarchical settlement systems; some degree of craft specialization; centralized control of resources and labor; and construction of public works (Peebles and Kus 1977). Of course, these categories are attempts to come to grips with the continuum of scale and complexity in nonstate societies (Feinman and Neitzel 1984). It is this organizational variability that establishes the chiefdom as the fulcrum of cultural evolution.

Archaeologists who wish to understand the organization and development of prehistoric societies face a difficult challenge. Their reconstructions are derived from empirical observations of material remains that, in turn, must be interpreted through inferences based upon arguments of analogy. Two sets of information provide useful analogies for Mississippian societies: (1) general models of cultural evolution drawn from anthropology; and (2) specific historical descriptions of southeastern chiefdoms written by the earliest European observers. Like archaeological data, these parallel pathways to the past defy easy synthesis. But it is useful to begin with a brief survey of these sources for clues about Mississippian organizational variability and the basis for leadership in these societies. Chiefdom size, degree of social ranking, and control of economic resources are identified as key variables in the developmental cycle of chiefdom formation and fragmentation. In the following chapters these insights are applied to the archaeology of the ancient agricultural communities of western Alabama and adjacent Mississippi.

Chiefdoms and Ranked Society in the Southeast

The early historical observations of southeastern societies are a productive source for the reconstruction of Mississippian social order (Hudson et al. 1985). They may provide a means to move beyond broad categorizations to encompass the specific form, content, and variability revealed by archaeologists. Nevertheless, it is often difficult to interpret these observations or apply them to the archaeological record. In addition, the early historical documents do not form a continuous written record. Instead, two sets of observations are available, separated by an interval of about 150 years in the late sixteenth and seventeenth centuries for which there are few or no known written descriptions of native life in the interior Southeast.

The sixteenth-century expeditions of De Soto, Luna, Pardo, and others produced descriptions of Late Mississippian societies with populous fortified towns, powerful chiefs, and complex interrelationships of tribute, alliance, and warfare. These descriptions depict southeastern chiefdoms prior to later disruptions. The conquistadores traveled through a social landscape composed of native populations that varied greatly in polity size and social complexity. They encountered not only chiefs who exercised military or political dominance over large territories, but also smaller, independent horticultural communities.

The most powerful chiefs exacted tribute from subordinate chiefs of other towns located within their domain and were able to marshall hundreds of warriors to oppose the Spaniards. Chiefs wore special dress and insignia of office (Bourne 1973:I:81, 88), maintained residences atop earthen mounds (Bourne 1973:I:87, II:28, 101), and some chiefs were conveyed in a litter carried by a retinue of prominent individuals (Bourne 1973:I:81). Taken as hostages, chiefs were instrumental in providing the Spaniards with food and goods as the expeditions moved from town to town within their territory.

While these descriptions indicate considerable chiefly power, the presence of the Spanish army potentially distorts interpretations of native political authority and organization. The very language of the narratives tends to obscure as much as it illuminates. The native political situation is described in such terms as *lords, vassals, provinces,* and *tribute.* Some readers assign to the southeastern chiefdoms the same political order that these terms ordinarily suggest. But it is equally possible that the Spanish inaccurately imposed their own profoundly hierarchical, feudal worldview upon societies they never understood; societies organized along quite different principles. The Spanish tendency to portray chiefs as autocrats is probably more the product of ethnocentrism than actual circumstance (Swanton 1979:6). In the narratives are hints that, when not prevented by the Spanish, chiefs conferred with a council to make decisions (Bourne 1973:I:75, 113). The physical strength and demeanor of Tascalusa and other chiefs suggest charismatic personality and prowess in warfare as important sources of authority (Swanton 1979:652).

The more perceptive eighteenth-century French and English observers, who often lived with their native hosts, penned detailed interpretations of southeastern social organization and political leadership. (E.g., Du Pratz, Charlevoix, Milfort, Penicaut, Adair, Bartram, Hawkins, and Romans are frequent references for this period. They are most accessible to the nonspecialist in Swanton [1979], and in reprints such as Adair [1968] and Bartram [1958].) As in the earlier Spanish accounts, the eighteenth-century native polities exhibited a considerable range in size and political complexity. Most groups, such as the Choctaws, Chick-asaws, and Muskogees, are described as relatively "democratic" societies with a strong egalitarian ethos, composed of autonomous demographic units organized into informal, politically decentralized confederacies or "nations." But there were a few groups, such as the Natchez and their neighbors in the Lower Mississippi Valley, that impressed the Europeans with sumptuary ritual, sacrifice of retainers, and a social hierarchy of "nobles" and "commoners."

Natchez society consisted of ranked kin groups, of which the most prominent were the Suns, a "noble" rank with ascribed privileges. The top-ranking Natchez authority figures, the Great Sun and the Great War Chief, were drawn from the Sun kin group. There was a gradient of social positions based on genealogical nearness to the Great Sun, but social mobility through merit had considerable latitude (Swanton 1911:100–108). Furthermore, the French noted that the Suns did not conform to European conceptions of an aristocracy because of a rule of exogamy that forbade Suns to marry other Suns.

The Great Sun and his retinue resided at a central community, where they were supported with food and labor from subordinate chiefs in outlying towns (Swanton 1911:118–121). Like some of the chiefs encoun-tered by the Spaniards 150 years before, the Great Sun was treated with deference, carried in a litter, resided atop an earthen mound, and wore special dress or insignia of rank. The Great Sun's authority was ex-pressed through appeals to the sacred, and he directed a ritual cycle of subsistence activities. His political power was limited by the other Suns, by a council, by the town chiefs, and by tightly prescribed custom (Swanton 1979:650; Lorenz 1988).

In the 150 years that separate these two sets of European commen-taries, native southeastern peoples experienced severe depopulation and social disruption caused by the ravages of introduced disease epidemics (Dobyns 1983; M. T. Smith 1987). Thus, in addition to the ethnocentric bias and other limitations inherent in ethnohistoric sources, an inter-pretive dilemma arises because the two sets of observations describe societies that lie on opposite sides of a watershed of important cultural transformations. The apparent discrepancy between sixteenth-century Spanish descriptions of complex, ranked societies and simpler, more-egalitarian eighteenth-century "tribes" points to a dramatic decline in southeastern sociopolitical complexity. For this reason scholars have been by turns cautious, ambivalent, or pessimistic about whether eighteenth-century social and political organization provides useful analogies for Mississippian societies. In the most extreme view population decline and social collapse were so catastrophic that continuity of cultural tradition, custom, or organization is not merely interrupted but impossible (Dobyns 1990).

One response among southeastern archaeologists to the social variation in the ethnohistoric sources and the archaeological record has been to refine their evolutionary categories. The most widely used typology subdivides the chiefdom continuum into "simple" and "complex" (Steponaitis 1978). Simple chiefdoms are small, autonomous political units with a single level of political decision making above the individual household, and institutionalized in the permanent office of chief. Complex chiefdoms consist of a paramount chieftain who exacts tribute from subordinate chiefs located in scattered communities. Thus complex chiefdoms represent a larger, more centralized organization with at least two levels of decision-making hierarchy above the household level.

Since the simple/complex chiefdom scheme implies a potential developmental continuum, it has encouraged some archaeologists to interpret the differences in the sixteenth- and eighteenth-century native societies as a stagelike evolutionary change (M. T. Smith 1987), with an apparent devolution from highly ranked to more-egalitarian societies or from complex to simple chiefdoms or tribes. This creates a problem, however, because the continuation of societies such as the eighteenth-century Natchez becomes something of an anomaly.

Preoccupation with the specific and irrevocable changes sparked by the Europeans should not obscure the fact that a network of small-scale and large-scale chiefdoms waxed and waned throughout the precontact Mississippian era. Many of these prehistoric chiefdoms appear to fall within the same range of sociopolitical complexity as that claimed to separate the sixteenth- and eighteenth-century southeastern societies. Archaeological indicators of chiefdom organization that decline or disappear in the eighteenth century, such as large, multiple-mound centers and burials with elaborate artifacts that demarcate a strong superordinate segment of society (M. T. Smith 1987), are also absent from many precontact Mississippian societies. Some regional examples include the Appalachian summit of western North Carolina and eastern Tennessee (Dickens 1978) and adjacent Georgia Blue Ridge (Wynn 1990); the Georgia coast (Crook 1986); south-central Georgia (Snow 1990); the northern Florida Gulf Coast (Milanich and Fairbanks 1980); the Big Black River valley, central Mississippi (Steponaitis 1989); and much of northern Alabama above the Fall Line (Walthall 1980; Jenkins 1982).

It is also common for such signs of complexity to appear briefly in certain areas, then revert back to simpler arrangements (Anderson 1990).

This organizational variability is placed in long-term perspective when the simple-to-complex-to-simple oscillation is viewed as an inherent condition of kin-based political formations.

There is no doubt that southeastern societies underwent significant cultural change from the sixteenth to eighteenth centuries. Depopulation and major demographic movements point to the fragmentation of powerful Mississippian polities. A brief examination of social institutions, however, reveals the possibility of both change and continuity in the new order.

Eighteenth-Century Southeastern Political Organization

Certain cultural continuities persisted despite the dramatic changes and transformations of the postcontact Southeast (Hudson 1976). There is reason, therefore, to examine eighteenth-century native social structure for insights into Mississippian societies. Two basic social forms are widely recognized in the eighteenth-century sources: (1) ranked exogamous kin groups (lineages, clans, and moieties); and (2) ranked exogamous kin groups with the additional creation of a "noble" rank with ascribed privileges and responsibilities (Swanton 1911, 1979:641–657; Hudson 1976:184–196; Knight 1990). Knight (1990), expanding the thesis of Josselin de Jong (1928), stressed that the system of exogamous clan and moiety, long considered an evolutionary dead end because of supposed egalitarian leveling mechanisms (e.g., Kirchhoff 1959), has a potential hierarchical structure. Knight argued that the hereditary chiefs and nobility/commoner distinctions found in groups such as the Natchez are anticipated in the implicit ranking system of clan and moiety. He proposed that the exogamous ranked clan systems of the historical era have the evolutionary potential to expand into social hierarchies with hereditary nobility and chiefs, and that Mississippian social organization took this form.

In the kin-based societies of the historical Southeast each person was a member of a localized matrilineage as well as a member of a non-localized, matrilineal exogamous clan. Ranking at the individual clan level can be recognized in the ethnohistoric sources in several ways. Sometimes specific clans consistently promoted strong leaders, which implies a nascent ascriptive principle at work (Gatschet 1969:156–157; Swanton 1928:192–197). In many groups a graded order of clan rank or prestige, sometimes with associated privileges or ceremonial roles, is explicitly recognized (Swanton 1928:114, 1979:662). If concepts of kin-group rank are fundamental to southeastern society, then the hierarchical Natchez system of "nobles and commoners" is best considered an amplification of the basic, widespread social structure (Josselin de Jong 1928; Hudson 1976; Lorenz 1988; Knight 1990). The structure of Natchez society differs from other southeastern groups only to the degree to which the Great Sun and the Sun kin group enjoyed greater veneration, respect, and authority (Hudson 1976:208–209).

Ranked kin groups found symbolic expression in the dualism of southeastern societies. Dual organization expressed itself in white/red institutions, ideas, and symbols. At the most fundamental level, white was associated with peace or order, and red was associated with war or disorder (Hudson 1976). Furthermore, this dualism had an asymmetry in that white was more esteemed than red. Clans were grouped into moiety divisions that assumed this duality (Swanton 1931:78; Hudson 1976:234–239). White/red dualism was an ideological construct to express political competition within the kinship idiom (Hudson 1976:234–239; Lankford 1981:50–54).

Although kin groups such as clans acted as competitive interest groups, they were part of larger political formations. The minimal political unit or polity of the historical Southeast was the *okla* (Choctaw) or *talwa* (Muskogee) (Gatschet 1969:156–158; Swanton 1928:242; Lankford 1981:53). The okla consisted of a population that participated in political, economic, and ceremonial activities at a common center. The leadership structure consisted of a civil chief, a war chief, a retinue of minor functionaries with largely ceremonial or religious duties, and a council of elders and warriors. As with social structure, the white/red dualism mediated okla organization and defined spheres of influence. One side of the okla organization, the civil chief and council of elders, was white and associated with peace and domestic affairs. The other side was red and concerned with war and affairs external to the okla. Red leadership roles were the war chief and body of warriors. Assertion of dominant leadership vacillated between the two principal offices, the civil, or okla, chief and the war chief (Hudson 1976:234–238), but consensus was the rule and the actual decision-making body was the council of elders and warriors. The civil chief presided over the council and shaped policy by persuasion or promotion of prevailing opinion (Adair 1968:459; Swanton 1979:652–654). Responsibilities of the civil chief varied somewhat but usually included ritual roles, mediation of certain disputes, and coordination of public activities and ceremonies. Perhaps most importantly, he supervised storage of surplus food through maintenance of a public granary.

The war chief was the military leader of the okla. The political power of the war chief was equal to or surpassed the civil chief's in times of war or external difficulties (Hudson 1976). Because prowess in warfare was a major path to status enhancement for young men, the war chief could draw on this support to sway decisions. He advocated, organized, and initiated raids against enemies. He was appointed by the council in recognition of his military abilities and achievements (Gatschet 1969:159; Hudson 1976:225).

Given the separate spheres of influence and the white/red conceptual framework, white leadership had theocratic qualities, while the red male military body was graded by age and accomplishments. Yet the amplification of kin-group ranking and the ascriptive principle clearly influenced this basic organization. So among those groups such as the Natchez the two chiefly offices were hereditary positions filled by the highest-ranking kin group, the Suns. For even the most "egalitarian" Muskogees, Chickasaws, and Choctaws, hereditary chieftainship was not unknown (Swanton 1931:76–79; 1979:663; Gatschet 1969:96, 104). Yet it is also clear that even hereditary southeastern chiefs ruled by consent of their peers and kinsmen, among whom rivals were ready to assume the rule should the chiefs prove incompetent (Swanton 1979:650). Whether rule by peer consensus characterized the earlier Mississippian societies is unknown.

There is general correspondence between the okla polity and the simple chiefdom. Both constitute a recognizable settlement hierarchy of domestic and public organizational units—households and a local center. Households may be dispersed around the local center to take advantage of very local resources, or houses may cluster at the local center for mutual defense. In the late prehistoric and early historical Southeast the dispersed pattern is by far the most common (Smith 1978). The minimal Mississippian political unit—a simple chiefdom—should consist of a two-tiered settlement system composed of (1) farmsteads or small settlements, affiliated with (2) a local center with one or two mounds. Complex chiefdoms are reflected in a three-tiered settlement hierarchy of (1) farmsteads or small settlements, associated with (2) a number of local centers that, in turn, are affiliated with (3) a large, multiple-mound regional center (Steponaitis 1986).

In this brief survey of the documentary evidence certain characteristics of southeastern chiefdoms have been emphasized. Two forms of social ranking have been discussed: ranked kin groups; and ranked kin groups with an additional top-ranked group with ascribed privileges and responsibilities. These degrees of social ranking varied with chiefdom size. The minimal political unit in the eighteenth century was the okla. This unit bears a close resemblance to the Mississippian system of local-center settlements archaeologists identify as a simple chiefdom. Ethnohistoric sources suggest that these minimal political units—okla or simple chiefdom—were building blocks for larger political formations. Simple chiefdoms existed as independent polities, articulated with other polities in decentralized confederations, or were united into complex chiefdoms. To the extent that European contact fragmented or reduced the size of chiefdoms in the early historical period, eighteenth-century political structure can be interpreted as attenuated institutions that originated in prehistoric times. If this assumption is correct, it suggests that the sociopolitical organization of many Mississippian chiefdoms was no more hierarchical or complex than their historical counterparts of a similar size.

The ethnohistoric documents suggest ways in which southeastern societies used the kinship idiom to create political formations and how kinship placed limitations on political power; but how did such chiefdoms originate? As in all ranked societies, southeastern political organization was kinship writ large. However, the form of kinship relations is not as important (and perhaps impossible for archaeologists to reconstruct) as the question of how kinship permits or denies access to resources and political influence. The dual leadership roles in southeastern chiefdoms represent two domains of responsibility and influence: civil chiefs, concerned with the pooling and disbursement of resources through the sanctified authority of ritual; and war chiefs concerned with acquisition and defense of resources.

Was the development of an elite dependent upon the ability to control access to resources or wealth? This question has been at the center of investigations into the rise of chiefdoms and social ranking (Service 1971, 1975; Peebles and Kus 1977; Wenke 1981; Wright 1984; Earle 1987). Again we turn to the archaeological and historical sources, this time to consider how competition for resources on the local and regional scale affected organizational variability and social ranking.

Organizational Variability and Resource Control

The principal material resources of surplus wealth in the Southeast, aside from human labor considered alone, were subsistence products and craft products, especially prestige goods. As the term is used here, prestige goods are those artifacts that served as symbols to express rank, status, or wealth. Food is a basic source of disposable wealth. The rise of the Mississippian chiefdoms coincides with intensive maize production. While often linked to population pressure, the increased maize production in the Eastern Woodlands around A.D. 1000 may have begun as a way to create a surplus for disbursement to enhance prestige, expand influence, and accelerate social ranking (Bender 1985; Steponaitis 1986).

The role that historical southeastern civil chiefs had in the management of public granaries and the allocation of stored maize is a strong clue that the origin of this formal office is tied to the ancient move toward intensive maize cultivation.

Native southeastern peoples did not live by corn and venison alone. Individuals, kin groups, and polities competed for access to prestige goods and the raw materials to make them. Many anthropologists have suggested that prestige goods may have become symbols with which to validate the ideology of chiefly authority. Copper, shell, and stone artifacts (and their European substitutes) served in the historical Southeast as prestige goods. Much of the Mississippian Southeastern Ceremonial Complex paraphernalia appears to have functioned in such a manner (Howard 1968).

Tribute is often used as a catch-all term for the mobilization of material goods or labor by the elite, and I will so use it here. Southeastern chiefs impressed Europeans with their ability to command tribute. In particular, the Spanish interpreted the political relationships of the sixteenth-century chiefdoms as akin to their own feudal system of lords and vassals, but exactly how native tribute functioned is difficult to determine. Involving the circulation of both subsistence products and prestige goods, tribute can be considered at two levels: (1) local resource mobilization emphasizing foodstuffs; and (2) external resource mobilization emphasizing prestige goods. A historical example of local resource mobilization was the movement of maize from dispersed households or communities to a civic and ceremonial center for storage and consumption. In these cases movement from household to center was governed by a ritual cycle of ceremonies, met communal economic needs, and may have served as a political strategy to reinforce chiefly authority.

Late prehistoric and historical subsistence economies were a mix of hunting, gathering, and cultivation. Analysis of food remains from archaeological sites shows a heavy dependence on wild resources. This meant a significant part of the economy was beyond the control of a would-be elite, and access was open to all. Similarly, people and soils were dispersed across the landscape. Horticultural production at the household and matrilineage level conferred a degree of subsistence autonomy. Only when food was amassed at a center was manipulation of surplus possible. Much more research is required to understand local resource mobilization between farmstead and center, and that is one focus of this study.

Local-surplus mobilization can be contrasted with external-resource mobilization. The ritual cycle of local-surplus mobilization may induce kin-group ranking, create demand, and intensify surplus production (Friedman 1975), but the limitations mentioned above may direct the search for wealth elsewhere. If yet more corn and venison cannot be obtained from kin and friends, at least in the wider world treasure awaits. This is, perhaps, why warfare plays an impressive and, some argue, pivotal role in the rise of chiefdoms (Carneiro 1981).

Warfare and its corollary, alliance/exchange, were important activities of Mississippian and historical southeastern chiefdoms. Prestige goods of nonlocal materials, and new ideologies, such as represented by the Southeastern Ceremonial Complex, became a medium through which to express political and competitive relationships (Peebles and Kus 1977; Helms 1979; Steponaitis 1986; Earle 1987; Anderson 1989). To judge from the Spanish accounts, access to distant resources was dependent on a complex mix of warfare, alliance, and exchange, and therefore the flow of wealth was difficult to control. A polity's position in the regional struggle for prestige goods determined how much was available to parcel out within the polity (Steponaitis 1989; Earle 1989). Changes in polity size and degree of social ranking were propelled by competition for resources. At the local level, demographic success permitted the generation of more surpluses, and no doubt larger communities held the military advantages needed to acquire distant resources (Carneiro 1967). When viewed over time, the ever-changing outcomes of these regional contests produce boom-and-bust oscillations in chiefdom size and political complexity in a region (Peebles and Kus 1977; Welch 1991; Steponaitis 1989; Anderson 1989).

Much of the tribute mentioned in the sixteenth-century accounts apparently served as ritualized gift exchanges to seal alliances between antagonistic populations (Anderson 1989). Some interpret this kind of tribute as a form of taxation within the complex Mississippian chiefdoms and evidence of political centralization (Hudson et al. 1985). The size of a number of sixteenth-century chiefdoms has been mapped based on the estimated spatial distribution of communities identified by the Spanish as payers of tribute to a powerful chief (Hudson et al. 1985). Some reconstructed boundaries, such as those of the Coosa chiefdom, encompass an enormous territory.

I suggest an alternative interpretation. These reconstructed boundaries may delineate only the effective "threat zone" of a powerful chief, not political centralization. If Mississippian polities were as hostile and insular as the Spanish accounts indicate, then it is likely that political relationships within many of these reconstructed boundaries were largely military. Complaints to the Spanish about nonpayment of tribute were so frequent as to suggest a chronic situation (Bourne 1973:I:70, 101, 154). On the regional scale Mississippian political relationships appear to have been highly decentralized.

It seems likely that tribute was a primary way to move valued products from point A to point B, across chiefdom boundaries. Instead of political centralization, the historical accounts of tribute relations may indicate just the opposite: that the ability to extend political administration in Mississippian societies was exceedingly limited. They could only resort to bouts of warfare until the weaker polity sued for peace, and a one-sided, ritualized presentation of goods created an alliance. Beyond the local level of competition defined by the kinship idiom, and appeals to sacred authority, external relationships involved non-kin, and so "negative reciprocity" held sway (Sahlins 1972). The farther away from the strong polity the weaker polity was located, the more likely that tribute demands could be ignored until the next round of harassment and extortion. If this interpretation of limitations on the ability of elites to control distant resources is correct, competition within and between polities would produce continuous regional oscillations in polity size and degree of social ranking (Sahlins 1958:114; Carneiro 1967; Wolf 1982:94; Earle 1987:297).

If through the changing fortunes of war and alliance the flow of prestige goods (or the distant materials to make them) to a polity was slowed or disrupted, the influence of established leaders and kin groups could weaken. Political influence might shift to new leaders and new kin groups who could "deliver the goods." Genealogies are easy to remake to legitimate an ascendant kin group's claim to special privileges on behalf of sacred authority. If the dearth of prestige goods was prolonged, then the chiefdom might decline and perhaps fragment into smaller units.

It is the inability to exercise independent control over the production of resources that is the weakness of chiefdoms and contributes to their well-known instability. A critical threshold in cultural evolution occurs when a chiefdom can break out of the reciprocal leveling mechanisms of kinship. Would-be elites have to say no to others, limit resource control to a minority, concentrate wealth, and, in effect, transform rank into true economic classes (Wolf 1982:72–100). How this was actually done is a subject of great debate, but control over the means of production must be central. In ancient states this involved, minimally, control of land and thus agricultural production, and the replacement of appeals to sacred authority with coercion as the means of last resort to enforce political decisions within a polity (Wolf 1982:79–83; Whitehouse and Wilkins 1986:94–97). Almost certainly neither were sustained in the native

Southeast. The fragility of the external prestige-goods economy and the limitations of the local subsistence economy are an unlikely foundation for state organization.

While it appears unlikely that even the most complex Mississippian societies established economic classes, specific kinds of resource control may have played a pivotal role in the development of Mississippian chiefdoms. To pursue this issue further, we must briefly consider the archaeology of Mississippian origins.

The Rise of Mississippian Chiefs

Archaeologists have long been concerned with understanding the nature and development of social ranking in kin-based societies. In eastern North America this interest has focused on late prehistoric Mississippian societies because they appear to represent a developmental transition from acephalous tribal units to more-hierarchical polities considered to be chiefdoms or ranked societies. Widespread intensification of maize horticulture accompanied this Mississippian emergence, and the two processes are thought to be linked. These two criteria, together with distinctive ceramic traditions and a characteristic iconography, constitute what is defined as Mississippian (Smith 1978; Griffin 1985; Muller 1983).

The Late Woodland–Mississippian transition (A.D. 700–1100) was a time of cultural innovation, population growth, and expanded crop production that culminated in an increase in sociopolitical complexity on a scale greater than had existed in previous Eastern Woodlands societies. Interpretation of this change is currently the subject of extensive research efforts (Kelly et al. 1984; Smith 1986; Steponaitis 1986). The explanatory frameworks that have been offered reflect the full range of concerns that enliven discussions of the evolution of chiefdoms (Earle 1989).

Theories of chiefdom development in the Eastern Woodlands are generally cultural-materialist in orientation, at the core of which is the idea that formal mechanisms for decision making above the household level appeared in response to stresses on the social group. Leaders are conceived of as "managers" who process and channel the increased information load created by technological, economic, or demographic change (Peebles and Kus 1977). The predominant form this explanation has taken can be reduced to the argument that stress is caused by imbalances between population and resources (Ford 1974).

While there are variations on this theme, the basic stress model portrays a gradual population increase that led to reduction of resource territories and restricted mobility caused by intergroup competition for food sources. This, in turn, is said to result in nutritional stress. The response was to diversify the resource base, to incorporate "second-line" fauna, and ultimately, by the Late Woodland period, to expand cultivation. Increased production of native starchy seeds by midwestern Late Woodland and Emergent Mississippian societies may have been a "preadaptation" for the rapid intensification of maize after A.D. 1000 (Smith 1986).

Yet the inadequacies of population growth as a primary causal force for cultural change have been widely acknowledged (Cowgill 1975). The counterargument follows from the observation that population growth is not an automatic variable independent of cultural perceptions. Since humans can and have controlled their reproduction, it is necessary to document the conditions under which families would find it to their advantage to produce more children. In Eastern Woodlands research gradual population growth is usually merely asserted, leaving questions of cause or consequence ambiguous.

Dissatisfaction with the limitations of demographic or environmental stress factors as the primary cause of cultural change has led to a greater interest among Eastern Woodlands archaeologists in how internal social demands may stimulate status differences and resource intensification (Nassaney 1987; Scarry 1986, 1988). In one influential "social" model (Bender 1979, 1985) the mobilization or production of food sources need not be a demographic or ecological imperative. Instead, dynamic social relations may act as an independent causal mechanism. The generation of a food surplus becomes a social strategy to extend alliances, reinforce obligations, and promote prestige (also see Hayden 1990).

Recently it has been suggested that competition among kin groups may have led to increased crop production to provide a surplus to fuel the various activities that promote prestige. Inherent limitations on the ability to amass surplus wild foods may have constrained such activities until crop production fostered new possibilities. Prior constraints were removed, and social hierarchies increased in scale (Steponaitis 1986). Kin groups that generated more food held the advantage in the competitive arena of feasts and gift giving that serve to bind together households in small-scale societies.

The rapid intensification of maize cultivation after A.D. 1000 has usually been explained in terms of this grain's capacity to sustain greater yields than locally native starchy seed crops (Smith 1989). However, several investigators suggest an ideological motivation for intensified maize production (Scarry 1988; Rose et al. 1991). They observe that, prior to A.D. 800–900, maize is recovered in only minor quantities and sometimes occurs in contexts that may imply a ceremonial significance. Maize may have been promoted as a "food of the gods," and its production and disbursement manipulated as a symbol of sanctified authority (Scarry 1988). To speculate further, maize may have been linked to an entire complex of new symbols and beliefs, access to which served as a source of power and prestige (see Helms 1979). New iconographic themes that accompany the Mississippian emergence may reveal such a connection (Prentice 1986).

Put in simplest terms, maize production may have been intensified because of its potential as an exchangeable, storable commodity, with or without the additional attraction of supernatural sanctity. The expanded maize production that marks the Mississippian emergence perhaps began as a household or kin-group "specialization" within a locale, not so much because of a pressing need to survive demographic stress but for the social advantages it conferred. Corn as commodity may have been an attractive alternative to traditional durable goods. As demand increased, and as more households generated surplus maize, aspects of production organization may have shifted from "entrepreneurial" to corporate or formal leadership on a communal scale.

The social hypotheses direct our attention to economic, social, and ideological strategies through which social rank or authority might be formed and legitimized. It is appropriate to stress the establishment of a formal office of leadership such as "chief" because the appearance of such positions seems to coincide with organizational shifts that promote social ranking. Both an increased degree of social ranking and positions of chiefly authority have been identified archaeologically with the Mississippian emergence.

Sanctified Authority, Group Ritual,
and Management of Pooled Resources

In many tribal societies the individual role of resource intensifier and coordinator of pooling, feasting, and gift giving falls to the "big man." The big-man role is not formally defined as a political office but is created through the personal initiative of a charismatic leader of temporary influence. Big men are "shrewd and able men who, through the manipulation of traditionally defined valuables, place people in their debt, create *ad hoc* followings or factions, build up networks of exchange relationships and thus temporarily exert influence in their local communities" (Meggitt 1973:194). The ambitions of the tribal big man are kept in check by the corporate nature of the lineages or other descent groups. Although big men are self-made leaders, ethnographers have sometimes noted a nascent ascriptive principle at work. Members of one descent group may assume the big-man role more consistently than members of other descent groups. So while big men themselves create personal followings, "the followers are the constant," and lineages may, in effect, promote their own big man so as to assert greater community influence as a corporate body (Meggitt 1973).

Perhaps at this social juncture, within specific historical circumstances such as the Mississippian emergence, the big-man role of intensifier and redistributor could become established as a permanent political office (Friedman 1975; Sahlins 1972; Feinman and Neitzel 1984:56). Probably big man and petty chief should be thought of as points along either a developmental or a descriptive continuum of increasingly formalized roles. Tribal big men and chiefs alike attempt to gain access to wealth and make it available to reward a body of followers. Such activities may initiate a complex interplay between ideological and material processes that may stimulate increased social ranking in cultural evolution (Sahlins 1972; Friedman 1975).

It was the ideology of chiefly authority, expressed through kinship, that legitimized the role that historical southeastern chiefs assumed in the management of public granaries, the allocation of stored maize, and direction of a ritual cycle of ceremonies. How did such a formalized office originate? Perhaps this leadership role emerged in concert with intensified maize cultivation. Aside from the possibility that intensification began as a social strategy, corn certainly became a basic commodity that promoted the cooperation of multiple households for communal storage.

Highest-ranked kin groups, such as the Natchez Suns, claimed their privileges by virtue of descent from mythical founding ancestors. Their authority was legitimized by appeals to the sacred, expressed through genealogical claims, and exercised by prescribed social custom. Dead ancestors may take an interest in the affairs of the living and communicate important advice. Therefore, one avenue to social and political influence is to claim access to supernatural sources.

Many anthropologists believe that these "mythological charters" can become a means to rationalize access to wealth or resources by a specific kin group (Wolf 1982:88–100). Success in extending control over wealth requires that chiefly authority be legitimated through ideological mechanisms because the kinship idiom usually curtails coercive force within the community (Peebles and Kus 1977; Earle 1987). On the one hand the reciprocal ethos of a kin-based society has a leveling effect, a strong mandate to redistribute wealth to "win friends and influence people." On the other hand kin may be able to make demands that are harder to ignore than others; consequently certain resources may (potentially) concentrate within kin groups to further political influence. It follows that the control of resources—ideological or material—must be a central focus of investigations into organizational variability and degree of social ranking in prehistoric and historical native societies.

The idea of chiefs as managers has been influential in studies of the evolution of ranked societies or chiefdoms. Service (1971) considered chiefdoms to be redistributive economies that emerged when chiefs took on the role of regulating reciprocal exchanges between communities to redress resource imbalances caused by environmental inequities. Yet it soon became apparent that many ethnographic examples of chiefdoms did not consist of economically specialized communities, and that local self-sufficiency was the rule (Earle 1987). Because some influential investigators failed to find evidence (in complex Hawaiian societies) that redistribution functioned to level out local environmental inequities, as Service proposed, they dismiss the possibility that redistribution may be a causal factor in the emergence of chiefdoms (Peebles and Kus 1977; Earle 1977).

However, the observation that redistribution is not central to some historically known complex chiefdoms does little to address the question of whether redistribution was a factor in the origin of such societies (Seeman 1979). Furthermore, ecologically or economically diversified communities need not be the only stimulus for redistribution. Changes induced by technological or social conditions—such as the need for central storage, shifts in the organization of labor, or ritual mechanisms to reinforce group solidarity—may make some form of redistribution a logistically desirable strategy for a group of cooperating households.

One problem is that the scale, emphasis, and meaning of "redistribution" varies in anthropological studies, and the term has become so loaded as to vitiate its usefulness. For the purposes of this study, I focus on redistribution in a rather restricted sense, to refer to the pooling and exchange of food between households that takes place during large-group aggregations, ceremonials, and feasts. To examine the origins of southeastern chiefdoms, it may be useful to subsume redistribution under a process previously referred to as local resource mobilization. An example of local resource mobilization in the historical Southeast is the movement of foodstuffs, especially maize and venison, from individual households to a local center as part of a ritual cycle coordinated by the civil chief.

Civil chiefs maintained a large storage facility for corn (Swanton 1979:379–381). Households would contribute a portion of their harvest to the "King's corn crib" as a "gift" (Bartram 1958:122–123). In actuality, the granary's store was communal in the sense that it was not the chief's to dispose of as he wished, although in some accounts he certainly had great latitude in doing so. The chief supervised the disbursement of corn to needy families, fed work parties for community projects, and, most importantly, provisioned ceremonial feasts (Swanton 1911, 1979). In the case of the Natchez, these feasts occurred monthly, or 13 times a year (Swanton 1979:260–261).

In addition to this overseeing of communal stores, ritual receipt of "first fruits," and other relatively benign ceremonial roles, many southeastern chiefs gained access to goods and labor from the populace in a process that appears "more akin to the collection of tribute than the institutionalized sharing of surplus" (Steponaitis 1978:420). This critical distinction identifies a scale of redistributive activities. "At one end of the scale we have the complete and equitable reassignment of a village's harvest back to its producers by a chief who is merely a temporary and benign custodian of it. At the other end there is enforced appropriation of a part of a society's food supply by a powerful ruler for his own benefit and that of a small ruling elite" (Carneiro 1981:59–60).

Carneiro insists that redistribution has little to do with chiefdoms or their origins. Instead, "we must seek the source of power that permitted a chief actually to tax his subjects and not just give back to them the goods they had previously brought him" (Carneiro 1981:63). For Carneiro, this coercive power and the origins of chiefdoms were brought about through warfare. He considers it unlikely that autonomous villages could be united into a single polity, his minimal criterion for the definition of a chiefdom, unless coercion played a role.

Yet in the Eastern Woodlands there were populations that manifested many characteristics that place them within the chiefdom social continuum, which consisted not of multiple, united villages, but a single, local center–dispersed household unit. There is both ethnohistoric and archaeological evidence that these units can be economically and politically autonomous (but not isolated) from other polities. Within such sociopolitical units the first critical step that may have led toward hierarchical forms of political control was the local emergence of a permanent decision-making office above the individual household level in response to common needs.

As caretakers of a communal storage facility, southeastern civil chiefs may have acted as primitive "bankers," the personification of an institution through which households could be protected against loss of surplus (Malinowski 1935). Nevertheless, southeastern chiefs were fed and supported by local resource mobilization, which must also be seen as a political strategy to reinforce chiefly authority.

The question of whether chiefs are "system-serving" or "self-serving" (Flannery 1972:423) must be placed in a developmental context. On the small social scale of local resource mobilization between farmsteads and local center, the system-serving advantages of pooled surpluses and the self-serving political strategy to extend personal authority must have been mutually reinforcing and coevolutionary.

As discussed previously, the inability of would-be elites to control directly the means of production in Mississippian societies meant that manipulation of resources was possible only after surpluses were stored in a central location. In other words, "in simple chiefdoms the amount of labor and goods being extracted from a dependent population was small enough to present a low cost of compliance; the question of economic coercion became moot, as the cost of refusal could be minimal and ideologically based" (Drennan, Feinman, and Steponaitis, in Earle 1989).

As mentioned earlier, it is probable that as the size of the polity expanded and the degree of social ranking increased, the mobilization of resources would become more coercive. So, for instance, while the Natchez Sun at the Grand Village received food from the local centers within the Natchez complex chiefdom, subordinate chiefs sometimes found this an imposition (Swanton 1911:110). For southeastern chiefdoms, this was the fragile boundary of scale where local resource mobilization dissolved into the "tribute" of external resource mobilization. To understand the development of these chiefdoms, we must first examine local resource mobilization in two-tiered settlement systems such as Lubbub Creek.

Ideological legitimation of leadership within a ritual format emerges as a central factor. The ritual format is of critical importance in the examination of how the big-man role of redistribution could become institutionalized in the formal office of chief. Ritual may be defined as "conventional acts of display through which one or more participants transmit information concerning their physiological, psychological, or sociological states either to themselves or to one or more other participants" (Rappaport 1971:63). A critical reinforcement present in ritual is "sanctity," a "quality of unquestionable truthfulness imparted by the faithful to unverifiable propositions" (Rappaport 1971:69).

Clearly, not all ritual communicates the same message to the same social entity. Rituals may be public or private, and individuals may participate differently. Furthermore, individuals do not merely react to the social idiom of ritual but continually create, alter, reinterpret, or manipulate its information content, with dynamic results. But whether ritual acts to support the status quo or, as in revitalistic or charismatic movements, serves as a force for social change, the sanctity principle remains a critical influence on social outcomes. Because kin-based societies rely on consensus rather than physical coercion to negotiate acceptance of political decisions, the sanctity principle may have been fundamental to the emergence of permanent political offices.

Moundville: A Prehistoric Chiefdom

It is necessary to connect the broad issues raised in this chapter—cycles of polity size; degree of social ranking; and the production, distribution, and control of resources—to archaeological investigations of Mississippian societies. Fortunately, the region examined in this study has received considerable research aimed at these issues, much of it focused on the regional center of Moundville, in the Black Warrior River valley in western Alabama.

Shortly after A.D. 1000, native populations in the Black Warrior valley intensified maize production and established several single-mound local centers and associated farmsteads. Toward the end of the twelfth century the Moundville regional center formed and eventually grew to a 100 ha site that included 20 major mounds arranged around an extensive plaza. From A.D. 1250 to 1400 Moundville was a center for the production and dissemination of prestige goods and distinctive Southeastern Ceremonial Complex paraphernalia. Moundville was at the apex of a three-tiered settlement hierarchy with a number of single-mound centers and their farmsteads distributed along the river. By the beginning of the sixteenth century Moundville's regional political domination had ended, the complex chiefdom structure had apparently collapsed, Moundville itself had been largely abandoned, and populations had reformed into dispersed villages (Peebles 1983b, 1986; Steponaitis 1989; Knight 1989).

Christopher Peebles's work (1971, 1978, 1983b, 1986) at Moundville has produced one of the most influential studies of Mississippian social and political organization. Peebles proposed that, if Moundville were a ranked society or chiefdom, it should have two fundamental social segments: (1) a high-ranking or superordinate segment based on ascribed or inherited status; and (2) a subordinate segment based on achieved status. To identify this structure, he grouped more than 2,000 burials into clusters defined by associated burial items and arranged the clusters into a hierarchy based on mound burials, cemeteries near mounds, and village burial locations. His superordinate segment consists of adults (Cluster Ia; sex unknown but assumed male) buried in mounds with copper axes, copper-covered beads, and pearl beads (N = 7), together with adult skulls or children/infants' skeletal parts that functioned as

ritual items; adult males and children (Cluster Ib) in mounds or cemeteries near mounds, with copper earspools, stone disks, bear teeth, and
mineral pigments (N = 43); and adults, children, and infants (Cluster II)
in mounds or cemeteries near mounds, with shell beads, galena cubes,
or oblong copper gorgets (N = 67).

Peebles's subordinate segment, composed of all age groups and both
sexes, represents 95% of the burial sample. This segment was buried in
cemeteries near mounds (and overlaps spatially a portion of the superordinate group) or in village areas. The largest burial cluster (N = 1,256)
contains no grave goods at all. Eight other clusters were created on the
basis of various combinations of artifacts such as ceramic vessels,
projectile points, bone awls, stone celts, and shell gorgets. Several categories (such as effigy vessels) were found with adults of both sexes.
Some artifacts (water bottles) were found with all age groups and both
sexes. Only adult males had stone celts, and some artifacts (shell
gorgets) occurred with adults and children but not infants (Peebles and
Kus 1977:438–439).

One of Peebles's superordinate clusters (Cluster II) contained all age
groups and both sexes. He concluded that membership in this group was
determined by ascription, because no evidence was found that associations of artifacts within this group formed patterns based on age and sex
(Peebles and Kus 1977). In his subordinate group, artifact associations do
form patterns based primarily on age and sex, and so Peebles concluded
that membership in this group would be determined by achievement as
shaped by the age and sex of the individual. Peebles's reconstruction
of Moundville social organization forms a status hierarchy: a majority
whose status was determined by age, sex, and achievement; a high-
ranking minority of ascribed status; and individual male paramount
leaders who are assumed to have arisen from the ascribed status group.

Peebles's identification of social ranking at Moundville is based upon
the assumption that differential distribution of artifact categories reflects
some sort of institutionalized restricted or preferential access. It is not
unreasonable to expect that Moundville, like historical southeastern societies, had a complex blend of ascribed and achieved status positions.
However, it cannot be assumed that all artifact associations map directly
onto positions of social status. Prentice (1987:198) has called attention to
the need to distinguish status items from wealth items:

> Status items are defined as those items which are restricted in use to a
> specific social segment. Ideally, they are symbols which are equated or
> identified with that social segment alone. Access to status items, by this
> definition, is determined solely by social position, *regardless of economic*

wealth. Wealth items, on the other hand, are distinguishable from status items in that wealth items are valued by everyone because they give the owner prestige. Unlike status items, wealth items are attainable by many people because they are not limited to a particular social status. . . . Thus, a person may be very wealthy and thereby gain access to many wealth items but still be prohibited from obtaining or exhibiting certain status items that some poorer man might possess [emphasis in original].

Peebles's identification of adult male formal leadership positions appears to isolate status items unambiguously. The presence of special copper artifacts—"supralocal" symbols with a widespread distribution during the Mississippian era—clearly marks individuals of rank or specific status, and burial of these individuals in or near mounds underscores their importance (Peebles 1971; Larson 1971). The most straightforward interpretation is that these items are insignia of formal office and, as insignia, are restricted to individuals who occupy those offices, but to what degree the basis for these positions is ascribed or achieved remains obscure.

Aside from the markers of male formal office, the specific status implications of the artifact associations and burial locations of the Moundville superordinate segment are open to other interpretations. Although burial location is an important organizational criterion for identification of superordinate status, with the exception of the male authority figures, the superordinate segment (Cluster II) at Moundville shares burial location in cemeteries near mounds with a portion of the subordinate segment, and so spatial segregation is not complete. Furthermore, some burials in both mounds and cemeteries near mounds have no grave goods at all (Peebles and Kus 1977:439), and therefore complete spatial segregation does not exist for the most numerous, subordinate cluster.

Drawing upon a large body of historical evidence, Prentice (1987) presents a convincing case that marine-shell beads functioned as wealth items in Mississippian society, possibly as a primitive medium of exchange. A substantial portion of the Moundville superordinate segment (Cluster II) is grouped on the basis of marine-shell beads, but if these are wealth items, as Prentice suggests, then they are not restricted to high-status individuals (Prentice 1987:206). Others have reached similar conclusions about associations in midwestern sites (Goldstein 1980).

In the Moundville case the identification of an ascriptive rank that crosscuts age and sex is dependent on the assumption, widespread in mortuary analysis, that infants and children who were too young to have achieved a status that merits the inclusion of elaborate artifacts in their graves, but who were nonetheless interred with such items, are individuals who belong to an ascribed rank. Many archaeologists do not accept this assumption. In one discussion of this issue in the prehistoric Southeast, a critical observation is offered: "Throughout much of native North America, status was achieved, or enhanced, by the distribution or destruction of wealth rather than by its accumulation. This distribution or destruction often took place at group ceremonials, burial among them. Hence, the wealth included with an infant might mark the status-striving efforts of a living relative, rather than the rank of the deceased" (Jenkins and Krause 1986:125).

Infants and children are often subject to special mortuary treatment through prescribed customs or religious beliefs that may function independently of social position (Hertz 1960). There is evidence that such traditions have great antiquity and continuity. In west Alabama and adjacent Mississippi infant/child burials that contain more grave goods (shell beads and ornaments) than most adult graves are not infrequent in the "egalitarian" Late Woodland phases that preceded the Moundville culture (Jenkins 1982).

Although large kin groups might be expected to have held the competitive advantage over their smaller counterparts in generating surpluses, unequivocal evidence of economic classes in Mississippian societies has yet to be discovered. In other words, while there may have been ascribed status positions at Moundville and elsewhere, the explicit (and often implicit) assumption that such positions were based on institutionalized wealth differences has not been demonstrated. Far more crucial to qualitative cultural change than the presence of ascriptive rank is the establishment of economically based social stratification, a society in which "members of the same sex and equivalent age status do not have equal access to the basic resources that sustain life" (Fried 1967:186). Certainly food is the most basic of resources. Perhaps the most compelling evidence that Mississippian society was not based upon economic stratification comes from osteological analysis. In a well-documented example an extensive comparison of elite and nonelite burials at the huge Moundville site failed to reveal significant differences in diet or health (Powell 1988).

Peebles proposed that the status hierarchy at Moundville would also have corresponding positions in the regional settlement system. Leaders at the single-mound centers, drawn from the superordinate segment of society, would be under the political control of the paramount at Moundville. Supralocal symbols, such as copper symbol badges, would indicate the rank of individuals in the overall regional system. Therefore, leaders and high-status individuals at local centers would have a subset of supralocal symbols at Moundville, but not those of the top leadership positions (Cluster I). Lacking an adequate sample, Peebles concluded that further archaeological investigation of Moundville's outlying sites was necessary to test this proposition.

Peebles's innovative analysis stimulated research in this direction. Welch (1991) attempted a reconstruction of the Moundville political economy. Basing his analysis on theoretical models of chiefdom economy (Service 1975; Peebles and Kus 1977; Wright 1977; Frankenstein and Rowlands 1978), Welch proposed that evidence for craft production and distribution, together with mobilization of subsistence resources, should conform to a distinct pattern at each level of the Moundville three-tiered settlement system: domestic unit; local center; and the regional center of Moundville. He then examined the distribution of artifacts and faunal remains at a local center and compared this with data from Moundville. From the observed pattern, he presented a model of the Moundville political economy.

In Welch's interpretation deer meat and maize produced by "commoner" domestic units (dispersed farmsteads) are supplied to "nobles" at a local center. In turn, elites at the local center send a portion of these subsistence products on up the settlement hierarchy to support a chiefly elite at Moundville. Welch interprets the pattern of craft production and distribution as a system under the centralized control of the chiefly elite at Moundville. While utilitarian items composed of local raw materials were produced in households, only at Moundville was there evidence that nonlocal materials, such as marine shell and greenstone, were converted to finished products. At Moundville there are locations of concentrated raw-material debris that may mark areas of specialized craft production of shell beads, fineware pottery, and greenstone tools (Peebles 1983b; Welch 1991). Prestige goods of nonlocal raw material were either imported whole or made only at Moundville, and their distribution is largely restricted to Moundville.

A few prestige goods, greenstone ceremonial celts and stone palettes (large disks), were passed from Moundville to local centers where possession was "restricted to the nobility" (Welch 1991:180). Utilitarian greenstone axes are found at all levels of the settlement hierarchy, but evidence of manufacture was found only at Moundville.

Welch concluded that outlying communities did not specialize in the production of utilitarian items as expected for a classic redistributive economy (e.g., Service 1975) or specialize in production of nonutilitarian items as expected in some models of tribute economy (e.g., Peebles and Kus 1977; Wright 1977). He summarized the Moundville political economy as "a form of prestige goods economy, in which most utilitarian items were produced domestically, most utilitarian items not produced domestically were produced at the paramount center, and most non-utilitarian items were produced at and/or restricted to the paramount center" (Welch 1991:178).

Welch's Moundville study is an extremely valuable contribution to Mississippian studies because it links political organization to expectations about artifact distributions and settlement hierarchies. However, this picture of the Moundville economy must be considered tentative. Small sample size and lack of adequate data prevented verification of several aspects of the model. Except for controlled surface collections and small test pits in mounds, data from local centers are limited to very small-scale excavations. Excavation data from one of the three levels of settlement—farmsteads—were unavailable. For this reason, mobilization of subsistence resources to elites could not be directly measured (Welch 1991:133). Provisioning of elites with meat was suggested from the composition of deer skeletal elements at a local center but could not be demonstrated because of inadequate or unavailable bone samples from farmsteads or Moundville (Welch 1991:92–98, 133). Much more work will be required to verify the model.

Lubbub Creek: Mississippian Organizational Variability in a Two-Tiered Settlement System

A number of issues have been raised about Mississippian organizational variability, social ranking, and resource control. What is the basis of leadership and social ranking in Mississippian societies? Does dual organization into civil and military leadership indicate parallel sources of political power with different developmental paths in the evolution of the chiefdom? If so, how can these roles be identified archaeologically? How does sociopolitical and economic organization vary with the size of the polity? Does management or control of surplus production support an economic basis for social ranking in Mississippian societies? What form will this take in a two-tiered settlement system—a local center and farmsteads—when compared to a three-tiered system such as Moundville?

As current interpretation of Mississippian social, economic, and political organization in the Southeast is based almost entirely on large mound centers, we need a greater understanding of the more common two-tiered settlement system. One such system is represented by the Lubbub Creek site, 33 miles (approximately 53 km) west of Moundville. Lubbub Creek is one of several Mississippian single-mound local centers

in the central Tombigbee River valley. These sites represent a local variant of the Moundville culture, and their location on the Moundville
periphery raises intriguing questions about interpolity relations.

Excavations at Lubbub Creek and four farmstead sites furnish a
data base with which to assess site variability, site economic interrelationships, and sociopolitical organization. If the Tombigbee sites were
organized as a part of the Moundville polity, or in a similar manner, then
artifacts that mark Peebles's superordinate rank would be expected to
occur only at local centers. Supralocal artifacts that identify a rank or
formal office at Lubbub Creek should not be equivalent to those that
mark the highest-status positions at Moundville. Artifacts associated
with the Moundville superordinate group would not be expected to
occur at farmstead sites. Similarly, if the Tombigbee sites conformed to
the proposed Moundville model of chiefdom economy, farmsteads
would be expected to provision an elite at the local center with food.
Production of craft items from nonlocal materials would be expected to
be restricted to the local center. Prestige goods of nonlocal raw materials
would not occur at farmsteads.

Of course, it is because the Moundville models were developed explicitly with a three-tiered complex chiefdom in mind that we would not
expect the Tombigbee social and economic patterns to be the same, but
the similarities and differences promise to be informative about organizational variability in Mississippian polities. To anticipate the following
chapters, the Lubbub Creek polity appears to be organized quite differently from the Moundville system and diverges from several en-
trenched concepts about Mississippian societies in general.

The initial step in this study is to present evidence that reveals the
social and economic conditions that led to the establishment of a local
center, Lubbub Creek, and connect these conditions to the emergence of
formal leadership institutions—a simple chiefdom. But before this can
be done, it is first necessary to introduce the cultural and historical
context from which these conditions arose.

The Cultural-Historical Context for the Mississippian Occupation Along the Central Tombigbee River

ALTHOUGH A SET of common characteristics identifies a Mississippian cultural pattern that is recognizable over a wide area of the Eastern Woodlands, it is equally clear that this way of life unfolded in various ways in different localities. Only by examining the Mississippian phenomenon in specific cultural-historical settings do we gain both the necessary comparative perspective and the realization that each cultural-historical context is laden with unique possibilities and constraints.

An outline of prehistoric cultural dynamics from A.D. 600 to 1600 in the central Tombigbee River area is presented in this chapter, and chronological, economic, social, and developmental factors are interpreted. In this region Mississippian horticultural populations were distributed in a series of single-mound-and-village centers and associated small, dispersed habitation sites or farmsteads. Each local center–farmstead aggregation appears to represent a minimal sociopolitical unit. Excavations at a single-mound center, Lubbub Creek, and four farmstead sites are summarized below. Together, the five sites furnish the data base, and a window through which to view site variability, site interrelationships, and sociopolitical organization in the region.

Physiographic and Environmental Characteristics

The archaeological sites examined in this study are located along the central Tombigbee River in western Alabama and eastern Mississippi (Figure 1). The sites extend from Tibbee Creek in Lowndes County, Mississippi, south about 58 miles (90 km) to the vicinity of Gainesville in Greene County, Alabama. This portion of the Tombigbee lies entirely

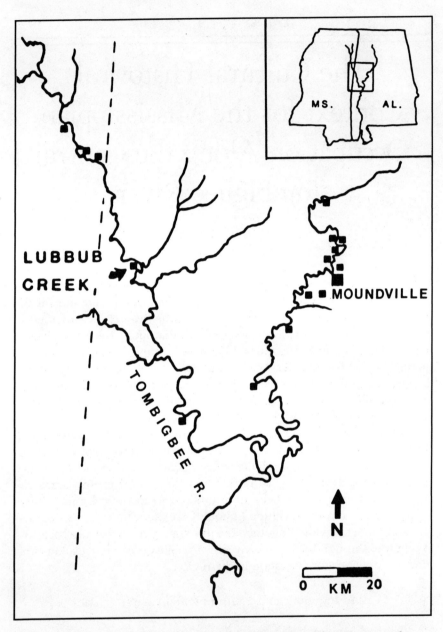

Figure 1　Location of Study Area. Squares represent Mississippian mound centers.

within the Gulf Coastal Plain, a region of Mesozoic and Cenozoic sedimentary deposits. In the study area the river flows along the interface of two physiographic zones (Lineback 1973; Cross 1974). East of the Tombigbee River valley are the Fall Line Hills, a dissected upland of low elevation but steep topography. To the west the Black Prairie (Black Belt) forms a flat-to-rolling region composed of dark fertile soils of the Selma Chalk deposit. The Black Prairie extends in a narrow arc from western Tennessee to central Alabama. From the vicinity of Aliceville, Alabama, the Tombigbee River cuts through the eroded chalk formations and flows southeast through the Black Prairie to meet the Black Warrior River.

In addition to the major transition zones of upland and prairie, the meander-belt zone of the river floodplain creates extensive alluvial soils subject to annual or regular flooding. Horizontal movement of the river channel shapes a landscape of terraces, swamps, and horseshoe bends. Through time, the river may cut off the narrow neck of a bend, leaving an isolated body of water or oxbow lake.

A detailed discussion of biotic communities in the study area can be found in Caddell (1981), Cole (1983), and Scott (1983), and will not be repeated here. While the concentration of Mississippian sites in major ecotones has been frequently noted, these Tombigbee studies indicate that more-immediate local conditions shaped prehistoric subsistence variability. Prairie, slope forest, upland forest, and floodplain forest present a mosaic of diverse biotic communities within a few kilometers of each site.

Cultural and Chronological Outline

Late Woodland Period (A.D. 600–1000)

The Miller III phase, composed of several subphases, is the Late Woodland period cultural entity in the central Tombigbee River valley (Table 1). Traditionally, Late Woodland in the Eastern Woodlands has been considered a cultural decline from the vigorous exchange networks and ceremonialism of the Middle Woodland period. It is now increasingly clear that social and technological processes occurred between A.D. 600 and 1000 that were of fundamental importance to Mississippian development.

For example, during Miller III small triangular projectile points appear that signal the adoption of the bow (Ensor 1981; Blitz 1988). While no changes in faunal remains can be directly attributed to the new technology, single and grouped human burials with embedded arrow points (Hill 1981) represent the earliest evidence of intergroup conflict in the region. As in other areas of the Southeast, maize becomes increasingly

Table 1   Regional Cultural Chronology

DATE A.D.	PHASE CENTRAL TOMBIGBEE	PHASE MOUNDVILLE AREA	PERIOD
1600	SUMMERVILLE IV	ALABAMA RIVER	EARLY PROTOHISTORIC
1500		MOUNDVILLE III	LATE
1400	SUMMERVILLE II/III		MISSISSIPPI
1300		MOUNDVILLE II	MIDDLE MISSISSIPPI
1200		MOUNDVILLE I	EARLY MISSISSIPPI
1100	SUMMERVILLE I		
1000	COFFERDAM GAINESVILLE		
900	CATFISH BEND	WEST JEFFERSON	LATE
800	VIENNA		WOODLAND
700		NO PHASES DEFINED	

visible archaeologically at this time, but it was clearly a minor dietary supplement (Caddell 1981). Another important change is an apparent growth in population and sedentism. In the study area the number of Miller III phase sites increases significantly over earlier components. Sites are larger and middens are more substantial (Jenkins 1982:110).

Ceramic and lithic artifacts are the basis for phase definition. The ceramic complex is dominated by two types, Mulberry Creek Cord Marked and Baytown Plain. There is a trend throughout the phase for grog (crushed sherd) temper to replace sand temper and for the proportion of Mulberry Creek Cord Marked to increase relative to Baytown Plain (Jenkins 1981). The lithic technology is characterized by the appearance of the small triangular arrow point, thermal treatment of locally available chert pebbles, and use of microlithic tools to work both freshwater and marine shell. A few simple flake and groundstone tools complete the inventory.

The Miller III settlement system consisted of large riverine base camps, occupied for much of the year, with seasonal dispersal to small transitory camps (Jenkins 1982). Riverine base camps have dense middens composed of mussel shell, animal bone, dark soil, ceramics, and lithic debris. Excavated base camps often reveal post molds, structure remains, graves, and large storage pits. Features often cluster and overlap, evidence of recurrent or long-term occupation, but no clear community layout is evident. Miller III houses are small, oval or rectangular structures of single-set posts. Significant reduction in house size from earlier periods (Jenkins 1982) suggests the emergence of the nuclear family as an important economic unit at this time. Transitory camps are found in both prairie and upland locations (Blitz 1984) as well as floodplain settings. These camps have little midden accumulation and light artifact densities. No Miller III mounds have been identified in the study area.

Miller III has been divided into several subphases, defined by the relative percentages of ceramic varieties rather than the presence of diagnostic types (Jenkins 1982). Frequency seriation of feature contents has permitted the identification of spatially distinct subphase components at sites. The available radiocarbon dates often exhibit considerable overlap and temporal range. Four subphases have been defined: Vienna (A.D. 600–900); Catfish Bend (A.D. 900–1000); Gainesville (A.D. 1000–1100); and Cofferdam (A.D. 900–1100).

The cultural and chronological implications of these subphases are controversial and open to various interpretations. Jenkins thought these subphases reflect subtle stylistic variations that correspond to distinct social groups. Gainesville base camps have small rectangular structures with sunken floors and hearths. In addition to the Mississippian-like structures, the Gainesville subphase has rare occurrences of grog-tempered loop handles and shell-tempered pottery that Jenkins and Krause (1986:84) interpret as a "move toward Mississippian norms." The Cofferdam subphase shows no evidence of Mississippian influence.

Welch (1990:200–203) presents an alternative interpretation: that Gainesville and Cofferdam subphase components represent, respectively, cold-season and warm-season camps of the same cultural group. He observes that the evidence for primarily cold-season use of Gainesville subphase camps is the presence of well-built houses with hearths, deer mandibles (evidence of winter venison procurement), and scarce representation of fish and turtles in the faunal samples. In contrast, the warm-season characteristics of Cofferdam components include insubstantial shelters, a higher proportion of turtles and fish, and less nutshell than found in Gainesville components (Welch 1990:202).

Welch suggests that the two subphases be consolidated into a single Cofferdam-Gainesville subphase that developed from the preceding Catfish Bend subphase.

Still other investigators doubt the validity of the Gainesville subphase altogether (Rafferty and Starr 1986). Futato (1987:228–232) notes that Gainesville and Catfish Bend subphase samples fail to seriate separately and suggests that the Gainesville subphase may possibly be Catfish Bend features with intrusive Mississippian sherds. The absence of radiocarbon dates for the Catfish Bend subphase merely adds to the uncertainty.

Miller III phase societies practiced a generalized hunting, collecting, and gardening economy. Based on frequencies of Miller III faunal remains, second-line foods such as mussels, turtles, and other small animals appear to have increased in dietary importance relative to deer when compared to earlier Woodland phases (Table 2). From Early Miller III to Middle Miller III (Cofferdam) there is a small but perceptible decline in deer remains, 88% to 70.9% of the total sample by weight, together with a corresponding increase in turtles and fish (Woodrick 1981:Table 37). This perceived trend toward the incorporation of smaller creatures apparently changes in Late Miller III (Gainesville) when proportions of deer increase and fish and turtles decrease. These changes have been interpreted as a response to subsistence stress induced by population pressure (Cole et al. 1982; Scott 1983; Futato 1987; Welch 1990).

Scott (1983:322) summarizes this argument with insights gained from zooarchaeology. She maintains that, faced with resource shortages, Miller societies could either diversify by adding new resources or intensify by increasing the yield of those resources they already exploited. The limits of diversification of wild food sources were reached in Middle Miller III with a maximum breadth of second-line foods. Late Miller III faunal remains, with a more focused emphasis on deer, signal the shift to the only alternative left—intensification through expanded maize cultivation. Labor-intensive cultivation became a less costly option than continued diversification with diminished returns. Scott (1983:324) concludes that, "in fact, the intensification of corn agriculture probably occurred in the subsequent Late Miller III period. The proportions from the Gainesville Lake sites show a relative increase in the quantity of deer and decreased emphasis on both turtles and fish—a trend that continues into the Mississippian period. This renewed emphasis on deer and the decreased importance of aquatic resources was probably made possible by a modification in trophic relationships in which, per capita, the

Table 2 Woodland Faunal Remains: Relative Contributions of Major Taxa by Bone Weight (Grams) and Percentage

Phase/Period	Deer		Other Mammal		Turtle		Bird		Fish	
	Wt.	%	Wt.	%	Wt.	%	Wt.	%	Wt.	%
Gainesville/ Cofferdam[a]	4,216.5	74.5	285.9	5.0	583.9	10.3	414.4	7.3	158.0	2.8
Gainesville	2,804.9	76.5	192.6	5.3	263.2	7.2	329.9	9.0	76.2	2.1
Cofferdam	1,411.6	70.9	93.3	4.7	320.7	16.1	84.5	4.2	81.8	4.1
Early Miller III	7,082.9	88.0	206.1	2.6	526.9	6.6	140.5	1.8	70.4	0.9
Late Miller II	7,075.3	89.0	91.1	1.1	496.0	6.2	177.3	2.2	11.6	1.4

Source: Adapted from Woodrick 1981:Table 37.
[a] Gainesville and Cofferdam samples combined.

human population consumed greater quantities of plant foods and correspondingly lesser quantities of animal protein."

I doubt that the current evidence is adequate to demonstrate that Miller III populations were "pushed" into becoming Mississippian farmers by resource stress. Nor is the argument for subsistence stress so compelling as to rule out other possible reasons for the modest frequency changes in faunal remains. The Middle Miller III and Late Miller III samples upon which these arguments are based (Woodrick 1981:Table 37; Scott 1983:Table 14) represent, respectively, Cofferdam components and Gainesville components (Jenkins 1982:105–108; Welch 1990:Table 23). The modest variation in deer frequencies between these two samples changes largely in relation to the proportion of warm-season remains (turtles and fish) in the sample.

If Welch's interpretation that the Cofferdam and Gainesville subphases represent warm-season and cold-season components of the same cultural system is correct, then the faunal frequency changes may reflect seasonal differences rather than absolute temporal trends. Thus the perception that Late Miller III Gainesville represents a narrowing of the use of wild resources is quite possibly an illusion. Even if the difference is not seasonal, it cannot be viewed as a temporal trend because the radiocarbon dates indicate Cofferdam and Gainesville are contemporary. Given the present uncertainty, related previously, as to whether Catfish Bend, Cofferdam, and Gainesville subphases represent sequential, overlapping, or composite constructs, the arrangement of the associated faunal sample into a sequence that purports to illustrate temporal trends in the Late Woodland subsistence economy is problematic. Rather than unequivocally demonstrating subsistence stress due to overpopulation, the only clear trend evident in the faunal remains is the effort to expand food resources through time.

Hickory nuts and acorns are the most abundant floral remains during Miller III. Seeds of herbaceous annuals increase in abundance in Miller III samples compared to earlier phases, probably an indication of expanded land clearance (Caddell 1981:46). This may indicate small-scale gardening, but commitment to a starchy-seed horticultural complex on the same scale as identified for the contemporary Midwest (Smith 1989) does not seem to be present in the Tombigbee region (Caddell 1981:47) or throughout much of the southeastern coastal plain (Scarry 1988). Maize is consistently present in Miller III flotation samples but in very small quantities.

There is no evidence of hierarchical social ranking in Miller III mortuary remains. Burials at base camps often cluster into groups and have been referred to as cemeteries. However, burial clusters correlate with the densest area of contemporary midden, post molds, and pit features, and exhibit no formal internal arrangement. Interments are frequently placed in used storage pit features. Most burials lack grave goods in Catfish Bend (71%) and Cofferdam-Gainesville (63%) (Welch 1990:205). As summarized by Cole and her colleagues (1982) and Welch (1990), 34 Catfish Bend subphase burials were found in two clusters at site 1Pi61. Age-and-sex composition of furnished and unfurnished burials was similar. Freshwater- and marine-shell beads and pendants were the only burial furnishings. Four shell pendants were placed with women. Subadults received more beads than adult females, and adult females received more beads than adult males. Eighty percent of the 3,094 beads were placed within two graves, each of which contained a single young woman interred in a seated position.

During the subsequent Cofferdam-Gainesville occupation at 1Pi61 thirty-three burials were found distributed in two clusters. Subadults continued to receive many shell beads but not as many as adult males. A few adult males were also furnished with additional materials such as bear canines; one male had a greenstone celt and one male had a shell pendant. No seated young female burials were found, and adult women had few grave accompaniments. Marine shell increased in frequency over freshwater shell as a source for ornaments. This increase in nonlocal items, and greater quantity and diversity of goods placed with adult males, may signal expanded exchange relationships in which these individuals (or their social groups) participated (Welch 1990:206).

Early Mississippi Period (A.D. 1000–1200)

Mississippian cultural development in the Tombigbee River valley cannot be fully understood without reference to the major regional site of Moundville, located in the adjacent Black Warrior River valley of western Alabama. Local Mississippian phases over a large area from the Middle Tennessee River valley south to the Alabama River of central Alabama and west to the Tombigbee River valley have been designated, based on material culture traits shared with Moundville, the Moundville variant (Jenkins and Krause 1986:91). Two phase sequences of the Moundville variant have been constructed for the central Tombigbee River valley: the Tibbee Creek–Lyon's Bluff–Sorrells phase sequence based on the unpublished Lyon's Bluff site excavations (Marshall 1977); and the Summerville I–IV phase sequence at Lubbub Creek (Peebles 1983a). However, the material content of several sites previously placed in the Tibbee Creek–Sorrells phase sequence (Tibbee Creek, Kellogg, Yarborough) is identical to the Summerville I–IV phase sequence. Perhaps with future research important distinctions will become apparent, particularly in the protohistoric materials. For now, because the primary descriptive data have not been published for the Tibbee Creek–Sorrells phase sequence at Lyon's Bluff, all sites discussed are in reference to the more extensively documented Summerville phase sequence.

The Summerville I phase represents the Early Mississippi period in the study area (Peebles 1983a). Ceramic technology, decoration, and vessel forms are sharply discontinuous with the Miller III ceramic tradition. Grog temper and cord-marked surfaces are no longer in use. All Summerville ceramics are shell-tempered and part of the same ceramic tradition as the Moundville I phase. Two ceramic types, Mississippi Plain *var. Warrior* and Moundville Incised *var. Moundville* constitute more than 90% of the ceramic complex. Globular jars, flaring-rim bowls, and subglobular bottles replace Miller III cylindrical beakers and conoidal jars. Diagnostic Summerville I ceramic attributes are small loop handles and strap handles decorated with two central nodes (Peebles and Mann 1983). The lithic technology is rather simple, with stone procurement from local gravels for manufacture of such items as arrow points and microdrills used to produce shell beads (Ensor 1991). Groundstone artifacts include greenstone celts, incised sandstone disks or palettes, discoidal or "chunkey" stones, abraders, manos, and adzes. Shell and bone were worked into a variety of tools and ornaments. Lubbub Creek produced a copper plate embossed with a falcon image, and copper arrow-shaped cutouts—symbol badges associated with the Southeastern Ceremonial Complex (Jenkins 1982).

As in other areas of the Southeast, the social dynamics of Mississippian emergence are open to various interpretations. Jenkins and Krause (1986:120) offer three possible scenarios for the central Tombigbee area: (1) Mississippian immigration and Miller III population displacement; (2) Miller III "Mississippianized" through diffusion of material culture and ideas; or (3) limited Mississippian immigration with acculturation of neighboring Miller III groups. Other investigators consider the Mississippian emergence an indigenous economic transformation, with social and material changes shaped by the shift to maize agriculture (Peebles 1983c).

It would be interesting to link this dramatic dietary shift with the seemingly simultaneous changeover in ceramic forms, remembering that so much of pottery is a culinary artifact. However, such a scenario should not exclude the secondary role of diffusionary imports. Similar shell-tempered vessel forms made an exceedingly rapid appearance across an enormous area of the Mid-South. For this reason alone it is unlikely that the radically new ceramic tradition in the Tombigbee region can be explained solely as a local technological change, as has been

Table 3 Selected Radiocarbon Dates from Tombigbee
Mississippian Sites

	Laboratory Sample	*Date* A.D.*[a]*	*Comments*
Lubbub	Beta-8968	980 ± 90	Pre-mound Surface Pit 13 cut by Structure 5A. Dates beginning of ceremonial precinct (Blitz 1983b:240)
Lubbub	Beta-1095	1190 ± 80	Summerville I structure, Household Cluster 2-1 (Blitz 1983c:260)
Lubbub	Beta-1097	1070 ± 125	Hearth in Summerville I structure, Household Cluster 1-1 (Blitz 1983c:269)
Kellogg	UGa-910	1195 ± 76	Feature 6 post mold associated with Moundville Incised *var. Moundville* (Blakeman 1975:Table 25)
Kellogg	UGa-2764	1185 ± 90	Feature 65, Summerville I (Atkinson et al. 1980:237)
22Lo507	UGa-680	1265 ± 105	Hearth on next-to-final stage, Coleman mound, early Summerville II–III (Rucker 1974:34)
Lubbub	Beta-1092	1290 ± 65	Household Cluster 4-2, Summerville II–III (Blitz and Peebles 1983:298)
Lubbub	Dicarb-1233	1410 ± 45	Structure 1, Household Cluster 1-2, Summerville II–III (Jenkins 1981: Table 1)
Lubbub	Beta-1104	1450 ± 70	Structure 3, Household Cluster 4-4, Summerville IV (Peebles and Mann 1983:77)

[a] All dates are uncorrected.

suggested (e.g., Peebles 1983a:396; Welch 1990:209). The presence of rare Early Mississippian attributes such as grog-tempered loop handles, together with shell-tempered sherds in Late Miller III contexts, indicates changes that are ambiguous enough to interpret as either prototypes of indigenous development or evidence of external interaction.

The radiocarbon dates do not clarify the situation. They bracket the Summerville I phase between A.D. 1000 and 1200 (Peebles and Mann

1983) and overlap with those of the Gainesville and Cofferdam sub-phases of Miller III (Table 3). The available dates are imprecise enough to permit Summerville I to begin at A.D. 1100, and so support indigenous development out of Miller III (Welch 1990:203) or provide time for over-lapping cultural traditions to interact (Jenkins 1982:117–122). In short, the Tombigbee River area encapsulates all the controversies that enliven investigations into the Mississippian emergence.

Maize expanded to 93% of recovered floral remains at the expense of wild nut species, almost the reverse of earlier Miller III proportions (Jenkins and Krause 1986:Table 2). Hickory nuts continued to be utilized while acorns, formerly the resource of highest carbohydrate content, declined sharply as maize production intensified (Caddell 1983:240–244). Both Miller III and Summerville I populations used the same array of game species but in slightly different proportions. As with earlier periods, deer contributed the bulk of protein in the diet (Table 4). There is a modest increase in the proportion of large animal remains, especially deer (compare Table 2 with Table 4).

It is difficult to assess the importance of such modest proportional changes. This shift has been interpreted as evidence of a more focused strategy to maximize large high-energy species, a least-cost decision made feasible by agricultural intensification (Scott 1983:361–365). Scott identifies this shift as taking place in Late Miller III, but if the interpreta-tion of the Miller III faunal data discussed above is valid, then this pro-portional increase in deer occurred in Summerville I concurrent with intensification of maize production. Alternatively, it is possible that em-phasis on deer is merely an opportunistic response due to localized increases in the edge habitats favored by deer, brought about by altera-tion of floodplain areas due to cultivation. Increases in other open-habi-tat floral and faunal remains may also reflect land-clearing activities (Ca-ddell 1983; Scott 1983).

Human health patterns are important indicators of cultural change. Osteological analysis reveals that the relative frequency of porotic hyper-ostosis—anemia due to health stress—was much higher in Catfish Bend and Cofferdam-Gainesville mortuary samples than in those from Summerville I (Cole et al. 1982:Table 14; Welch 1990:Table 25). Several investigators propose that this health stress resulted when population growth exceeded the carrying capacity that could be sustained through a hunting-gathering and low-level-gardening economy (Cole et al. 1982; Scott 1983; Welch 1990; Futato 1987).

However, because of its generalized nature, porotic hyperostosis in these Woodland populations cannot be simplistically equated with population pressure. It can result from disease vectors that arise from

Table 4 Mississippian Faunal Remains: Relative Contributions of Major Taxa by Bone Weight (Grams) and Percentage

Period	Phase	Deer		Other Mammal		Turtle		Bird		Fish	
		Wt.	%	Wt.	%	Wt.	%	Wt.	%	Wt.	%
Protohistoric/ Late Mississippi	Summerville IV	2,294.5	82.0	170.0	6.1	59.9	2.1	244.9	8.7	28.0	1.0
Middle Mississippi	Summerville II–III	1,968.2	86.7	50.6	2.2	142.0	6.2	90.0	4.0	20.1	0.9
Early Mississippi	Summerville I	324.1	83.1	23.6	6.1	17.4	4.5	21.0	5.4	3.5	0.9

Source: Scott 1983: Appendix A.

increased sedentism or aggregation (poor sanitation) or diets deficient in iron (Mensforth et al. 1978; Huss-Ashmore et al. 1982). Moreover, until uncertainties about the temporal relationships of the Catfish Bend and Cofferdam-Gainesville subphases are resolved, burial samples from these subphases cannot be arranged into a sequence that demonstrates a decline in health through Late Woodland times. Given the lack of mortuary samples from earlier phases, it is by no means certain that Miller III populations were any less healthy than their Woodland predecessors.

Clearly, Miller III groups were under considerable health stress, but it is unrealistic to claim that intensified maize cultivation and, by extension, the Mississippian emergence are to be explained primarily by a single, independent variable—population growth. Population and technology are interdependent variables mediated by human intentionality. Nor can an adequate understanding of long-term social change be gained by focusing only on local environmental conditions.

Jenkins and Krause (1986:123) express a broader, multicausal interpretation of the Late Woodland to Mississippian transition that attempts to integrate both local and external factors. They suggest that the adoption of maize by Late Woodland Miller groups stimulated population growth that in turn favored increased sedentism and increased use of second-line resources. Thus a mutually reinforcing feedback relationship between maize intensification and population growth amplified through time. The resulting changes in resource territories and established subsistence practices led to increased intergroup competition in which local social groups were more receptive to introduced "Mississippian" ideas and practices (Jenkins and Krause 1986:121).

Jenkins and Krause's model is more consistent with the available evidence than the ecological determinism of the advocates of population pressure. I would add that, rather than being driven by ecological limitations beyond their control, the Tombigbee populations transformed their local environment to suit newfound opportunities. These opportunities were actively created through acquisition of maize and the bow—the two most potent technological revolutions of the Late Woodland era—that diffused from original sources far outside the Southeast. The competitive context of individual and group interaction generated the principal motivations for acceptance of these new technologies. If, as Jenkins and Krause propose, the new technologies changed subsistence strategies and increased regional competition, then under these conditions population growth would become advantageous.

Minimally, the Summerville I settlement system consists of a local center, composed of a platform mound and habitation area, and dispersed small settlements or farmsteads. Summerville I and Miller III components are frequently present on the same site. Six local mound centers occur on the main channel of the central Tombigbee River. From north to south, these sites are Butler (22Lo500), Chowder Springs (22Lo554 and 555), Coleman (22Lo507), Lubbub Creek (1Pi33 and 85), Hilman, and Brasfield (1Gr15). An additional local center, Lyon's Bluff (22Ok1), is located on a secondary stream immediately outside the study area.

With the exception of Lubbub Creek (to be discussed later) and Lyon's Bluff, the occupation sequence at these centers remains unknown. Only a single radiocarbon date is available from one of the other five centers. A date of A.D. 1265 ± 105 obtained from a hearth on the next-to-last building stage of the Coleman Mound (Rucker 1974) suggests most of the construction occurred in Summerville I. Five centers have a single platform mound. At Chowder Springs there are two small mounds placed 100 m apart. Chowder Springs Mound B has a Summerville I component (Moore 1901), but no phase association is available for Mound A. The cultural association of Butler, Hilman, and Brasfield is uncertain. The Brasfield Mound is one of the larger mounds in Alabama (Sheldon et al. 1982:4). Summary data for the central Tombigbee platform mounds are presented in Table 5.

Many small, dispersed Mississippian sites have been found (Figures 2–3). Unfortunately, available surface collections are scant and mostly yield plain pottery that does not permit a phase designation. Survey in the study area has been limited largely to the main channel. Little is known about Mississippian use of secondary streams or areas away from the river. Viewed on a regional scale, Mississippian settlement in western Alabama appears to represent clustered populations surrounded by extensive buffer zones devoid of people. Extensive surveys south of the study area (Sheldon et al. 1982; Brose et al. 1982) have discovered that much of the lower Tombigbee River system above the Mobile delta area has few or no Mississippian sites. These broad floodplains appear to contain the environmental conditions preferred by Mississippian societies (see Smith 1978) but were not occupied. Similar clusters of Mississippian settlements have been recognized elsewhere in the Southeast (Anderson 1990).

This clustered pattern suggests a social landscape shaped by intergroup warfare that had the end result (if not the specific intent) of creating buffer zones that served as game reservoirs (see Hickerson 1965). While the physical environment has long been the primary explanatory device for Mississippian settlement patterns (Ward 1965; Peebles 1978), the distribution of local centers must also be understood as a response to social and political conditions. In other words, local Mississippian settle-

Table 5 Central Tombigbee Platform Mounds

Mound Site	Known Associated Components	Mound Dimensions in Meters			Relative Size Index (L × W × H)	Reference
		Length	Width	Height		
Butler	unknown	54.9	39.0	2.4	5,139	Moore 1901
Chowder Springs A	unknown	25.0	25.0	2.2	1,375	Moore 1901; Rucker 1974
Chowder Springs B	Summerville I	34.0	27.0	1.6	1,469	Moore 1901; Rucker 1974
Coleman	Summerville I, early Summerville II–III	45.0	30.0	4.0	5,400	Moore 1901; Rucker 1974
Lubbub	Summerville I–IV	49.0	49.0	3.4	8,163	Moore 1901; Jenkins 1982; Blitz 1983b
Hilman	unknown	insufficient data			—	Moore 1901; Welch 1990
Brasfield	unknown	68.6	45.8	5.8	20,865	Moore 1901; Sheldon et al. 1982

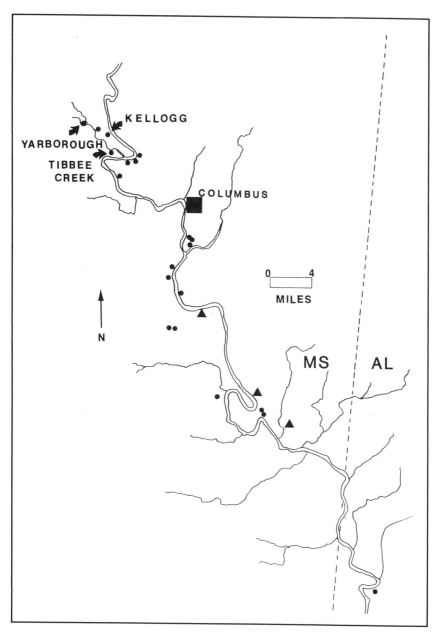

Figure 2 Mississippian Sites Along the Central Tombigbee River (North). Dots represent farmsteads or transitory camps. Triangles represent local mound centers.

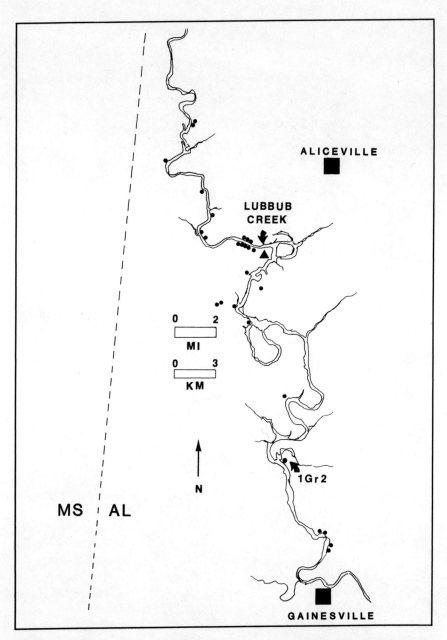

Figure 3 Mississippian Sites Along the Central Tombigbee River (South). Dots represent farmsteads or transitory camps; triangles represent local mound centers.

ment locations, abandonments, and clusterings may be responses to relationships with other population clusters (cf. DeBoer 1981).

Unfortunately, the lack of temporal control for the majority of known Mississippian sites and other limitations in the extant survey data currently restrict broader interpretations about settlement density and patterning. It is probable that all of the local mound centers along the main channel have been located. These centers exhibit no spatial or artifactual evidence of political centralization, and it is therefore unlikely that the local mound centers were united into a larger political entity beyond temporary, expedient alliance. A local mound center and associated farmsteads probably constitute the effective political unit, perhaps akin to the okla or simple chiefdom discussed in the preceding chapter.

It is quite possible, however, that the developmental and occupational histories of these sites will be more varied than the current data indicate, and that this variability will reflect political processes beyond the central Tombigbee River, such as connections with the powerful but localized chiefdom at Moundville. At first glance, however, it is surprising how independent outliers such as Lubbub Creek appear to be, and this raises critical questions about the extent of territorial or administrative control exercised by such famed polities as Moundville, often described as the second-largest site in pre-Columbian North America.

Middle Mississippi Period (A.D. 1200–1450)

The Summerville II–III phase is the local Middle Mississippi period occupation in the central Tombigbee River valley (Peebles 1983c). It represents a cultural-historical continuum with Summerville I, but new interregional social processes are perceptible, although as yet poorly understood. Summerville II–III is defined by the presence of all varieties of Moundville Engraved, a well-made fineware. The appearance of Moundville Engraved in the central Tombigbee and other areas of the Moundville variant corresponds to the formation of a three-tiered settlement hierarchy in the Black Warrior River valley. In the latter the apex was Moundville, the regional ceremonial center of a powerful polity. At Moundville, Moundville Engraved is considered to be the product of part-time specialists (Van der Leeuw 1981). Mold-assisted production, firing, and decorative methods are technically and artistically more elaborate than those of earlier wares. Engraved motifs often depict Southeastern Ceremonial Complex themes such as the winged serpent and hand-eye.

Varieties of Moundville Engraved provide sensitive chronological markers with which to subdivide the Middle Mississippi period in the Black Warrior valley (Steponaitis 1983). Such temporal resolution has not yet been possible in the Tombigbee area, and, for now, the Summerville II–III phase is an aggregate of these ceramic varieties. Other Summerville II–III ceramic attributes include rare terraced rectangular vessels (perhaps acquired from Moundville), restricted bowls, and notched lip treatment (Peebles and Mann 1983).

Floral and faunal analyses reveal a subsistence economy generally similar to that of the Summerville I phase. There is little change in lithic technology. Burials occur in small clusters or in association with domestic dwellings.

Investigation at the Tombigbee local centers, with the exception of Lubbub Creek and Lyon's Bluff, has been minimal, and therefore it is not known which of these were occupied during the Summerville II–III phase. As mentioned before, Coleman (22Lo507) seems to have been abandoned at the beginning of the phase. While Lyon's Bluff was apparently palisaded at this time (Marshall 1977), the Summerville II–III community at Lubbub Creek was unfortified for part or all of this phase. Site abandonment, cycles of palisade building, and the adoption of Moundville Engraved all suggest an intense period of social interaction between the local Tombigbee centers, engendered by the rise of Moundville 33 miles (53 km) to the east. Perhaps embedded in these changing relationships, but in a manner not yet understood, is the question of why a three-tiered settlement hierarchy formed in one river valley and not the other.

Late Mississippi/Protohistoric Period
(A.D. 1450/1500–ca. 1600)

Traditionally, the protohistoric period in the interior Southeast is defined as the hiatus in the historical record between the first recorded European contact (in the study area, the De Soto expedition in A.D. 1540) and the initial explorations and settlements of the French and English in the late 1600s. Discussions of this time period in the southeastern United States are dominated by two themes: (1) changes in the Mississippian cultural pattern that are characterized as a decline; and (2) the nature and effect of initial European contact. The dominant view that has emerged in recent years is that these processes are directly related: the decline of chiefdom organization is the result of massive depopulation from epidemics unleashed through European contact (Curren 1984; M. T. Smith 1987). Others observe that chiefdoms are unstable political constructs that fluctuate in size and duration, producing a cycle of rise and decline that has considerable prehistoric depth (e.g., Peebles 1986; Anderson 1989). A prerequisite to evaluating such propositions is an adequate chronological framework, which in the study area still requires a great deal of refinement.

In the central Tombigbee area Late Mississippi/protohistoric sites are designated the Summerville IV phase (A.D. 1450/1500–ca. 1600) (Peebles 1983c). Summerville IV mortuary practices include burial of subadults in large globular jars, or burial urns. Subsistence remains continue to indicate maize as a staple. At least one of the Tombigbee centers, Lubbub Creek, was fortified at this time.

Continuity from earlier ceramic forms is evident in Summerville IV but there are changes. Alabama River Applique is the characteristic ceramic type. There is a trend, beginning in Summerville II–III, for jars to have multiple strap handles, which increase in number to 10 or more in Summerville IV. Punctation, vertical incision from the lip, and rare painted decorative treatments appear (as they do in the late Moundville III phase) as part of a broad horizon style with origins in the central Mississippi Valley (Sheldon and Jenkins 1986). Moundville Engraved was no longer produced. As with the earlier Summerville phases, the vast majority of the ceramic assemblage is plain. The lithic technology changed little from earlier phases.

Summerville IV is poorly dated, and it is particularly uncertain when it ended. The protohistoric ceramic chronology in the central Tombigbee region still requires a great deal of basic sequence definition coupled with more-absolute dates. At the Lyon's Bluff site the Sorrells phase component produced a radiocarbon date of A.D. 1557 ± 65 (Marshall 1977). Changes in the ceramic complex throughout the region correspond closely in time to the collapse of Moundville's sociopolitical and settlement hierarchy. By early in the sixteenth century Moundville was largely abandoned (Peebles 1987). Absolute dates for the terminal Moundville III phase average in the first third of the 1500s (Welch 1991:Tables 3.3, 3.4). The subsequent Alabama River phase of the Black Warrior River valley shares many ceramic characteristics with Summerville IV.

The Alabama River phase has long been considered a postcontact phenomenon (Sheldon 1974). The few available radiocarbon dates for the Alabama River phase (also designated Moundville IV) in the Black Warrior valley suggest a span from the early sixteenth century to ca. 1700 (Curren 1984). Peebles (1986, 1987) argues that the terminal dates for the Moundville III phase fall too early to support the traditional contention that Moundville disintegrated because of epidemics spawned by Spanish explorations such as the De Soto expedition (1539–1543). Peebles (1986, 1987) contends, based on chronological and other evidence, that internal political and economic weaknesses inherent to chiefdom organization resulted in the decline of Moundville, and observes that, "like their neighbors to the north such as Cahokia, Kincaid, and Angel, many Mississippian centers in the Southeast devolved on their own, without help from Europeans. Likewise, many Mississippian polities, such as the Natchez and Appalachee, survived sustained contact with the Europeans without collapsing. In brief, one cannot blame Soto for all the bad things that befell the native peoples of the Southeast throughout the whole of the 16th century" (Peebles 1987:24). What role, if any, European epidemics played in the demise of the Moundville culture will remain unclear pending a more accurate absolute chronology.

A terminal date of A.D. 1600 for Summerville IV is an estimate. No European artifacts have been found in association with materials from the Summerville IV phase. Moreover, the headwaters and upland northern tributaries of the Tombigbee River in northeastern Mississippi have numerous sixteenth-, seventeenth-, and eighteenth-century sites, at least some of which are Chickasaw (Marshall 1977; Johnson and Sparks 1986; Atkinson 1987). Immediately west of the Tombigbee River valley, in the uplands where the Pearl River, Pascagoula River system, and western tributaries of the Tombigbee form a watershed, there are numerous eighteenth-century Choctaw sites, but Mississippian sites are minimal or absent (Blitz 1985). Settlements in both areas may have formed as part of a demographic shift from the Tombigbee River floodplain. While the timing and cause of this shift remain uncertain, the main channel of the central Tombigbee River appears to have been abandoned by the seventeenth century.

The Excavated Sites

Each of the sites examined in this study was excavated by university-based research teams as a part of the Tennessee-Tombigbee Waterway, a massive public works project administered by the United States Army Corps of Engineers. In this section brief summary descriptions for each Mississippian site are presented.

The sites described below were chosen for excavation because of location, visibility, preservation, impending destruction, and other administrative concerns. The goal was to retrieve the maximum amount of information possible within temporal and funding constraints. Excavation techniques were generally similar. The site summaries supply the necessary background information for more-specific comparisons, presented in succeeding chapters, of ceramics, faunal remains, prestige goods, mortuary treatment, and architectural remains. Together, the five sites furnish the data base with which to assess hypotheses about site variability and sociopolitical organization in the region.

Detailed information for each site can be found in the original site reports. The following sources are the basis for the summary descriptions: for Lubbub Creek, University of Alabama investigations directed by Ned J. Jenkins (Jenkins and Ensor 1981; Jenkins 1982) and University of Michigan investigations directed by Christopher S. Peebles (Peebles 1983a); for Tibbee Creek, Mississippi State University excavations directed by John W. O'Hear (O'Hear et al. 1981); for Kellogg, Mississippi State University excavations directed by James R. Atkinson (Atkinson et al. 1980); for 1Gr2; University of Alabama investigations, directed by Ned J. Jenkins (Jenkins and Ensor 1981; Jenkins 1982); and for Yarborough, University of Alabama excavations directed by Carlos Solis (Solis and Walling 1982).

A Local Mound Center: Lubbub Creek

The Lubbub Creek site is located on a low terrace within a large horseshoe bend of the Tombigbee River in Pickens County, Alabama. The river cuts a loop that demarcates a 600 m × 1,000 m peninsula of floodplain and swampland. The wide meander-belt floodplain forms a boundary between the Fall Line Hills and Black Prairie physiographic zones. Within several kilometers of the site, multiple biotic communities can be found: floodplain forest; upland forest; grassland; swamps; mussel beds; and oxbow lakes (Caddell 1981).

The area's first archaeological investigations were those of Clarence B. Moore (1901) who examined an 11 ft high (3.5 m) prehistoric mound (1Pi85) situated on the narrow neck of the bend. In the 1970s archaeologists from the University of Alabama located and tested a series of middens (1Pi11, 12, 13, 33) within the bend. It became clear that the locality was a large multicomponent site.

In 1977 extensive investigations under the direction of Ned J. Jenkins focused on 1Pi33. Heavy sod was cut from six recovery strips 30 ft (9.14 m) wide and of lengths varying from 120 ft (36.60 m) to 420 ft (128.02 m). The strips were plowed, gridded into 10 ft (3.05 m) units, and surface-collected. The major effort focused on a 30 ft × 250 ft (9.14 m × 76.20 m) strip where midden was removed to expose features. Numerous pit features, post molds, two structure patterns, and a Mississippian cemetery with 27 burials were uncovered. The following year the University of Michigan began a 14 month excavation program under the direction of Christopher S. Peebles. An extensive sampling program of 1,079 auger and test pits over a 111 ha area determined that the principal Late Wood-

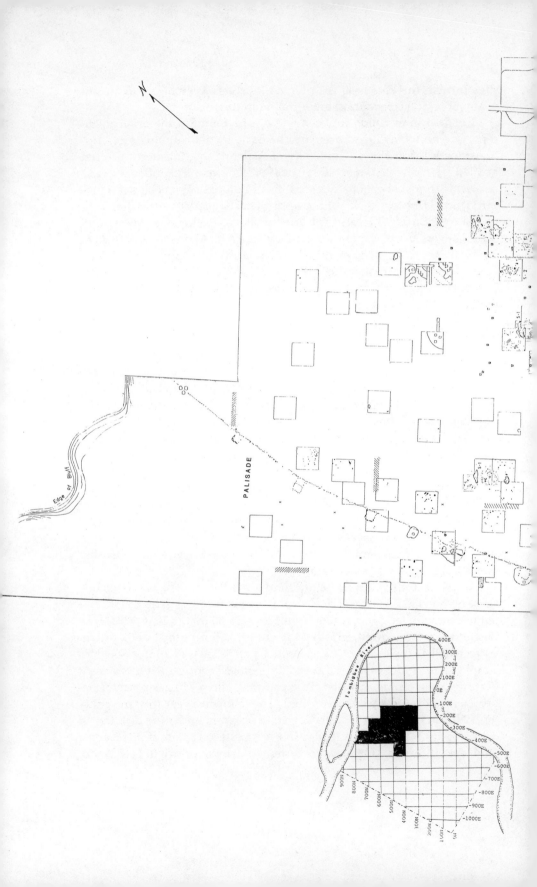

N

Edge of Bluff

PALISADE

Tombigbee River

400E
300E
200E
100E
0E
-100E
-200E
-300E
-400E
-500E
-600E
-700E
-800E
-900E
-1000E

900N
800N
700N
600N
500N
400N
300N
200N
100N
0N

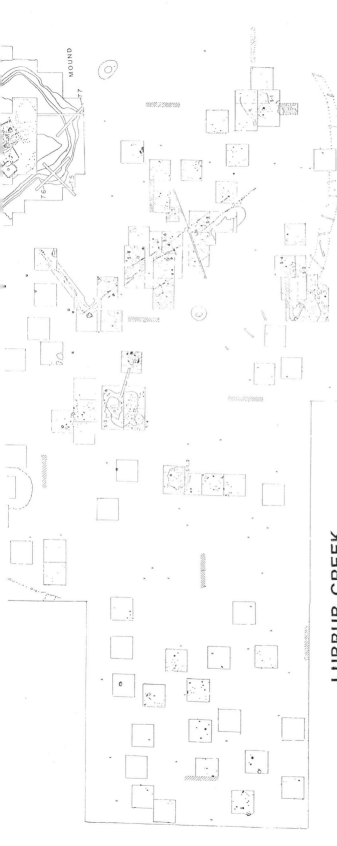

LUBBUB CREEK
ARCHAEOLOGICAL LOCALITY

PICKENS COUNTY, ALABAMA

MOUND

PREHISTORIC DITCH

○ Postmold   ◇ Pit   ⬠ Midden

× Phase I Auger Test   ⊘ Burial   ◯ Daub Concentration

⊘ Wall Trench   ⊚ Disarticulated Burial   ⤳ Phase I Transect

✳ Smudge Pit   ○ Hearth   Structure Outline

▨ Backhoe Trench   ◯ Depression Outline

▨ Prehistoric Ditch

0   5   10m   20

Figure 4   Lubbub Creek Site Map

land and Mississippian deposits were concentrated within a 23 ha portion of the bend. The Corps of Engineers elected to preserve half of this area. The other 12 ha, the densest expanse of Mississippian occupation, was the focus of a 20% sample by area. These efforts resulted in one of the largest archaeological site excavations in the Southeast since the Works Progress Administration (WPA) projects of the 1930s. More than 20,000 m² were excavated. Cultural features exposed included 25 structures, 425 pits, 43 burials, 3,984 post molds, and expanses of midden (Figure 4). An enormous collection of artifacts and floral and faunal remains was secured and analyzed.

From about A.D. 600 to 1000 the river bend was used as a Late Woodland Miller III phase base camp. Scattered clusters of midden, post molds, burials, and large pits for hickory nut/acorn storage were present. The Mississippian occupation at Lubbub Creek transformed the river bend into a permanent settlement that oscillated in size through several centuries. Changes in the community plan for each of the three phases were documented.

The Mississippian ceramics from Lubbub Creek have been classified following the type-variety method commonly used in the Southeast (Mann 1983). Temper, surface treatment, and decoration are the criteria for type designation. Variations in secondary attributes within each type are grouped as varieties. Diagnostic type-varieties were used as time markers to construct a relative chronological order (Peebles and Mann 1983). Seriation of the sample, supported by a series of radiocarbon dates, permits the Lubbub Creek occupation to be divided into a three-phase sequence:

Summerville I   A.D. 1000–1200
         II–III   A.D. 1200–1450/1500
         IV   A.D. 1450/1500–1600

Presence or absence of diagnostic type-varieties was the basis for assigning features to specific phases. Summerville I was defined primarily by the presence of Moundville Incised *var. Moundville*. Summerville II–III is characterized by all varieties of Moundville Engraved. Summerville IV is marked by the type Alabama River Applique. A basic characteristic of the ceramic tradition is the predominance of plainware (94%).

Jar, bowl, and bottle forms are the basic vessel shapes at Lubbub Creek (Figure 5). Identification of vessel forms from rim sherds was performed by Baxter Mann and John Blitz. This task was made easier by Steponaitis's (1983) excellent study of whole vessels from Moundville, as

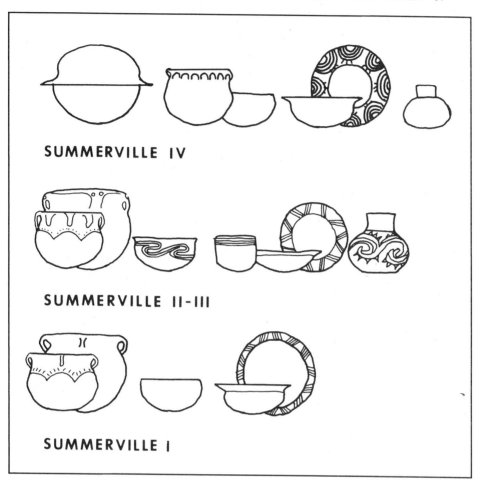

Figure 5 Representative Vessel Forms of the Summerville Phases

well as a number of whole or nearly complete vessels from Lubbub. Recent southeastern studies provide a basis for inferring functional uses from vessel shape (Hally 1986). However, evidence applicable to Summerville ceramics permits only very general inferences about cooking, serving, and storage uses.

The Summerville I phase community (A.D. 1000–1200) represents the Early Mississippi period component. A central ceremonial precinct was established. It consisted of a sequence of paired buildings within an enclosed compound that over several decades was transformed into a low platform with adjacent plaza. The Summerville I community spread out in an arc around the mound. Four single-set post structures of this component were excavated. A series of bastioned palisades fortified the community. One set of walls enclosed the central ceremonial precinct, and an outer palisade line formed a barrier across the neck of the bend. Based on the extent of features, the Summerville I community covered 8.5 ha. Density of houses was very low. No more than six houses are estimated to have been occupied at any one time (Peebles 1983a:399–401). Faunal remains indicate a mixed economy of maize production, gathering, and hunting. Deer, bear, and turkey were the important large food animals.

No fortifications were present during the Summerville II–III phase (A.D. 1200–1450/1500). The site area expanded to 11.3 ha. Six structures with associated features were uncovered. Based on the density of house remains, it is estimated between five and 18 houses were present at any one time (Peebles 1983a:399–401). The platform mound and plaza remained the central focus of the community. Several construction stages raised the mound to maximum height, and two ramps were added. No significant change occurred in subsistence practices.

During the Late Mississippi/protohistoric Summerville IV phase (A.D. 1450/1500–ca. 1600), the Lubbub Creek site was again fortified, this time with a ditch 230 m in diameter and 1 m deep. This construction demarcated a 4.2 ha community. Five single-set post houses and associated features were found, with an estimated two to seven houses in use at the time (Peebles 1983a:399–401). Little change took place in the faunal assemblage, but the proportion of recovered maize decreased and acorns increased.

Human burials from all three phases were found, often in association with a domestic dwelling. Health, as indicated by osteological analysis, was generally good for all three phases (Powell 1983). Graves in the partially excavated 1Pi33 area were arranged in rows. Four Summerville I burials appeared to be associated with an oval post-mold pattern. One of these burials contained two adult males, one with a copper plate embossed with a falcon symbol, copper headdress ornaments, a greenstone celt, marine-shell ornaments, and portions of other individuals believed to be war trophies (Jenkins 1982). The copper ornaments are similar to other Mississippian iconographic materials thought to function as symbol badges of a specific status or office of leadership (Larson 1959). Children interred within large jars marked the Summerville IV phase. A pit that contained the stacked, disarticulated remains of 43 individuals appeared to represent the final stages of an intricate mortuary process, perhaps redeposition from a charnel structure (Powell 1983) (a more comprehensive examination of mortuary evidence is presented in Chapter 7).

Lubbub Creek was a local center of ceremonial and social activities for several centuries. Interestingly, the population of the settlement was apparently quite low. Rough estimates based on phase time span, arbitrarily set at five persons per house, generate a maximum population range of under 100 people at any one time (Peebles 1983a:399–401). Furthermore, the site does not appear to be a densely nucleated settlement in the usual sense of the term. Although there are concentrations of features and midden, surprisingly large expanses within the community are devoid of both. Indeed, the resident population was probably not large enough to have constructed or maintained the fortifications unless aided by the dispersed farmstead population. (Evidence that these farmstead residents regularly aggregated at Lubbub Creek is developed further in Chapter 6).

Dispersed Small Settlements

Tibbee Creek (22Lo600). The Tibbee Creek site is an extensive midden deposit situated on Tibbee Creek at the edge of the Tombigbee River floodplain in Lowndes County, Mississippi (O'Hear et al. 1981). The site was discovered in 1976 during clearing operations prior to construction of the Columbus Lock and Dam complex on the Tennessee-Tombigbee Waterway. Artifacts, mussel shell, and dark midden soil extend along a low alluvial terrace about 300 m in length and cover a 2 ha area.

Two kilometers north of the site the Tombigbee River cuts a large meander loop that creates a broad floodplain dotted with sloughs, swamp, and old natural levees. The site is located at the point where the smaller floodplain of Tibbee Creek meets the Tombigbee meander-belt zone. In the vicinity of the site, Tibbee Creek creates shoals with abundant freshwater-mussel beds. Immediately to the west is the Black Prairie. Thus, within a 2 km radius of the site a diversity of rich habitats can be found (Figure 6). A series of ten 1 m × 1 m test units revealed two major cultural strata that varied in depth from 30 to 70 cm. The thicker deposit was a black organic layer of mussel shell, animal bone, and Late Woodland and Mississippian pottery. Beneath this midden was a thin stratum with earlier components. These earlier occupations were interpreted as locations of short-term, small-group encampments from about 1000 B.C. through the Middle Woodland period. The most intensive occupation and much of the midden date to the Miller III phase when the site was a large base camp. The final prehistoric component was a small Mississippian farmstead (Figure 7).

Because of temporal and funding limitations, only a small part of the site, approximately 70 m × 40 m, was mechanically stripped to expose

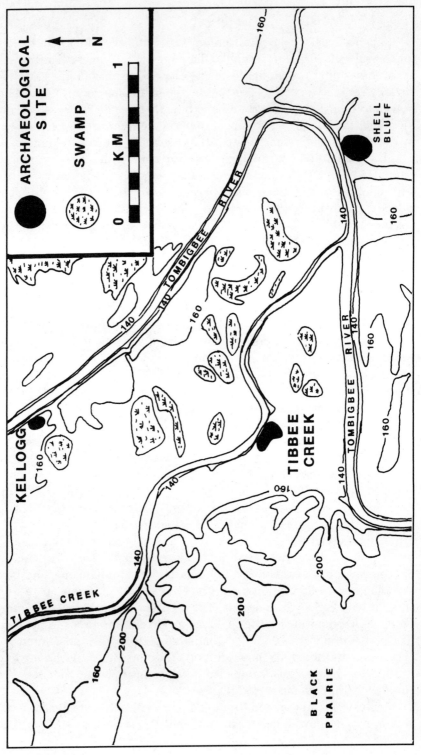

Figure 6 Environmental Setting of Tibbee Creek and Kellogg (Adapted from O'Hear et al. 1981)

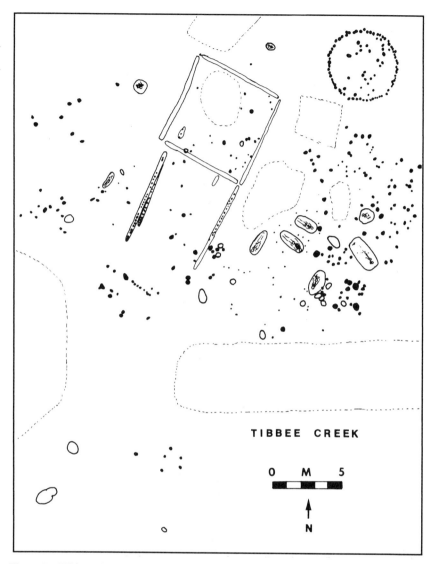

Figure 7   Tibbee Creek: Mississippian Features. Dotted lines enclose
unexcavated or destroyed areas. (Adapted from O'Hear et al. 1981)

features intruding into the sterile subsoil. The major Mississippian feature, Structure 1, was a large, two-room wall-trench building. One room
was completely enclosed. The other "room" appeared to be a porchlike
extension of the first compartment with one open side, although a line of
single post molds 2 m directly in front of this open side may indicate a
screen. The two rooms enclosed an area of 72 m², unusually large for a
Mississippian domestic dwelling in this region. However, the lack of

definite floor levels and the clear evidence of wall rebuilding make it unclear whether the two rooms were part of a single building (O'Hear et al. 1981:243).

Structure 2, a circular post-mold pattern 5 m in diameter, was uncovered adjacent to Structure 1. While this structure produced a radiocarbon date of A.D. 965 ± 55, one post mold contained a Mississippian sherd. Noting the unreliability of the radiocarbon assays from the site, the excavator suggested that the two structures belonged to the same Mississippian component (O'Hear et al. 1981:245). To the south and west of Structure 1, 13 pit features were excavated. Most were round or basin-shaped holes dug for small-volume storage, but one pit with fired walls served an additional, but unknown, function. Three "smudge pits" were also found.

Eleven Mississippian burials were uncovered. A small cemetery was established a few meters east of Structure 1. In it were five burial pits that contained two adult males and four subadults. An additional grave held a young man with an antler-tine projectile point lodged in the left shoulder. This grave was deeper and larger than the others and crosscut the two rows. After interment the grave had been reopened, and several long bones removed. On the opposite side of the house were placed three individual burials of infants or children under the age of two, separated from the cemetery group.

Both floral and faunal remains were recovered by water-screening through fine mesh, but poor preservation and small sample size limits interpretation. Bone, shell, and lithic artifacts were recovered from feature contexts. The presence of early ceramic attributes such as strap handles with one or two nodes in the middle of the handle and the absence of later types place the component in the Summerville I (Tibbee Creek) phase.

To summarize, the Mississippian component at Tibbee Creek appears to represent a single farmstead with associated features. Although other Mississippian features may have escaped detection because of the limited excavated exposure, the Mississippian component seems to have been quite small, if the minor amounts of Mississippian sherds recovered in surface collections can serve as a guide (O'Hear et al. 1981:17).

Kellogg (22Cl1527). The multicomponent site of Kellogg is located about 1.5 km north of the Tibbee Creek site, directly on the west bank of the Tombigbee River in Clay County, Mississippi (Figure 8). Kellogg shares the same general environmental setting as Tibbee Creek, with easy access to diverse upland, bottomland, and prairie habitats. Like Tibbee Creek, the site is subject to periodic flooding. Situated on a slight

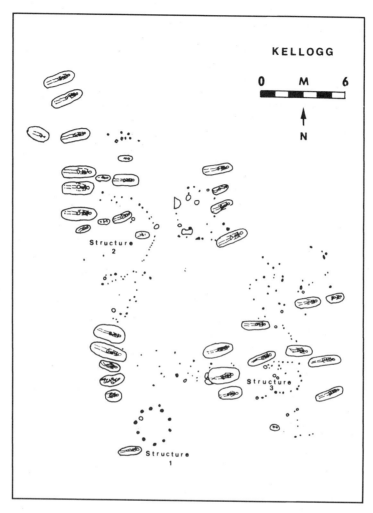

Figure 8 Kellogg: Mississippian Features (Adapted from Atkinson et al. 1980)

rise, Kellogg covers an 80 m × 60 m area. It was first recorded during an initial survey of the Tennessee-Tombigbee Waterway (Rucker 1974). The following year Blakeman (1975) dug three 2 m × 2 m units and found a deep deposit of Archaic through historic period artifacts. Carbonized material from a Mississippi period post mold was radiocarbon dated to A.D. 1195 ± 76, but no structure pattern was uncovered.

Major investigation began in 1978 using two excavation strategies. Two excavation blocks (4 m × 4 m and 4 m × 2 m) were gridded into 1 m units. Materials were recovered by water-screening fill and by hand recovery. A dense midden of mussel shell, lithic debris, animal bone, and sherds, extending to 20 cm below surface, was formed entirely during the Woodland and Mississippian occupations. Beneath this layer was a 25–100 cm deep accumulation of Archaic period artifacts. An area approximately 500 m² was mechanically stripped of the upper midden layer to horizontally expose features (see Figure 8).

Mississippian features were abundant. Post-mold patterns of three distinct structures were revealed. Structure 1 was a tight circle of single-set posts associated with Mississippian ceramics. Only 2.8 m in diameter, the building is very small for a dwelling, but a small, associated fire basin suggests some type of shelter, perhaps a sweat lodge (Atkinson et al. 1980:197). The postholes average 30 cm in diameter, which is quite large. Structure 2, a circular post pattern 5.5 m in diameter, was located 7 m north of Structure 1. Two small pits and three Mississippian adult burials appear to be associated with the house. Seven meters east of Structure 1 was an oval single-set post building 2.25 m in diameter: Structure 3. This small structure was open along one edge, the posts having been obliterated by the grader operation; or, possibly, the structure was open-ended. Post molds were not excavated, making cultural affiliation uncertain, but Mississippian burials and pits clustered closely around it.

Thirty-two Mississippian pit features were distributed around the three structures. Nine features were small smudge pits commonly encountered at Mississippian sites. However, most were small round pits that presumably functioned in some storage or food-processing capacity. A considerable amount of well-preserved floral and faunal remains were screened, floated, or retrieved by hand from these features, and provide data on subsistence activities and site seasonality. Abundant bone, lithic, and ceramic artifacts were recovered from feature contexts. Two radiocarbon dates, A.D. 1185 ± 90 and A.D. 1195 ± 76, complement the relative ceramic chronology and place the Mississippian component in the Summerville I (Tibbee Creek) phase.

Thirty-three Mississippian burials were found at Kellogg. Graves were dug side by side in rows to form four distinct clusters. These were primary interments with most individuals extended in supine position, and the head consistently oriented between due east and east-northeast. Males and females from infancy to 50 years of age were present. Examples of both traumatic injuries and infections or developmental pathologies were few, and the population was healthy (Gilbert 1980:30). Pottery vessels, marine-shell beads and gorgets, greenstone celts, and other items were included as grave goods.

In sum, the Mississippian component at the Kellogg site appears to represent a farmstead or hamlet. While the site is referred to as a village in the excavation report, the distribution of Mississippian features indicates a very small social group. The burials, pit features, and post-mold patterns could easily have been produced by one or two families living at the site at any one time during the 200 year phase interval.

Yarborough (22Cl814). The Yarborough site is located on the left bank of Tibbee Creek in Clay County, Mississippi. It is situated on a natural levee about 4 km upstream from the Tibbee Creek site. Within walking distance of Yarborough, uplands, terraces, valley slopes, prairie, and bottomlands promote diverse plant and animal communities (Gyllenhal-Davis 1982). Cultural debris was concentrated on two small knolls on the highest part of the levee. Periodic inundation had scoured a low area between these two points, and artifact deposits had been subject to erosion and alluvial processes. As a result, only a few cultural features remained intact. Although artifacts from as early as the Early Archaic period were discovered, there were two major occupation episodes. A few pit features and a large sample of Alexander ceramics indicate a small Late Gulf Formational period encampment (ca. 600–100 B.C.), and the remains of a Late Mississippian/protohistoric farmstead were found (Figure 9).

Excavation procedure consisted of profiling the site along the eroded stream bank for 60 m, a series of 2 m × 2 m units, removal of recent alluvium over an 8 m × 7 m area to expose a burned wattle-and-daub structure, and vertical sampling of a 50 cm deep refuse dump directly south of the structure. The burned Late Mississippian structure was a large irregular mass of daub. One half of this structure had been destroyed by heavy machinery at the time the site was cleared. No intact floor surface was detected, and there was ample evidence of fluvial disturbance. A scatter of single-set post molds was present, but the shape of the building could not be determined.

The refuse dump was more informative. A small gully or depression had been used as a disposal area by the Mississippian occupants. Subsequent slumping had protected the dump from major erosion. Large, well-preserved samples of ceramics, floral and faunal remains, and other artifacts were recovered by the water-screening through fine mesh. This feature was the best preserved depositional context at the site and yielded abundant information about the Mississippian subsistence economy (Scott 1982).

The greater portion of the ceramic assemblage conforms to the Summerville IV (Sorrells) phase (A.D. 1450/1500–ca. 1600), and the three radiocarbon dates from the dump average A.D. 1480. However, some

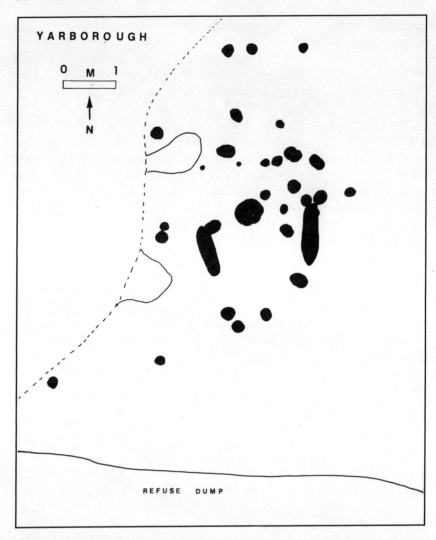

Figure 9   Yarborough: Mississippian Features. Solid black features are post molds and wall trenches; dotted line indicates destroyed portion of structure. (Adapted from Solis and Walling 1982)

Summerville I ceramics were also recovered from the dump, indicating a mixed deposit. Yarborough represents a small habitation site that was occupied, perhaps more than once, as a single-household farmstead.

1Gr2.   Site 1Gr2 is situated on an old alluvial terrace 170 ft (52 m) from the east bank of the Tombigbee River in Greene County, Alabama. An old river meander encloses the site on three sides to isolate an exten-

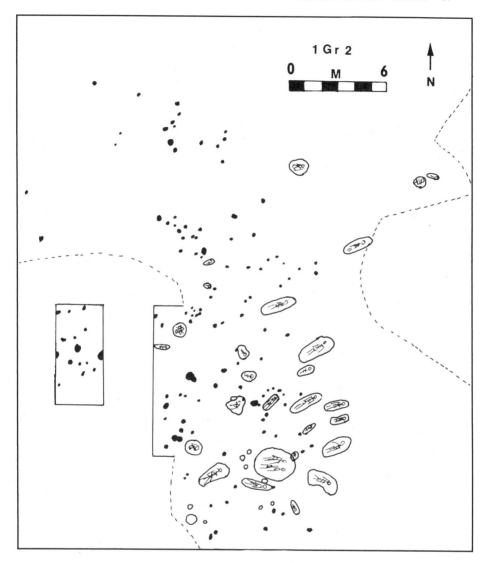

Figure 10 1Gr2: Mississippian Features. Dotted lines demarcate unexcavated areas. (Adapted from Jenkins 1982)

sion of upland forest adjacent to the floodplain. A dark midden 61 m in diameter (3,600 m²) defined the limits of the site. A perennial spring flows from the base of the terrace, which is the highest point of land for three miles along the eastern side of the river. Site 1Gr2 is about 10 miles (16 km) south of the Lubbub Creek site, but by river the distance is approximately 21 miles (33.8 km).

Site 1Gr2 may be the Craig's Landing site recorded by Clarence B. Moore (1901). The site was tested by the University of Alabama in 1972 and 1974. Major excavations in 1976 were conducted in two stages. Ten 10 ft × 10 ft (3.05 m × 3.05 m) excavation units were established to sample the deep deposits. Six well-defined cultural strata demarcated 10 components, and the site stratigraphy played an important role in the establishment of the prehistoric chronological sequence in the central Tombigbee River valley (Jenkins 1982). The thickest layer of midden and shell accumulated during the Late Woodland and Mississippi periods. This layer was mechanically removed over the entire site.

Mississippian features were concentrated within a 36 m × 36 m area in the southeastern quarter of the site (Figure 10). A small cemetery contained 28 burials, although only 24 of these can confidently be assigned to the Mississippian occupation. Remains of males and females from infancy to 50 years of age were exposed. Most were single, primary interments, but three graves with multiple, secondary burials were present. Several interments represent only fragments of individuals, and overall preservation was poor. An oval pattern of post molds approximately 2 m across surrounded a single burial, Burial 17. Burial 17 was an individual whose skull and specific long bones were retrieved after the initial interment, and so perhaps the post molds are from a screen or mortuary facility (Jenkins and Ensor 1981:40).

Numerous other post molds, some of which are undoubtedly attributable to the Mississippian component, were noted but not excavated. No other structure patterns could be defined. Ten smudge pits and three basin-shaped pit features were also excavated. However, the major Mississippian feature was a mass of midden deposited adjacent to the cemetery area. This midden was sampled by the earlier strategy of 10 ft × 10 ft units and produced most of the artifacts and floral and faunal remains from this component.

In short, the Mississippian presence at 1Gr2 consists of a midden deposit, a cemetery, one structure, and evidence of others. The relative ceramic chronology places the occupation within the Summerville II–III phase (A.D. 1200–1450). Since the features cluster into a small area, it seems probable that the social group was correspondingly few in number. Yet the midden deposit and accumulated graves suggest the site was occupied for at least several decades. The site is interpreted as a farmstead of one or two families.

CHAPTER 4

Platform-Mound Excavation at Lubbub Creek

H OW IS IT POSSIBLE to derive evidence from archaeological remains that would reveal a developmental relationship between
management of pooled resources, group ritual, and the emergence of
chiefly authority? Limitations on the ability to model complex cause-and-
effect processes render archaeological data particularly ill suited to identify social relations and individual actors, an important focus in history,
cultural anthropology, and other social sciences (Trigger 1982; Benson
1983). However, it is possible to identify a social context that gave meaning and power to individual actions. Because ritual involves standardized, repetitive activities in a restricted spatial locus, archaeologists can
recover patterned associations of artifacts and features that will identify
this social context (Flannery 1976). The establishment of a specialized
facility, a ceremonial precinct such as a platform mound within a community, is one of the most visible remnants of such processes. A mound,
after all, is objectified ritual.

Sanctified Authority, Group Ritual, and
Mississippian Platform Mounds

If ritual and political spheres of activity are localized in such places,
one might concede that "society's central decision-making organization
should be reflected in the morphology, distribution and functional associations of its public architecture" (Spencer 1982:137). Commenting on
the appearance of public architecture in Formative Mesoamerica, Drennan (1983:48) observes that it may "be related to the increasingly complex
group decision-making structure of sedentary agriculturalists through

the process of *sanctification*, whereby the privileged access of some people to the sacred renders them particularly effective in influencing the behavior of the social group as a whole" (emphasis in original).

Earthen platform mounds were the principal form of public architecture in Mississippian societies. Through extensive archaeological investigations and early historical observations, southeastern archaeologists have gained important insights into uses of Mississippian platform mounds. A detailed examination of these data cannot be considered in this study, but two basic points will be established: (1) mounds were closely identified with the ideology of chiefly authority; and (2) mounds were the focus of ritual activities that sometimes included food disbursement.

Earthen mound construction is ancient in the Southeast. As tumuli, they may have existed as early as Middle to Late Archaic (pre–Poverty Point) in the Lower Mississippi Valley (Gibson and Shenkel 1988), and as raised platforms for ritual activities, they occurred widely in the Middle Woodland period (Mainfort 1986). These early ceremonial platforms remain poorly known. However, distinctive platform mound–and–plaza arrangements first appear around A.D. 700 in the Coles Creek culture of the Lower Mississippi Valley (Williams and Brain 1983), and soon after A.D. 1000 they are a ubiquitous characteristic of Mississippian societies. Coles Creek and Mississippian platform mounds were repeatedly enlarged in a series of construction episodes over a considerable span of time. Each stage typically forms the substructure for buildings. It has been suggested that the placement of Coles Creek structures or residences atop platforms structurally similar to the earlier Woodland prototypes permitted elites to co-opt a sacred symbol to reinforce their authority (Steponaitis 1986:386).

Sixteenth-century Spanish observations of Late Mississippian platform mounds, and eighteenth-century French and English accounts, indicate two basic mound functions: (1) as elite, chiefly residences; and (2) as temple/charnel structures. Sometimes the chief's residence and the temple/charnel structures occupied separate mounds or locations within the community (Swanton 1911:59, 159, 167; Bourne 1973:I:87, II:101). In other cases the two buildings were placed together atop a single mound (Bourne 1973:II:28). This pairing of the two buildings to create a ceremonial precinct may account for the discovery of paired buildings on Mississippian mounds, those at Hiwassee Island being perhaps the best-known examples (Lewis and Kneberg 1946:Plates 15–19). Apparently, chiefs' residences were merely larger versions of the common domestic dwelling. More-detailed comments on temple/charnel structures are available. While southeastern temple/charnel structures and associated ceremonialism exhibit temporal and regional diversity, some fundamental characteristics can be traced back into prehistory.

Platform mounds were central to Mississippian ideology. Mississippian iconography has been related to three ideological themes: (1) chiefly/warrior-cult insignia, notably falcon and weapon symbolism (Brown 1985); (2) an ancestor cult associated with temple/charnel structures (Waring 1968; Brown 1985; Knight 1986); and (3) earth/fertility themes (Waring 1968; Knight 1986; Prentice 1986). These latter two themes are closely associated with platform mounds.

Both historical period and Mississippian mound temple/charnel structures contained, in addition to the dead, wooden or stone statues of ancestor figures (Waring 1968). Sanctified authority based upon genealogical claims promoted an ancestor-oriented component in the belief system. In this sense, temple/charnel structures may have become shrines for descent groups (Brown 1985).

It has long been recognized that temples, shrines, and ceremonial centers may represent a world symbol, an *axis mundi* (Eliade 1959). In these places the community may symbolically assure the cyclic renewal of both the natural world and the continuity of cultural traditions (Eliade 1959; Wheatley 1971). Backed by ethnohistoric data, Knight (1986:678) interprets Mississippian mounds as symbols of the earth, the periodic addition of earthen stages being a cycle of world renewal that functions to cover older "polluted" surfaces in a "communal rite of intensification."

The earth/fertility theme is further reinforced by the historical connection between intensified maize cultivation and mound ceremonialism. Mississippian mound construction episodes have long been considered antecedent to the annual "busk" or green corn ceremonialism in the Southeast (Swanton 1928). The historic busk ceremony revolved around the rekindling of the sacred fire and a communal feast of the new corn (Howard 1968). Waring (1968:54–58) tried to demonstrate that compound structure patterns discovered atop Mississippian platform mounds were a prototype of the Muskogean square-ground. He argued that the annual refurbishing of the square-ground was a historical transformation of earlier mound construction episodes.

Another interpretation links the periodic addition of mound construction stages and succession to chiefly office or some equivalent change in community or kin-group status (Waring 1968; Swanton 1911; Krause 1987; Hally 1987; Anderson 1989). Like the basic elements of the historical busk (new fire, new corn), the death and replacement of a chief represents a transitional crisis in community continuity, a crisis that may demand that the mound as earth, temple, and shrine be renewed.

In the historical Southeast, temple/charnel structures were the scene of food disbursement activities. Feasts were a central focus of eighteenth-century Choctaw mortuary ceremonialism (Halbert 1900; Swanton 1931), the best documented example. These feasts were of two types, which anthropologists classify as critical and calendrical ceremonies (Titiev 1960). The first was a funeral feast among the deceased's relatives upon the placement of the deceased's bones, bundled within a cane casket, into the local temple/charnel structure, or "bone house." In some accounts members of the opposite moiety also participated. The second type of mortuary feast was a large-scale semiannual or annual ceremony (accounts differ on the schedule) in which the multiple kin groups that composed the two moieties ate, to honor the dead, in the presence of the cane caskets at bone houses (Bossu [1768], Milfort [1802], and Cushman [1899], cited in Swanton 1931).

An important study by Seeman (1979) links mortuary ceremonialism to redistribution in the Eastern Woodlands. Seeman noted the common occurrence of faunal remains, especially deer bone, together with pot-sherds in association with Ohio Hopewell charnel-house mounds. He advanced a functional interpretation of historical southeastern charnel-house ceremonialism, in particular the detailed information available for the Choctaw, as an analog to Ohio Hopewell charnel-house practices. The principal food consumed at these feasts was meat. Seeman (1979:45) proposes that in the Eastern Woodlands "meat was the critical resource," even more than cultigens subject to short-term fluctuations, and that the frequent charnel-house feasts "provided a means of equalizing the effects of local surpluses and scarcities of this key resource."

Seeman's hypothesis can be placed within the developmental context of maize production intensification in the Mississippian subsistence economy. The greater investment of energy, labor, and time that presumably accompanied maize horticulture would place a premium on the most efficient possible manner of hunting deer (Seeman 1979:45–46). Archaeologically, this might be manifested in evidence for intensive seasonal hunts, patterns of the sort that have been identified in the Tombigbee faunal data (Scott 1983).

Whether one interprets such an intensive shift as the inevitable result of the inability to diversify resulting from population-resource imbalances or as a logistical necessity to accommodate a new mode of production, intensification of deer hunting and the pooling of meat would have had advantages. Furthermore, the historical southeastern subsistence cycle of small-game hunting and fishing in the local vicinity of the farmstead maize fields in the warm months, and intensive group hunts in the cold months, may reflect this pattern. I hasten to add, on a cautionary note, that historical patterns of hunting were also affected by Euro-American market forces (Hudson 1976).

If intensification of maize production fostered new patterns of labor cooperation such as intensive seasonal hunts, perhaps the pooling of meat and other critical resources at the local center was mediated through group ritual. Through such a process, feasts in and around a special facility situated upon a platform mound may have become a common form of Mississippian community organization. Not only would these activities establish a social context in which pooled surpluses and group ritual could stimulate the amplification of sanctified authority, but, most importantly for archaeologists, it would create an identifiable location where evidence of such activities could be recovered.

If the establishment of platform mounds provided a social context for the ideological legitimization of leadership, in a ritual format based upon the management of pooled resources, then testable expectations about mound activities and their physical evidence can be summarized as follows:

1. If the mound were the location of food-pooling activities, then artifacts, ecofacts, and architectural features should be present that can be linked to feasting and storage. Such evidence might include contrasting patterns between mound and village food remains, vessel size and function, and post molds of storage facilities.
2. If the mound were the location of ritual activities, then nonutilitarian artifacts of ritual paraphernalia or costume, and unique architectural features associated with the sacred fire and temple layout, should be present.
3. If the mound were the location of institutionalized activities, then architectural arrangements should be patterned, repetitive, and extend over a time span longer than a single generation.

Evidence for a developmental relationship among feasting, group ritual, and the emergence of sanctified authority was uncovered at the Lubbub Creek site through excavation of the community's earthen platform mound. Originally the mound was a square, flat-topped platform 40 m at the base and 3.35 m tall. Unfortunately, the upper portion of the mound could not be directly investigated because it had been bulldozed away in the 1950s. Despite this destruction, our excavations determined the sequence of construction, secured material remains with which to reconstruct mound-related activities, and documented the initiation of a ceremonial zone on the premound surface around A.D. 1000, at the very beginning of the Mississippian community (Blitz 1983b). Before proceeding to a broader interpretation, it is necessary to describe the premound buildings, features, and mound construction stages, and to summarize their sequence of development.

Mound Excavation

At the turn of the twentieth century Clarence B. Moore conducted an archaeological exploration of the Tombigbee River in his steamboat, the *Gopher.* He visited the "mound at Summerville," dug a few shallow pits, found "here and there fireplaces and refuse material," and concluded that the mound was "a living site and a place of refuge" (Moore 1901:504–505). The mound did not again attract the attention of archaeologists until the 1970s when the University of Alabama conducted surveys of the area as part of the Tennessee-Tombigbee Waterway project. The mound was named the Summerville Mound and given a site number, 1Pi85. Because at the time of our investigation only the general location of the mound was known, the excavation was undertaken in three distinct stages: (1) test trenches were cut to define the extent of the in situ deposit; (2) the plowzone was stripped and the mound dimensions were mapped; and (3) the premound surface was extensively excavated.

The plowzone was removed from a 3,475 m^2 area over the low mound. What remained of the mound foundation was composed of alternating zones of clay and sand. This surface represented the cleavage plane from which the bulldozer had sliced away the upper portion of the mound in the 1950s. It revealed the mound construction stages in a manner similar to concentric growth rings exposed when a tree is cut (Figure 11). These remnant stages showed that the Summerville Mound was a platform with sides of roughly equal length that formed a square base with sharp, angular corners. The dimensions at the base of the final construction stage were 39 m × 40 m.

Three distinct episodes could be seen in the horizontal plan. In each episode sand fill was used to increase the height and breadth of the mound, and heavy clay was used as the stable surface foundation for buildings. Two ramps provided access to the summit. The bulldozer had truncated the mound at the surface of the first construction episode, destroying all above this juncture.

Test-trench profiles revealed that the intact base of the mound covered the old ground surface to a depth of 60–100 cm. We hoped that a careful examination of the premound surface might provide an insight into the initiation of mound use at Lubbub Creek. A bright yellow clay,

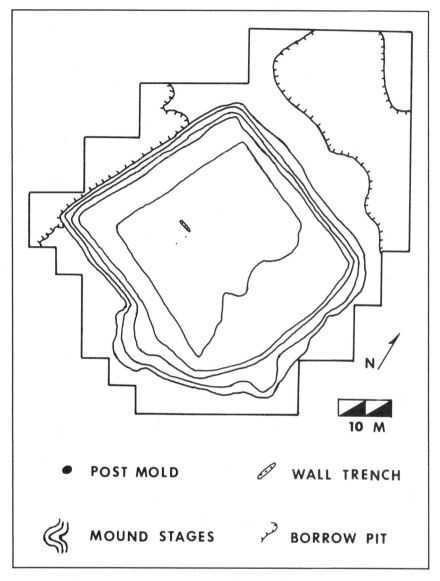

● POST MOLD   ✍ WALL TRENCH

〰 MOUND STAGES   ↗ BORROW PIT

Figure 11   Intact Mound Remnant Beneath Plowzone

designated Zone O, was encountered at 50 cm below the plane of bull-dozer cleavage. Zone O proved to be a rectangular clay platform that capped a series of structure features. These features were a complex sequence of six superimposed structures or buildings, which had been erected on the original ground surface prior to the construction of the mound (Figures 12 and 13). An area of 650 m^2 was exposed on this

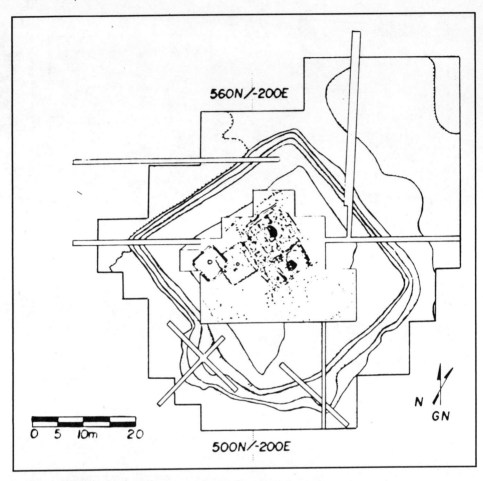

Figure 12   Superimposed Features on Premound Surface

premound zone. Superposition and intersection of wall trenches and other features, together with a single radiocarbon date and associated ceramics, permitted us to place the sequence of premound structures and subsequent mound construction stages in their relative chronological order.

The two earliest structures constructed on the premound surface were Structures 4 and 3 (Figure 14). Structure 4 was a small circular cluster of post molds 3.5 m in diameter. The very small size and lack of hearth or floor staining suggest a nonresidential function, such as a storage facility, but there is no direct evidence to support such an interpretation. Structure 3 was a rectangular structure 6.5 m × 4 m with deep, closely set post molds and a prepared clay floor. The Structure 3 post-

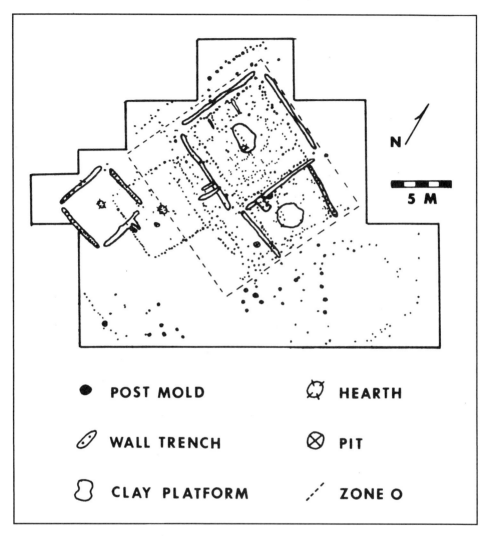

POST MOLD   HEARTH

WALL TRENCH   PIT

CLAY PLATFORM   ZONE O

Figure 13   Sequence of Structures on Premound Surface

mold pattern could not be completely traced because it had been destroyed by subsequent building activity. No diagnostic artifacts were found associated with either structure, and most of the surface was remarkably devoid of artifacts. Structure 3 post molds occurred nearly 10 cm higher than those of Structure 4, a possible indicator that the two buildings were not contemporary, but truncation by later activities is just as plausible. The only other features were two shallow pits that appeared to be contemporary with Structure 4. They contained charred corncobs and wood charcoal. A sample from one was radiocarbon dated to A.D.

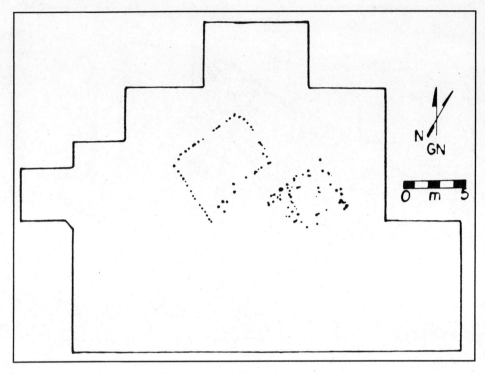

Figure 14   Structure 4 and Structure 3 on Premound Surface

970 ± 90. These structures represent the initiation of a more elaborate architecture that marked the Late Woodland to Mississippian transition.

Soon after the abandonment of Structures 3 and 4, two wall-trench buildings, Structures 2 and 5A, were erected (Figure 15). The smaller building, Structure 2, was a square pattern of four deep trenches that defined a floor area of 30 m². There was a small circular clay hearth near the center. The other wall-trench structure, Structure 5A, was a large rectangular building with two compartments. The largest was a 9 m × 9 m square formed by four wall trenches with open corners. These wall trenches were as much as 60 cm deep. Two other trenches formed a second compartment or portico with one open side. The total length of this building was 13.6 m. In the center of the larger compartment was a circular depression, probably a hearth, filled with ash and fired clay.

Structures 2 and 5A were probably contemporary, since both occurred at the same elevation, displayed the wall-trench construction technique, and obviously postdated Structures 3 and 4 but predated Structures 1 and 5B. Both the small and large wall-trench structures were intentionally razed, and all debris completely removed from the entire

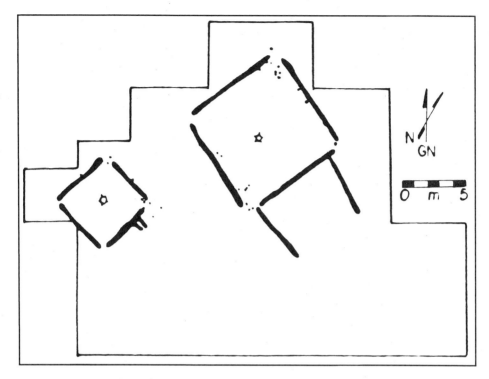

Figure 15 Structure 2 and Structure 5A on Premound Surface

area. Small bits of fired daub that escaped this clearing operation indicate the possibility that the buildings burned. After these structures were destroyed two new structures were erected over the remains of the earlier buildings. Like the earlier buildings, there was one smaller, square structure—Structure 1—and one larger, rectangular building with two compartments—Structure 5B—but this time they were constructed of single-set posts (Figure 16).

Structure 1 was a square pattern that enclosed 36 m² of floor space. Two parallel wall trenches formed a narrow vestibule entranceway 2 m long. There was a central clay hearth and a mass of clay packed against the outside walls. Perhaps this clay feature functioned as a clean, elevated platform or bench for social activities. This outside benchlike feature had the architectural effect of insulating the structure foundation and creating a sunken floor area.

Structure 5B was a long building constructed directly over the earlier wall-trench structure (Figure 17). One difference between them was that instead of the second compartment's remaining open on one side like a portico, here it was closed off to make two rooms. This structure was

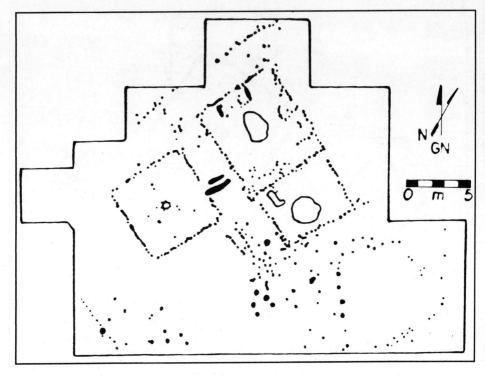

Figure 16   Structure 1 and Structure 5B on Premound Surface

14.1 m long and enclosed an area of about 81.7 m². A large raised clay platform dominated the center of each room. The platforms had been intensely heated to a bricklike consistency and probably served as raised hearths. Another feature, located against the interior wall, was a raised platform of packed, unfired clay of a type sometimes referred to as a "seat" by archaeologists but that probably served as a step up to an opening into the other room. Perpendicular to the northern wall was a pattern of two small wall trenches and several post molds at the upper end of the building. This feature may represent a third small compartment or some kind of substantial furniture.

Although both of the buildings were sparse in artifacts, the presence of Moundville Incised *var. Moundville* sherds indicates use during Summerville I (A.D. 1000–1200), the initial Mississippian phase. Structures 1 and 5B were the last buildings constructed on the premound level. Both appear to be contemporary with each other. These final two buildings were razed, just as Structures 2 and 5A had been before. Once again most debris was removed, but potsherds, ash, and faunal remains formed small sheets of midden around the perimeter of the structures. A

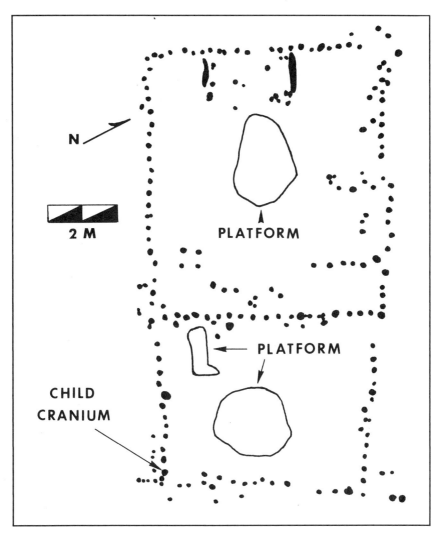

Figure 17 Structure 5B

number of post molds in the premound precinct could not be assigned to a specific sequence of buildings. Some post molds clustered together in a manner that may have resulted from screens, racks, or elevated storage facilities (see Figure 16). Unfortunately, they formed no clearly discernible patterns, and it was not possible to determine their function.

After the destruction of these last buildings a layer of yellow clay was packed down upon the newly cleaned surface, forming a rectangular platform that covered all of the Structure 5B and part of the Structure 1 post-mold pattern. This platform, Zone O, initiated the first stage of mound construction (Figure 18). Zone O was not exposed for very long before being covered by Zones L and M, because Zone O showed no evidence of erosion or any indication that it had functioned as a foundation for buildings. Instead, Zone O was quickly covered by Zone M, which supported a wall-trench structure upon its summit. The configuration of this structure could not be determined, for it was at this surface that the bulldozer cleaved away the upper portion of the mound and redeposited it into the adjacent borrow pit from which earth used to construct the mound had originally been procured. The presence of large amounts of fired daub suggests that the Zone M building may have burned.

With the termination of occupation on Zone M, the mound was again increased in size with the application of sand fill, Zone K. The lack of erosion in Zone K indicated that it was rapidly constructed and capped over with the clay stage, Zone J. Not surprisingly, Zone K was nearly devoid of cultural material because this stage merely served to increase the mound dimensions. However, a 1 m^3 sample of Zone J produced a large amount of Summerville II–III phase sherds. This material was concentrated on the western side of the mound parallel to the borrow pit. The mound stood at this height for some time, and presumably it supported an important building. Next the mound was expanded once more with the addition of sand fill, Zone I, and a final clay construction stage, Zone H. The artifact content of Zone I was negligible, but Zone H contained abundant Summerville II–III phase ceramics. It was also in this final configuration that we found evidence for one and probably two mound ramps. From each mound zone a measured volume of soil was water-screened to recover a sample of artifacts.

Sometime after the completion of the final stage, a large quantity of debris—sherds, mussel shell, animal bones, and ash—was deposited in the apex of an angle formed by the south ramp and the south edge of the mound. This material was apparently dumped from the mound summit, since an approach from the direction of the village would have been prevented by the open borrow pit.

Patterned Continuities in Mound Architecture

The premound complex of structures represents the establishment of a special-activity precinct centrally located within the community, yet spatially demarcated and architecturally distinct from it. The premound structures were continually rebuilt, renovated, and enlarged in place over many years. There is a striking regularity in architectural orienta-

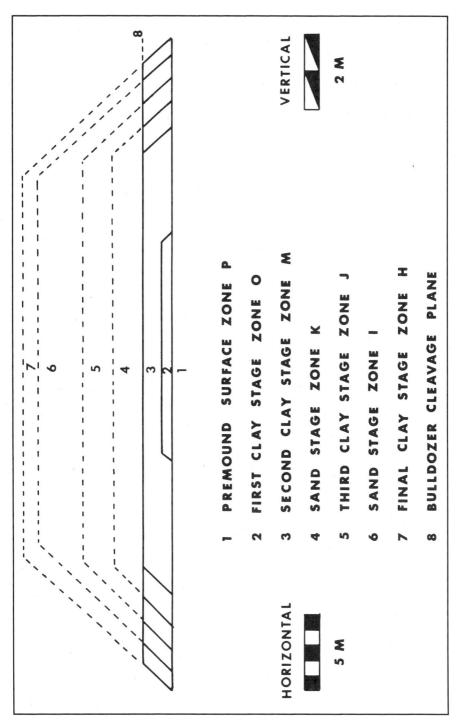

HORIZONTAL

5 M

VERTICAL

2 M

1   PREMOUND SURFACE ZONE P

2   FIRST CLAY STAGE ZONE O

3   SECOND CLAY STAGE ZONE M

4   SAND STAGE ZONE K

5   THIRD CLAY STAGE ZONE J

6   SAND STAGE ZONE I

7   FINAL CLAY STAGE ZONE H

8   BULLDOZER CLEAVAGE PLANE

Figure 18 Major Remnant and Reconstructed Mound-Building Stages of the Summerville Mound, 1Pi85. Zone L is included as part of Zone K.

tion. With the exception of Structure 4, all premound structures were rectangles with the long axis oriented about 26 degrees south of true east. Later, when the premound zone served as the surface for initial mound construction, each new and larger construction stage retained this orientation. Mound ceramic samples indicate construction spanned several centuries. This expansion can be compared to a series of nested boxes.

This creation of a ritual space became the focal point around which a community formed. The separateness of the premound structures from the residential part of the community was emphasized by a line of post molds that surrounded the perimeter of the premound zone and maintained the same orientation as the buildings. This partition or fence formed an enclosed compound. Furthermore, the orientation of the premound compound and initial mound stages was replicated in the layout of a series of palisade lines that represent several sequential episodes of construction. Unlike the defensive bastioned palisade 200 m west of the mound, only one of the other four palisade lines (the inner palisades) had an obvious bastion, so perhaps their purpose was to demarcate symbolically a special social space. Therefore during the Summerville I phase an inner palisade line (rebuilt several times) enclosed a fenced-off premound compound.

The premound structures are different in size and form when compared to the domestic dwellings. The initiation of the premound precinct begins with a slightly more elaborate version of a domestic dwelling, Structure 3. Structure 4 may be contemporary or slightly earlier. The next two building sequences (Structures 2 and 5A, Structures 1 and 5B) represent paired contemporaneous buildings. The smaller structures appear to be more substantially built versions of domestic dwellings, but the adjacent large buildings are clearly specialized structures. The paired building arrangements span what must be at least several decades at the beginning of the Mississippian occupation.

This creation of a ceremonial precinct on the premound surface provides support for the theme of world renewal that some scholars have associated with mound ceremonialism. There were no structures built upon the surface of Zone O, the first construction stage. This implies that the primary symbolic function of this initial stage of mound construction was to cover a previous "polluted" surface, rather than serve as a foundation for an important building.

What social processes produced this architectural pattern? Perhaps an influential individual sponsored and maintained a ceremonial precinct that became the ritual focus for a number of surrounding households. Such an authority figure could have stimulated kinsmen and others to produce surpluses to be consumed in ceremonial feasts over which the individual presided as host. The sequence from the initial pair (Structures 3 and 4) to the paired Structures 2 and 5A could be interpreted as the transformation of a domestic household into a specialized ritual facility. Alternatively, the facilities may have been established by a descent group or other corporate unit that then either promoted a member (or through which a member promoted himself) to a formal role in the associated activities.

While I see no way to establish which of these scenarios led to the observed architectural layout, I propose that an individual or individuals associated with the smaller structure had a central role in the activities that took place in the larger building; the physical proximity of the smaller structure to the large ceremonial building may have had the symbolic effect of utilizing the sacred to legitimate a position of authority; and the continuity of architecture indicates that these activities and, perhaps, the roles associated with them became formalized and institutionalized through time. This patterned, repetitive architectural arrangement was not idiosyncratic or temporary but clearly transcended the influence or lifetime of a single individual. If the continuity of the paired structures and construction episodes over time does indicate the institutionalization of mound activities and the social roles associated with them, what were these activities?

The architectural and spatial layout alone does not provide sufficient information. It is necessary to reconstruct mound-related activities through analysis of associated artifacts. If the mound zone was the location of specialized activities, then some material correlates should survive. Further, the artifact pattern at the mound should differ from that of artifacts recovered in other community or domestic contexts. Only through comparison of artifact variability in different community contexts can the broader social implications be perceived.

Evidence of Mound Activities: Artifacts, Ecofacts, and Features

Artifacts recovered from the mound did not appear on initial inspection to differ remarkably from materials found in the village domestic refuse. Still, there is evidence to connect some of these items to the themes of ritual and feasting. The most abundant items were potsherds and animal bone. Lithic debris and artifacts, never abundant in Summerville domestic contexts (Allan 1983), are even less plentiful and diverse in mound contexts. The few lithic artifacts included a number of tools: two shaft drills; a single microdrill (< 3 cm long); one bifaced perforator/graver; and several unretouched Madison arrow points that were deposited prior to any use that would necessitate resharpening. The minute amount of debitage recovered from structure floors indicates that very occasional tool maintenance (but not production) occurred at the mound. Of three whole and 12 broken greenstone celts recovered at Lubbub Creek, the largest (14.4 cm) was found in the mound fill, together with four celt fragments.

Several artifacts imply special-purpose items that might be consistent with a ritual format. The only lithic materials unique to the mound were unmodified mica (muscovite) fragments associated with Structure 5A. A nonlocal resource, mica is probably an element of costume or ornamentation. A ground sandstone disk fragment was found on the floor of Structure 5B. The edge of this disk is notched and incised with concentric circles. The only other disk fragments came from Structure 7 in the village. Ground sandstone disks with notches, circles, and Southeastern Ceremonial Complex motifs have been found most often at Moundville, the probable source of their regional dispersal, either in mounds or burials (Webb and DeJarnette 1942:287–291). Specimens have been recovered with traces of pigment, thus the interpretation that they are "palettes" (Walthall 1980).

Numerous large lumps of chalk, hematite, limonite, and breccia capable of producing white, red, and yellow pigments were present. Although the size and density of these mineral lumps found at the mound were exceptional, they were commonly encountered in village contexts as well. In short, while the mica, the stone disk fragment, and pigments may indicate ritual paraphernalia, only the tiny scrap of mica was unique to the mound context. In addition, an awllike implement made from the ulna of a bobcat *(Lynx rufus)* recovered from the mound was a unique item found nowhere else on the site.

Faunal remains, analyzed by Susan Scott (1983), are perhaps more revealing about mound activities than the limited number of lithic artifacts. Bones of several bird species were unique to the mound: Carolina parakeet *(Conuropsis carolinensis);* cardinal *(Cardinalis cardinalis);* bluejay *(Cyanocitta cristata);* crow *(Corvus brachyrhynchos);* mockingbird/brown thrasher *(Mimidae);* and a merlin *(Falco columbarius).* Rather than being food items, these remains are most likely parts of costume or ritual paraphernalia. Interestingly, the French observers mention bird symbolism in connection with Natchez and Taensa temples: carved wooden birds affixed to the roof and stuffed birds around the "altar" (Swanton 1911:164).

Scott notes that the colors red, white, black, and blue represented in the birds' plumage symbolized the cardinal directions in a pervasive historical southeastern cosmology, and goes on to observe:

Remains of a crow were recovered from the sand fill of the fourth building stage (USN 4534). Blitz interprets the layers of sand fill as building stages, with superimposed clay strata lending stability to the final shape of the mound and serving as the surface upon which structures were erected. Among the Choctaw, "crow feathers indicated mourning and were the only ones that could be put on when there had been a death in the family. It was principally the chiefs who used them, however, the others confining themselves to black cloth" (Swanton 1931:44). The inclusion of this species in the sand fill suggests a possible impetus for the periodic accretion of the mound [Scott 1983:349–350].

Scott's symbolic interpretations can be expanded further. Several of the bird species played central mythological roles in the Southeast. The falcon was a widespread southeastern symbol of chiefly authority and military prowess (Hudson 1976:129; Brown 1985:140). Carolina parakeet remains have been recovered from unusual depositional contexts at various prehistoric Eastern Woodlands sites and connected to ritual paraphernalia associated with smoking (Gernet and Timmins 1987).

The cardinal remains are also of interest. According to La Page du Pratz, "they said that a great rain fell on the earth so abundantly and during such a long time that it was completely covered except a very high mountain where some men saved themselves; that all fire being extinguished on the earth a little bird named *couy-ouy*, which is entirely red (it is called in Louisiana the cardinal bird), brought it from heaven. I understood by that that they had forgotten almost all the history of the deluge, etc." (Swanton 1911:177). Themes of fire-bringer and the perpetuation of fire on earth revealed in the Natchez myth find a possible material referent in the unique association of cardinal remains with pre-mound structures that contain large raised hearths suitable for sacred fires.

Food consumption is also implicated in the faunal remains. Scott compared faunal samples between mound and village contexts. By bone weight, large mammals (principally deer) dominate both mound and village samples. However, deer mandibles, hind limbs, and especially forelimb skeletal elements were overrepresented in the mound debris. Similar overrepresentations in the distributions of deer skeletal elements have been interpreted as differential access by an elite at other Mississippian sites (e.g., Bogan 1980; Belmont 1983; Cleland 1965; Penman 1983; Rudolph 1984). Because observed differences between mound and village samples were not great, and bone fragmentation presented comparative problems, Scott (1983:356–357) advised caution in interpreting this pattern as evidence of preferential high-status access to choice cuts of venison. The only other important difference in the two faunal samples was the much higher relative frequency of fish (particularly catfish) and turtles in the mound sample. Clearly, differences in the social context of food consumption are indicated in the mound and village samples, but it cannot be assumed that access was restricted to an elite. Finally, almost half of the mouse or rat bones recovered at Lubbub Creek came from the mound. Perhaps this concentration is "a subtle indication of the location of village stores" (Scott 1983:356).

Two elements of historical southeastern mound ceremonialism expected to leave some physical evidence, if present in this early period, are (1) the eternal fire; and (2) placement of the disarticulated bones of deceased chiefs or other members of the descent group into baskets or wooden containers, deposited upon a small "altar" within a compartment inside the temple/charnel structure.

Reference to both may be found in a description, by La Page du Pratz, of the interior details of a Natchez temple/charnel house situated on top of a mound:

> The interior of this temple is divided into unequal parts by a little wall which cuts it from the rising to the setting sun. The part into which one enters may be 20 feet wide and the other may be 10, but in this second part it is extremely gloomy, because there is only one opening, which is the door of the temple itself, which is to the north, and because the little communicating door is not capable of lighting the second part.
>
> There is nothing remarkable in the inside of the temple except a table or altar about 4 feet high and 6 long by 2 broad. On this table is a coffer made of cane splints very well worked, in which are the bones of the last great Sun. The eternal fire is in this first part of the temple. In the other and more secluded part nothing can be distinguished except two planks worked by hand on which are many minute carvings *(plusiers minutes)* which one is unable to make out, owing to the insufficient light [Swanton 1911:162].

There are architectural elements in the Lubbub premound buildings that correspond to a remarkable degree with La Page's description: internal subdivision; raised hearth platforms as would be expected for an eternal fire; interior post-mold pattern at the northern end of Structure 5B that duplicates the "altar" for the bone caskets; and an interior clay step in Structure 5B that possibly marks the location of the "little communicating door."

The only human burial found in the mound area was the cranium of a one- to two-year-old child placed in a small pit or posthole within the foundation of Structure 5B without any accompanying artifacts (see Figure 17). The placement within the wall alignment suggests a dedicatory sacrifice. Infant and child crania, apparently intended as ritual accompaniments, have been found in other mound contexts at Moundville and at Seven Mile Island, a Moundville variant site in the middle Tennessee River valley (Peebles 1971; Webb and DeJarnette 1942).

A connection between infant sacrifice and the cycle of mound/temple construction is established historically through a strange incident witnessed by Iberville. Iberville was present in 1700 among the Taensa when lightning set their temple afire. "These savages, to appease the Spirit, who they said was angry, threw five little children into the fire of the temple. . . . An old man of about 65 years, who appeared to be the principal priest, was near the fire, crying in a loud voice: 'Women, bring your children to sacrifice them to the Spirit in order to appease him.' . . . The action of these women was regarded by them as one of the finest one could make" (Swanton 1911:266–267).

No associated multiple, disarticulated human remains were located that would support an interpretation that the premound structures had a charnel function, but it is possible that, if bone baskets were once present, they were ultimately removed elsewhere with new construction episodes. Mortuary evidence that suggests such a scenario was found in two different interments adjacent to the mound. A deposit of disarticulated, stacked bundles of bones (Burial 9, USN 7840), referred to as an ossuary (Figure 19), contained portions of 37 adults, three infants, two children, and one adolescent (Powell 1983:460). These stacked bundles had the appearance of having been placed in some perishable containers or bound together, but no remains of these were found. The second interment (Burial 5, USN 6310) was a cache of stacked adult calvaria (top portions of crania) placed over the disarticulated bundled remains of an adult female who in turn was placed atop the calvarium of a child (Figure 20).

A direct historical analogy provides insight into this pattern. The physical remains were analyzed by Mary Powell (1983) who calls attention to parallels between these burials and the elaborate mortuary program of the eighteenth-century Choctaws. As related in the definitive compilation by Swanton (1931), the Choctaw mortuary program included temporary scaffolding, defleshing and bundling of the bones, funeral feasts involving representatives of opposite moieties, and conveyance of the bones within a basketry or wooden container to a temple/charnel structure (the word *Tombigbee* is a corruption of the Choctaw *itombi*, "box" or "coffin," and *ikbi*, "makers" [Byington 1915]). Under circumstances not entirely clear in the early accounts, the bone containers were periodically removed from the charnel house and buried

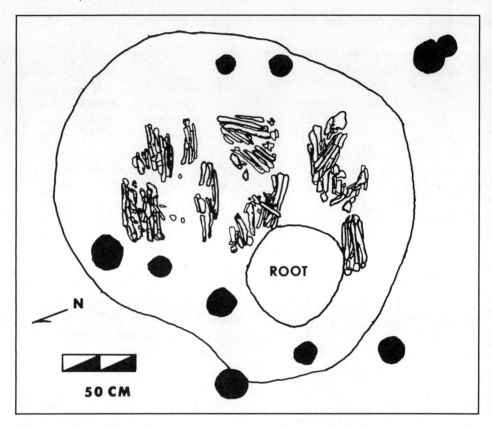

Figure 19   Ossuary Deposit of Stacked Bundles of Disarticulated Human Bone (Adapted from Albright 1983)

together. Powell suggests that the two mass burials are the final stage of a similar mortuary program.

Ceramic Variability as a Measure of Mound-Related Activities

If the mound were the location of specialized activities—feasts or storage—then the mound and village pottery samples might be expected to vary in an informative way. In order to explore this possibility, the total sherd sample from Lubbub Creek was subdivided into a mound sample (N = 5,992) and village sample (N = 50,152) for comparative purposes. Two characteristics of the ceramic assemblage were considered to be the most sensitive indicators of use-related activities: serving, cooking, and storage distinctions; and vessel size.

In ethnographic examples of small-scale kin-based societies a com-

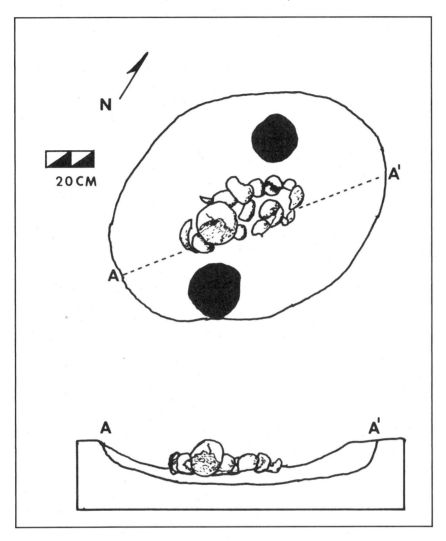

Figure 20 Cache of Human Calvaria

mon responsibility of community leaders is to supervise the pooling of food and to host large-group feasts that are the principal setting for ritual and political activities. Differences in the ratios of serving, cooking, and storage vessels at various community locations might indicate an emphasis on such activities (Drennan 1976). The serving, cooking, and storage distinctions in the Lubbub Creek pottery can be identified by coarse-ware/fineware categories and by vessel shape.

Two basic ware categories are defined by a coarse-temper/fine-temper dichotomy in paste composition and by a burnished/unburnished distinction in surface treatment. Technological studies indicate coarse shell temper is resistant to thermal shock, whereas fine shell temper facilitates production of thin, durable walls in various shapes (Steponaitis 1983:33–45). In addition, coarse shell temper highly correlates with unburnished ware, and fine shell temper highly correlates with burnished ware. The burnished category used in this case also includes a dark surface treatment (black-filmed) that is the result of smudging and reduction during firing. Because the black-filmed surface is destroyed when exposed to fire, it is unlikely this ware was used for cooking (Steponaitis 1983:33). Based on these observations, the ratio of burnished to unburnished sherds should provide a measure of serving/cooking activities. If the mound were the scene of feasting, then it was expected that a greater proportion of fine serving ware would be discarded there than in more-mundane domestic contexts elsewhere in the community.

Vessel-shape classes provide further functional clues (see Appendix, Figure 52). Recent southeastern studies provide a basis for inferring functional uses from vessel shape. Following the morphological and use-wear criteria outlined by Steponaitis (1983) and Hally (1986), bottles and flaring-rim bowls are considered to have predominantly a serving function, standard jars a cooking or storage function, and simple bowls a cooking or serving function.

When the ceramic sample was divided into burnished and unburnished categories that reflect the serving/cooking distinction and compared between mound and village contexts, it was discovered that, although the mound has a slightly higher proportion of serving-ware, as expected, this difference is not very dramatic (mound = 0.08; village = 0.06). Similarly, when a chi-squared test was conducted to determine whether the four major vessel-shape classes—standard jar, bottle, flaring-rim bowl, and simple bowl—are independently distributed across mound and village samples, no important difference in the distribution of vessel shapes was revealed ($x^2 = 4.77$; $df = 3$; not significant at .05 level). The composition of mound and village ceramic assemblages is similar. Ratios of ware categories and vessel shapes vary little throughout the community wherever serving, cooking, and storage activities took place.

Given that mound and village ceramic samples share a similar composition of vessel shapes, ware categories, and decoration, vessel size might be more informative about mound activities. Differences in vessel size may be more directly related to the volume of food prepared and served, and, by implication, the size of the serviced social group; and the variety of food-processing tasks.

Presumably, the greater volume of food consumed by a large group will necessitate larger cooking and serving vessels than required for a smaller group of people (Turner and Lofgren 1966). Of course, it is also possible that the needs of large-group food consumption could be met merely with more vessels, rather than larger vessels. There are ethnoarchaeological studies that have discovered a weak but positive correlation between vessel size and social group (household) size (e.g., Nelson 1981).

The variety of food-processing tasks is also expected to influence vessel-size ranges. Ethnographic observations have noted the correlation between the diversity of food preparation and other household activities that involve pottery and the use of different vessel sizes (Nelson 1981, 1985). These needs are met in the manufacture of various sizes within each shape class, frequently designated by specific names (DeBoer and Lathrap 1979). If these observations were generally applicable, domestic contexts would be expected to represent the most diverse set of activities and thus have the greatest range of sizes. Specialized contexts, with a limited set of activities, would be expected to have a more restricted range of sizes. These observations are not offered as universal principles. This is an empirical question to be examined anew in each case. If differential distributions of vessel size occurred, then it would be a justified inference (when supported by parallel lines of evidence such as faunal remains) to conclude that the social context of food consumption had shaped this distribution.

If the mound were a special-activity location of large-group food consumption and if the village ceramic sample primarily reflected small-group household use, then a higher relative frequency of large vessels would be expected in mound contexts when compared to village contexts; and there should be a correspondingly narrower size range in the mound sample than in the village sample. In order to evaluate these expectations, the first step was to gather information on vessel size.

Because the ceramic data consist almost entirely of sherds, orifice diameter was used as an indirect estimate of vessel size. In testing this assumption, correlation coefficients revealed a positive relationship between orifice diameter and vessel height for a sample of 17 complete standard (globular) jars and 10 complete simple bowls from Moundville.

Orifice diameter and height relationships for other bowl forms were not tested with whole vessels; however, it is expected that orifice diameter can be used as an indirect measure of vessel size for these forms as well, because orifice diameter and height relationships (also orifice diameter and maximum diameter relationships [Nelson 1985:313–314]) are a function of the relatively simple geometric forms represented. This

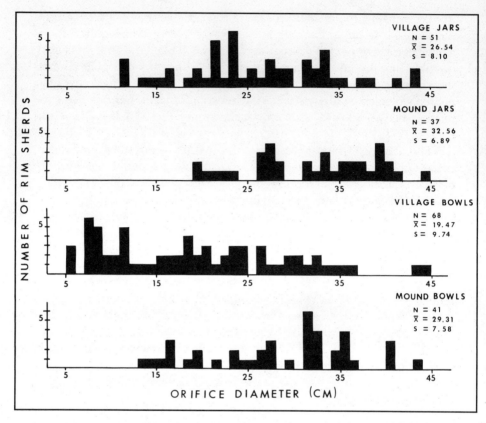

Figure 21   Size-Frequency Histograms of Mound and Village Jars and Bowls

orifice-height relationship would not be expected to hold for the highly restricted orifices of bottle forms, and, as few bottle rim sherds of a measurable size were recovered, this vessel-shape class was excluded from the samples.

For each rim sherd sufficiently large to determine vessel shape, orifice diameter was measured by matching the curvature of the rim arc with a series of concentric circles separated by 1 cm increments. Generally, it was discovered that small sherds with an arc of less than about 10 degrees could not be as precisely measured on the template as could larger sherds, and were excluded. Because of the fact that function can be attributed to vessel shape in only the most general sense, the basic jar/bowl distinction presents the clearest functional contrast. Size-frequency histograms of mound and village jar and bowl forms are shown in Figure 21. Median orifice diameters for jars (mound = 34.0;

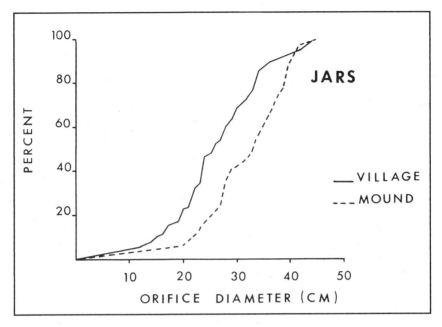

Figure 22 Cumulative Frequency Curves of Orifice Diameters: Village and Mound Jars

village = 26.0) and bowls (mound = 32.0; village = 19.0) differ substantially.

Are there size-range differences for jars and bowls between mound and village contexts? For jars (cooking/storage), a greater size range is found in village than in mound contexts. Specifically, the mound has an overrepresentation of the largest vessels, with the smallest sizes absent. For bowls (cooking/serving), the same pattern holds. Large bowls are overrepresented and the small end of the range is absent.

Another way to perceive these differences is to examine cumulative curves of orifice diameters of jars and bowls in the village and mound samples (Figures 22 and 23). The distributions of both jar and bowl rim diameters were compared using the normal approximation for Mann-Whitney's U statistic, appropriate when sample sizes are large or there are ties across classes (Blalock 1972:259–260). For both jars ($Z = 3.38128$, $p < .01$) and bowls ($Z = 4.9799$, $p < .01$), mound samples are significantly different from village samples. Mound jars and bowls are missing the lower tails of the village distributions. This is particularly dramatic for bowls less than 13 cm in diameter, but I am unable to determine how or for what purpose these small vessels were used.

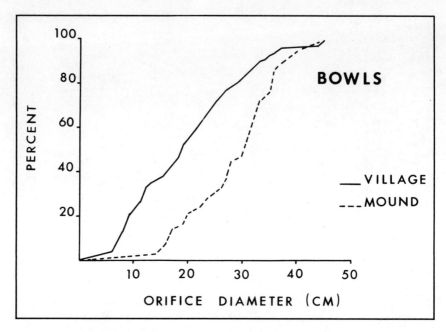

Figure 23   Cumulative Frequency Curves of Orifice Diameters: Village and Mound Bowls

It is clear that there are significant differences in the sizes of mound and village vessels. These results are interpreted as evidence that the broad range of vessel sizes in the village samples reflects a variety of domestic household activities, while the narrower range in the mound suggests primary emphasis on large-group food consumption and perhaps storage.

Summary

Evidence for a possible developmental relationship among ritual, feasting, and the emergence of sanctified authority was uncovered at the Lubbub Creek site through excavation of the remaining portion of the platform mound. A sequence of paired, specialized buildings created a ceremonial precinct early in the center's history. The structure pairs are interpreted as analogs or prototypes of the chief's residence and temple/charnel buildings associated with historical southeastern mound ceremonialism.

Mound-related activities are linked to ritual and feasting through analysis of artifacts and ecofacts. Remains of costume and ritual paraphernalia were identified. Faunal remains reveal a distinct social context of food consumption on the mound when compared to the village. Functional characteristics of ceramic samples from mound and village contexts were compared. There are no significant differences in the distribution of vessel shapes, nor are there important differences in the ratio of serving to cooking wares. However, the mound sample has a more restricted range of vessel sizes and disproportionately larger vessels than the village sample. These results suggest that mound activities included feasts in a ritual format. The rebuilding and continuity of mound architecture over generations is interpreted as institutionalization of the activities and associated roles.

CHAPTER 5

Storage, Defense, and Chiefs

W E TURN NOW to consider the Summerville settlement system in detail. It is an axiom of archaeological research, and perhaps obvious to the reader, that in order to understand a past way of life researchers must examine a representative range of locations—archaeological sites—where people conducted their daily activities. To forward this goal, I will attempt to sketch (if sometimes in rather tentative, broad strokes) aspects of Summerville site seasonality, site permanence, and subsistence activities. The picture presented in the following pages is no doubt incomplete, but the cumulative result is the perception of the farmstead–local-center settlement system as an interdependent social, economic, and political unit.

In another aspect, however, the comparison of site categories helps to isolate those social and economic conditions that may have led to the establishment of the farmstead–local-center system, and serves to focus attention on how these conditions perhaps shaped the emergence of formal positions of leadership. I argue that the logistics of maize production, defense, and food storage created two potential sources of political influence: (1) authority over pooled food surpluses sanctioned through appeals to the sacred authority; and (2) leadership in war.

Storage and Defense

As reviewed in Chapter 3, the archaeological evidence of population-induced resource stress in the Tombigbee River valley is equivocal. Maize was used at low levels in Miller III and then rapidly intensified to become a staple with the transition to Summerville I after A.D. 1000.

While it is important to determine which processes were active in a specific historical context, it should be emphasized that the population-resources stress hypothesis and the social "corn as commodity" hypothesis are not mutually exclusive. If surplus maize conferred social advantages, then this was doubly so under any conditions of subsistence stress.

Whatever the cause, there are logical reasons to suspect that intensifying maize production demanded changes in the organization of subsistence practices. Such changes may be reflected in the appearance at this time of dispersed households or farmsteads, each composed of a small number of people. Farmsteads apparently provided the optimal conditions (or at least the preferred situation) under which to practice a mixed economy of cultivation, hunting, and gathering. If maize permitted a smaller work group such as a family to generate food at productivity levels that had previously required larger work groups, then dispersed households may reflect this greater independence. But new problems were possibly created that make it unlikely that these farmsteads were socially or economically autonomous. Farmstead maize fields had to be tended in the warm months, and the harvest stored. However, the individual farmsteads were vulnerable to attack. There is direct evidence that the introduction of the bow in the Miller III phase created a more dangerous social environment. For the first time there is unambiguous evidence of violent conflict among Tombigbee Woodland populations. Miller III burials include multiple interments with embedded arrow points (Hill 1981). Evidence of violent traumatic injury, as indicated by "parry" fractures or embedded projectile points, is present in 24% (19 of 78) of the Miller III population and 18% (6 of 33) of the Lubbub Creek Summerville I population (Cole et al. 1982; Welch 1990: Table 25; Powell 1988:487–489). Parry fractures of the ulnae were also present among farmstead adults (Gilbert 1980:301–304; O'Hear et al. 1981:137–144), and at Tibbee Creek a young man died when an antler arrow point penetrated his upper torso (O'Hear et al. 1981:145).

The escalation of group conflict that accompanied the bow need not be interpreted as a response to stress from population growth. As I have argued elsewhere (Blitz 1988), the large-scale, time-transgressive pattern of bow adoption in the Eastern Woodlands represents a rapid chain-reaction mechanism of competitive advantage that crosscuts local environmental conditions. The external introduction of the bow may have presented new possibilities of resource exploitation or territorial expansion and perhaps even fostered demographic changes in the Late Woodland period, rather than having been a response to such changes.

The threat of attack raises questions about storage and defense.

There is a change in storage technology in the transition from Miller III to Summerville I that may be related to the increase in maize production. Miller III groups dug large, deep storage pits to hold acorns and other nuts gathered in the fall. Although often interpreted as an indicator of sedentism, such underground pits are particularly useful to conceal surpluses for a period of time while the social group is absent (DeBoer 1988). At Miller III base camps some of these pits are very large, as much as 1.5 m in diameter and 1.3 m deep (Jenkins and Ensor 1981; Blitz 1983a).

While both Miller III and Summerville I populations dug a variety of small pits that probably served short-term food-storage functions, the Summerville I populations ceased to construct the presumably longer-term, large-basin, cylindrical and belled pits favored in Miller III. A similar disappearance of large underground storage pits from the archaeological record marks the Late Woodland–Mississippian transition in the Moundville area (Mistovich 1988). Paradoxically, at a time when storable maize rapidly increased, as is clearly documented in the botanical remains (Caddell 1983), there is a dramatic decrease in the volume of visible underground storage facilities. Apparently, the preferred storage method changed to the aboveground granary or corncrib widely observed in the Southeast during the early historical period. For whatever reasons it was adopted, the highly visible aboveground granary was a security risk at farmsteads.

In an atmosphere of increased sedentism, agricultural intensification, and warfare, a group wishing to protect its food surpluses and to avoid being dislodged from favorable localities can be expected to resort to fortifications. I propose that the creation of a local center as the focus of social and economic integration for dispersed households was, at least in part, a response to these problems. The Mississippian people needed a centrally located fortified place, such as the site at Lubbub Creek, where they could protect their maize harvest and themselves from attack. Unfortunately, it is not possible to verify this proposition through the direct investigation of storage facilities because aboveground cribs are very difficult to identify archaeologically with any degree of certainty (for possible examples see Emerson and Jackson 1984:157; Milner 1984:30; Polhemus 1987:241). Small post-mold patterns or clusters, some with associated daub, charred corn kernels, and lack of floor staining, were found at Lubbub Creek (Blitz 1983c:261). These appear to be small ancillary structures that may include storage facilities, but clear evidence of function remains elusive (see Figure 37 below).

Nevertheless, that communal storage facilities were utilized by Mississippian societies in the Southeast is abundantly documented by the early Spanish observers. De Soto, Luna, and others depended heavily on the large stores of maize in the fortified communities in order to feed their hungry armies and often sought local centers primarily for this purpose. The later French and British observers describe how the communal stores were used for feasts and ceremonials that drew the farmstead populations in from the surrounding countryside to the local center (Swanton 1979:379–381; Bartram 1958:122–123, 326).

To summarize, a settlement pattern of farmsteads dispersed around a fortified center coincides with the Mississippian emergence in the central Tombigbee River valley. Dispersed households may have had advantages in a mixed economy of cultivation and wild food sources but left farmsteads and their surpluses exposed to attack. I propose that the solution to this problem was the creation of a centrally located fortified place where some portion of the household's maize harvest could be stored and protected. This solution implies regular or frequent aggregations of farmstead populations for a variety of social, economic, and ceremonial activities. A supporting body of artifactual and faunal evidence that clarifies the farmstead–local-center interaction is presented in detail below.

For now, I wish to establish that communal or centralized storage of harvests, perhaps with new forms of labor organization between cooperating households, may have created conditions under which responsibilities would have to be delegated to preside over pooling and disbursement of resources. The need to arrange a consensus of decision making above the household level may have stimulated an increasingly "corporate" character in kin groups and provided an atmosphere conducive to the emergence of political office. The platform-mound excavations at Lubbub Creek, which suggest that consumption of pooled food in a ritual format provided a social context for the amplification of communitywide authority, are consistent with the proposed changes in labor cooperation. But delegated responsibility for communal storage need not have been the only strategy for the advancement of ambitious personalities. If increased warfare and defensive concerns were a potent force for change, is there evidence for a social status or formal office based upon leadership in war?

Evidence for a Formal Office of Leadership at Lubbub Creek

Mortuary evidence of a formal office of leadership at Lubbub Creek was uncovered by the University of Alabama excavations in 1977. A small cluster of Mississippian burials (1Pi33) was found, some of which formed a series of short, parallel rows of three or four graves with similar orientations. Summerville I and II–III phase burials composed the rows, which suggests the formation of a small cemetery over a considerable period of time. The excavator, Ned Jenkins, proposed that the 1Pi33 cemetery provides clear evidence that a formal office of leadership and ranking of descent groups was present by Summerville I (Jenkins 1982:130–132).

Within the cemetery cluster a single Summerville I phase grave (Burial 20) contained the primary interment of two adult males in their midthirties. The two individuals were placed one atop the other in an extended position. In association with the bottommost male were a copper plate embossed with a falcon symbol and a dozen copper arrow-shaped ornaments, probably used as components in a headdress (Figure 24). The uppermost male had a triangular projectile point in the right chest area, apparently a fatal wound. A set of arms and legs and a pair of feet were placed with the individuals. These limbs were articulated in a manner that suggested interment in the flesh (Hill 1981:278) and were interpreted as war trophies. Other items placed in the grave were a Moundville Incised *var. Moundville* vessel, a chert arrow point, mineral pigments, a drilled pearl bead, and 165 marine-shell beads (Cole et al. 1982:Table 2).

Jenkins (1982:130–132) notes that the copper artifacts are similar to other Southeastern Ceremonial Complex paraphernalia that have been interpreted as symbol badges (Larson 1959) and argues that these symbols are representations of an institutionalized office or rank. Copper emblems associated with adult males, with a complex but consistent thematic content, have been identified at several Mississippian sites as probable markers of chiefly status (Larson 1971; Peebles and Kus 1977). Brown (1985:140) has identified the distinctive Southeastern Ceremonial Complex symbols, the falcon and falcon impersonator, as important symbols of chiefly authority and of military leadership. In short, there are several clues as to the basis for leadership represented by Burial 20: (1) the symbolism of the copper badges implies that the formal office was reinforced by ideological sanctions (Jenkins 1982:130); (2) possession of the nonlocal copper badges suggests the individual had the ability to negotiate within a wider exchange-and-information network beyond Lubbub Creek; and (3) the falcon symbolism, strongly identified with warfare in the Southeast (Howard 1968:43–45; Brown 1985:140; Hudson 1976:128–129), together with the human "trophies" and evidence of violent death in Burial 20, underscores Jenkins's contention that the office was associated with leadership in war. Burial 20 is the only Mississippian interment to contain such items yet discovered in the central Tombigbee area.

Figure 24 Copper Emblems from Lubbub Creek (From Jenkins and Krause 1986: Figure 26c)

Burials within the 1Pi33 cemetery had the majority of nonlocal grave goods (marine-shell ornaments and copper-covered earspools) found at Lubbub Creek. Jenkins (1982:130) argues that this cluster represents the intentional spatial segregation of an "elite" descent group to be contrasted with less well-adorned burials widely scattered within the community. While it is certainly possible that the 1Pi33 cemetery cluster may represent a descent group, the evidence is rather ambiguous. Since the 1Pi33 cemetery contained 60% (19 of 33) of the Summerville I phase burials recovered at Lubbub Creek, it is not remarkable that the majority of nonlocal grave goods should be concentrated there. Nonlocal items are not restricted to these burials only. An individual with copper-covered earspools (together with a unique rectangular vessel) was located elsewhere in the community (see Figure 41 below), and marine-shell ornaments are found with interments at farmsteads (the distribution and social implications of prestige items are considered further in Chapter 7).

Only Burial 20, with the copper headdress and falcon symbol, contains artifacts that are likely to be the prerogative of a specific leadership role. Burial 20 strongly suggests that at least one basis for a formally defined office was leadership in war. Perhaps this position was the prototype of, or structurally similar to, the role of war chief in the historical Southeast.

Toward the Summerville Settlement System

Mississippian farmsteads, when excavated, often exhibit a remarkable degree of similarity in size and composition. They are small sites of one or two structures suitable for nuclear/extended-family use. Typically, artifact assemblages indicate a common range of basic hunting, fishing, collecting, horticultural, and raw material–processing tasks. As more of these sites are excavated, it is becoming increasingly clear that Mississippian farmsteads represent "the domestic level of production at its social minimum" (Muller 1986:204).

Mississippian populations had social and economic requirements that created oscillations in population nucleation and dispersion. Settlement nucleation favored defense and social integration. Settlement dispersal favored efficient utilization of natural resources. Under these conditions "many, if not all, Mississippian populations could be generally characterized as having a settlement system consisting of dispersed farmsteads surrounding a local center, with this system representing a flexible compromise solution to the opposing pressures of optimum energy utilization and optimum social-cohesion-boundary-maintenance-abilities" (Smith 1978:491).

This characterization matches the Summerville settlement system quite well. Many small, dispersed Mississippian sites have been located in the study area (see Figures 2–3). Site survey has been broad but opportunistic, and largely limited to the unforested portion of the floodplain within boundaries imposed by project impact areas. For this reason it is not possible to assess farmstead densities without further survey, but the general settlement pattern is known. Typically, small Mississippian sites are oval artifact concentrations 20–40 m in diameter, located on well-drained sandy or loamy soils scattered across the floodplain. Based on surface inspection, sites with sherds, lithics, mussel shell, and sometimes daub and midden were classified as farmsteads; and sites with fewer than 15 recovered sherds and no daub or midden were classified as transitory camps (Jenkins et al. 1975:74).

Farmstead Subsistence Activities

Informative similarities and differences in subsistence activities are evident when artifacts and ecofacts are compared between farmsteads and the local center at Lubbub Creek. Because the four farmsteads considered here are widely distributed, they did not all articulate with the Lubbub Creek center. Tibbee Creek, Kellogg, and Yarborough are closest to the Butler or Lyon's Bluff local center, while 1Gr2 is closest to Lubbub Creek. Regardless, artifact and ecofact assemblages can be compared as representative of site settlement categories: farmstead and local center. When this is done, utilitarian artifacts of stone, bone, shell, and pottery are highly comparable.

Lithic assemblages at both farmsteads and local center exhibit rather low quantity and diversity of tools and debitage. Farmstead lithic tool types are few and simple, and locally available stone predominates. This is true of contemporary Moundville phase farmstead lithic assemblages as well (Mistovich 1987). The most likely explanation is that many cutting tools and other implements were made of perishable cane, wood, bone, and shell. This was the case for the early historical native societies in the region (Swanton 1911:58).

Perhaps a reflection of this lack of emphasis on lithic technology is the fact that many Mississippian tools are morphologically similar to Late Woodland artifacts that also occur at these sites. For this reason tools and especially debitage are not easily assigned to components, and the potential for mixed samples limits assemblage comparison to simple presence/absence observations. Comparison of tools from Mississippian features, which probably represent the least contamination from earlier components, reveals that farmstead and local center share highly redundant inventories (Table 6).

Groundstone plant-processing implements—pitted stones, mullers,

Table 6 Utilitarian Artifacts Common to Both Lubbub Creek and Farmstead Domestic Contexts

Flake tools:	Projectile points
	Preforms
	Shaft drill
	Microdrill
	Perforator/graver
	Cobble knife/biface
	Chopper
Ground tools:	Greenstone celt (axe)
	Hammerstone
	Abrader
Bone/shell tools:	Antler projectile point
	Fishhook
	Awl/perforator
	Beaver-incisor chisel
	Mussel-shell hoe/scraper

and mortars—are only rarely found in clear Mississippian contexts at either site category, but recovery of groundstone fragments from features and house floors suggests their use was not uncommon. The large wooden mortar and long-handled pestle, widespread in the historical Southeast, was probably the principal Mississippian plant-processing implement. The use of this tool by Mississippian populations in northern Alabama is implicated in activity studies of osteological remains (Bridges 1989). Flaked-stone scrapers and hoes are also largely absent, but large freshwater mussel shells, perforated for hafting and exhibiting edge-wear, were probably used for these tasks (Curren 1981; Williams and Brain 1983:282–284).

Potsherds are the most abundant artifacts at both farmsteads and the local center. The function of ceramic vessels, as measured by variation in vessel-form categories, is a potential source of information about site activities. Identification of vessel form requires great quantities of large rim sherds, but the farmstead samples tend to be highly fragmented. Consequently, sample size is greatly reduced. However, identifiable vessel forms can be grouped into a composite farmstead sherd sample (N = 85). When this is done, the most abundant vessel forms are standard jars (62%), simple bowls (27%), and flaring-rim bowls (10%). The only other forms that can be identified are one bottle and one outslanting-rim bowl, both from the Summerville II–III phase farmstead, 1Gr2. This relative order of abundance (but not the same proportions) is identical for these same forms in the Lubbub Creek aggregate village sample. Perhaps this is a rough indication that the basic domestic vessel assemblage does not vary greatly between site types. Even if that is the case, however, it does not necessarily mean that storage, cooking, and serving activities at the sites were identical.

In sum, utilitarian artifact inventories are similar. The same array of hunting, fishing, cultivation, and raw material–processing tasks occurred in and around households at both farmstead sites and at Lubbub Creek. There is no indication of site or household specialization in terms of basic subsistence activities.

Cultivation and Plant Utilization

To label these small dispersed sites farmsteads implies that cultivation was a primary activity at these locations. That farmsteads were directly involved in cultivation is supported by the ubiquitous presence of maize and evidence of deforestation at farmstead sites.

In the Summerville I and II–III phase floral samples at Lubbub Creek, maize represented the largest proportion of food-plant remains (90%), but nutshells were found in more features than was maize (Caddell 1983:270). In the Late Mississippian/protohistoric Summerville IV phase samples these proportions changed. Nutshell composed the majority of food-plant remains (85%), and maize was no longer dominant (15%). If these proportional changes indicate an economic shift away from maize, the reason for this change is unknown. In addition to maize, Mississippian cultigens recovered in small quantities at Lubbub Creek were sunflower *(Helianthus annuus)* and the common bean *(Phaseolus vulgaris)*. Common wild food plants were persimmons, plums, grapes, and maypops (Caddell 1983:270). Starchy edible seeds were present but not in sufficient quantities to suggest they were important.

The same range of cultivated and wild food-plant remains occurs at farmsteads. Remains of maize, nuts, and edible fruit were recovered at all farmsteads (Caddell 1981, 1982; Scarry 1981; Crane 1980). At Tibbee Creek maize was present in four of seven feature samples (Scarry 1981:215). About half of Mississippian features at Kellogg (18 of 37 samples) contained maize (Crane 1980:333). In all 10 Summerville II–III phase features at 1Gr2 maize was present. Maize was the only cultigen at these three farmsteads. At the Yarborough farmstead, in Mississippian contexts of uncertain phase affiliation, maize represented 8.6% of food-plant remains (Caddell 1982:139). In addition to maize, sunflower and common bean were also present at Yarborough. By both weight and count, hickory nuts were the most abundant food species at Tibbee Creek, Kellogg, and Yarborough.

Taken at face value, the relative frequency of maize is lower at three of four farmstead sites when compared to Lubbub Creek samples. The exception is 1Gr2, where feature samples were exclusively from cob-filled smudge pits. Unfortunately, because of differential preservation biases inherent in plant remains, differences in sample processing, and limitations on samples analyzed, the proportional contribution of maize and wild food plants to the diet cannot be accurately assessed at farmsteads or compared to Lubbub Creek (Caddell 1981:50, 1983:231; Scarry 1981:213). Even a simple comparison such as percentage of features with maize is inadequate for this purpose, since it is clear that feature function, such as use of cobs as fuel in smudge pits, will affect preservation and recovery (Caddell 1981:33–34). For these reasons it would be unwise to conclude, based on the relative frequency of maize, that people on farmsteads participated in horticultural production or consumed maize to a lesser degree than residents of local centers.

That farmsteads were close to cleared garden plots is supported by several sets of evidence. Pollen and floral remains associated with both arboreal climax forest genera and weedy subclimax forest genera were recovered at Yarborough (Caddell 1982:139), Kellogg (Crane 1980:336; Fish 1980:338–339), Tibbee Creek (Scarry 1981:217), and 1Gr2 (Caddell 1981:44). The recovery of nonfood microfauna at Yarborough, such as white-footed mouse, pine vole, wood rat, and certain land-snail species, indicates the close proximity of hardwood forest, but the presence of cotton rat and rice rat suggests some open habitat as well (Scott 1982:151). Bone-count ratios of cottontail rabbit to swamp rabbit (field:swamp species) and grey squirrel to fox squirrel (climax:subclimax forest species) suggest more forest cover at Yarborough than at Lubbub Creek (Scott 1982:151). This variation in forest cover may indicate either a qualitative difference in the kind of cultivation practices—small garden plots at farmsteads, large-field planting at Lubbub Creek (Scott 1982:152)—or it may merely reflect the greater population concentration and resultant long-term occupational impact at the local center.

To summarize, it can be concluded that the same cultivated and wild food plants were consumed at farmsteads and the local center. Maize is ubiquitous at all farmsteads and certainly of dietary importance. Faunal and floral remains indicate land clearance in the immediate vicinity of farmsteads. Clearly, cultivation was a major activity at farmsteads.

Size of Social Groups at Farmsteads

Mississippian farmsteads in the central Tombigbee River area, like those examined in other regions, are thought to represent the remains of nuclear-family households. The size of structure remains and the limited spatial distribution of features and midden imply small group size.

In an innovative study Shapiro (1984) used ceramic vessels' function and size to investigate Mississippian intersite variability in Georgia. Differences in size and frequency of storage vessels were considered an indicator of site permanence. Differences in size and frequency of cooking and serving vessels were used as an indicator of group size. Shapiro examined samples from four sites: a large, permanent mound/village site; a warm-season farmstead; and two extractive camps. As expected, the larger and more permanent the site (as indicated by site size, faunal seasonality markers, midden development, etc.), the greater relative frequency of storage vessels and the larger the size of serving and cooking vessels.

This method is applicable to the Tombigbee sites. If Tombigbee sites exhibited some of the variability of Shapiro's sites, one would expect Lubbub Creek to have larger jars and bowls than the farmstead sites. Sample size (measurable rim sherds) was too small to permit useful comparison of individual farmsteads. Instead, jars and bowls from all four sites were combined to form a composite farmstead sample. Because all extant collections of farmstead potsherds could not be examined in the time allotted for measurement, the farmstead composite sample represents a subsample of total recovered rim sherds. The Lubbub Creek sample represents all measurable jar and bowl rim sherds from both village and mound contexts. As in Chapter 4, orifice diameter was used as an indirect measure of vessel size. Size-frequency histograms of Lubbub Creek and farmstead standard jar and simple bowl forms are shown in Figure 25.

For jars, with a cooking/storage function, a greater size range is found at Lubbub Creek than at farmstead sites, and these vessels are larger. For bowls, with a serving/cooking function, vessels with orifice diameters greater than 25 cm are more frequent at Lubbub Creek. These differences may be examined as cumulative frequency curves (Figures 26 and 27) and tested with the Mann-Whitney U statistic to determine the probability that they represent samples drawn from the same population. In each case the U-value was transformed into a normally distributed Z statistic and the probability level corrected for ties. For jars, significantly different distributions ($Z = 5.228$; $p < .0001$) are indicated. Significant differences in the two samples remain even when the mound

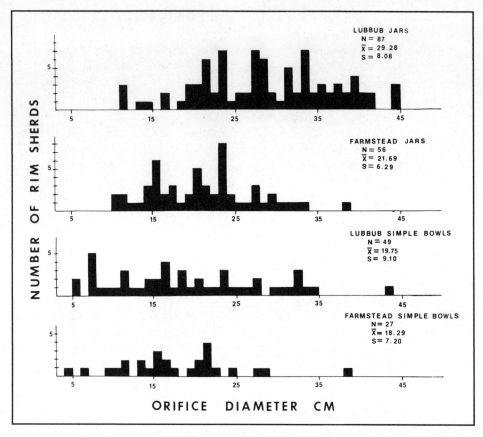

Figure 25   Size-Frequency Histograms of Lubbub Creek and Farmstead Jars and Bowls

jar sample, which contains large vessels concentrated at the mound, is removed from the Lubbub Creek aggregate sample ($Z = 3.400$; two-tailed $p < .0007$). For bowls, however, there is no significant difference in the two distributions ($Z = .733$; $p < .4633$).

Unless there are transformation processes at farmsteads that have created an unknown sample bias (the highly fragmented nature of the sample is of some concern here), the tentative conclusion is that farmsteads used a smaller size range of jars than the local center. With this caution in mind, differences in jar size between the farmstead and local-center samples are interpreted as a reflection of smaller group size at farmsteads; a lesser degree of site permanence at farmsteads compared to local centers and, consequently, a reduced storage capacity of vessels; and little variability in the social context of food consumption at farmsteads. Size differences among jar vessels probably reflect the addition

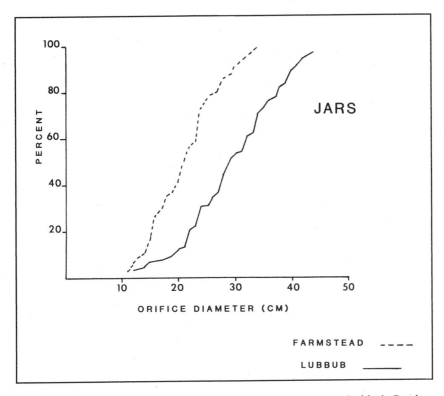

Figure 26 Cumulative Frequency Curves of Orifice Diameters: Lubbub Creek and Farmstead Jars

of certain activities specific to population aggregation at the local center. The lack of significant size differences in simple bowls for farmstead and local-center samples suggests no difference between site types in the kinds of serving and cooking activities specific to this vessel form.

There is an additional possible explanation for size differences of jar vessels. If farmstead and local-center inhabitants represented portions of the same population at different locations, or if some degree of residential mobility were a factor, the vessel-size differences may be due to transportation costs. In other words, families in transit from the local center took smaller vessels with them to farmsteads. This explanation depends on where and how often pottery was produced (see Chapter 7).

Seasonality and Permanence at Farmsteads

While Mississippian farmsteads are often considered self-sufficient domestic units that occupied a permanent year-round site, the cumu-

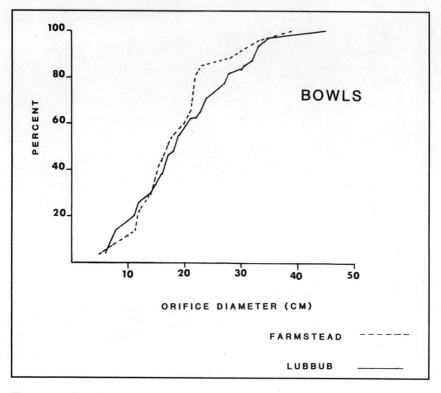

Figure 27   Cumulative Frequency Curves of Orifice Diameters: Lubbub Creek and Farmstead Bowls

lative efforts of several specialists' studies disclose a more complex situation in the central Tombigbee River area. It is clear that the excavated farmsteads are not merely transitory or limited-activity locations. All farmsteads have remains of substantially built structures. Internal hearths or daub (absent at Tibbee Creek) may denote cold-season occupancy. Human burials, moderate midden development, intersecting features, and rebuilding of structure walls are evidence of multiple-year occupation. However, it is the excellent studies of ecofacts that provide the most detailed picture of farmstead seasonality, permanence, and residential mobility.

Seeds of edible fruits, acorns, and nutshells from species available from summer through fall were recovered at all farmsteads. At Yarborough impressions of acorns and a cocklebur in daub point to the plastering of structure walls in the fall (Caddell 1982:140). Unfortunately, plants are rather poor indicators of seasonality because they are easily stored beyond the span of seasonal availability.

Faunal remains are more informative about site seasonality and permanence. Susan Scott compared faunal samples from Yarborough and Lubbub Creek. Her analysis led her to conclude that farmsteads "were not independent economic units" (Scott 1982:151).

Perhaps the most important food animal for Mississippian peoples was the whitetail deer. Scott compared the relative frequency of deer skeletal parts from the Yarborough farmstead to those recovered at the local center of Lubbub Creek and made an important discovery:

> With the exception of deer carpals, bones from the lower legs and feet of deer are far better represented at the Yarborough site than at the Lubbub Creek Archaeological Locality. The relative frequenc[ies] of skull and rib fragments are compatible at the two types of settlements. All other elements are relatively more abundant in the Lubbub Creek Archaeological Locality assemblage. The latter category includes all of the major meat[-]yielding anatomical parts. The complementary nature of these archaeological assemblages is strongly suggestive of a pattern of meat distribution in which deer were procured and butchered at outlying settlements with a large proportion of the meat being transported to larger villages with the bone still attached [Scott 1982:146].

Scott examined seasonal indicators on Yarborough deer antlers and mandibles, found that none had been procured in November or December, and suggested that the site was abandoned in the late fall. In contrast, most Lubbub Creek venison was obtained in November and December. In addition, "the quantity of turtle, snake, and amphibian in the Yarborough assemblage was exceptionally large when compared to materials from Lubbub" (Scott 1982:150). This greater emphasis on warm-season species at the farmstead suggests "seasonal differences in site utilization" (Scott 1982:150). From these discoveries, Scott arrived at the following cautious interpretations about farmstead-and-local-center interaction:

1. Farmsteads were abandoned for a period of time, perhaps as much as two or three months, in the late fall/early winter as families joined together in intensive deer hunts.
2. Because most of the Lubbub Creek venison was procured in late fall/ early winter, and given that deer were absent from the farmstead sample for this interval, the cooperative deer hunts probably coincided with some portion of the farmstead population's moving to the local center.

Scott's analysis, and the farmstead characteristics examined above, reveals that Tombigbee farmsteads do not conform to the dominant interpretation of Mississippian farmsteads as permanent, year-round, and self-sufficient sites. This perception is largely the result of midwestern excavations (Smith 1978; Yerkes 1987:112, 196), but farmstead investigations in Georgia suggest a degree of seasonal variability perhaps comparable to the Tombigbee sites (Shapiro 1984). Tombigbee farmsteads were permanent in the sense that families used the sites through many seasonal cycles, and in both warm and cold weather. But occupation was not continuous, and movement from farmstead to center must have been quite fluid. Farmsteads were self-sufficient in the sense that they must have produced and consumed some portion of their own food, but they were not economically or socially independent.

If, as the faunal data imply, there was a hiatus in farmstead occupation sometime in the late fall/early winter, what did families do with the stored surplus of their late summer/early fall harvest? Obviously they could not leave their stored maize at the temporarily abandoned site unless it was concealed in large underground storage pits. As previously discussed, suitable pits are absent at farmsteads. One possibility is that families had entirely consumed their harvest by fall. But it is far more likely that some portion was transported for storage at the local center. Transportation of maize would be easily accomplished by dugout canoe. An actual example of such a canoe has been recovered from the Tombigbee River and radiocarbon dated to the Middle Mississippi period (Stowe 1974).

Additional implications for site seasonality may be derived from human burials at farmsteads and local centers. At the Kellogg site, the excavator observed, all Mississippian burials were placed with the head oriented in an easterly direction, with the majority oriented to east-northeast. If burials were oriented to a solar position, then burial occurred in midsummer when the sun rises in that direction (Atkinson et al. 1980:169). Atkinson comments further, "If this hypothesis is viable and if this same patterned behavior also existed at such Moundville phase sites as Koger's Island and Snow's Bend, then interments at those sites more often took place during the winter solstice, for orientations there were predominately between due east and east-southeast (see Peebles 1971:74–75)" (Atkinson et al. 1980:169).

While Peebles interpreted these burial orientation patterns as supposed status indicators, Atkinson proposes that season of interment determines the predominant pattern. The Lubbub Creek burial data were unavailable to Atkinson, but following his argument, this idea can be applied to the seasonal cycles of aggregation and dispersal discussed above. If the greater portion of time spent at farmsteads were in the warm months, then we would expect summer orientations in the burials, such as those identified at Kellogg. Conversely, if Lubbub Creek were the scene of population aggregation in the late fall/early winter, and if such aggregations influenced interment frequency, then burial orientations would be expected to be predominantly oriented to the east and east-southeast, but not east-northeast. In Figure 28, the expected pattern of complementarity in the Summerville I phase burial orientation at farmstead and local center, while not absolute, presents a clear trend.

Similar comparisons of burial orientation for the Summerville II–III and Summerville IV phases were not made because of insufficient data on burial orientation. The Kellogg pattern was not replicated at the roughly contemporary Tibbee Creek site, where orientations were quite variable (Atkinson et al. 1980:169). However, the 11 Tibbee Creek burials represent a divergent sample in other ways as well. The absence of adult females, and the high frequency of infants and subadults (7 of 11), often flexed or positioned in reference to the house walls (O'Hear et al. 1981:150–151), may constitute an inappropriate situation to compare with the larger Kellogg and Lubbub Creek samples. At any rate, we should not be too quick to dismiss the complementarity in the Kellogg and Lubbub Creek orientations because Tibbee Creek fails to conform to expectations.

The burial orientation patterns are intriguing and worthy of further investigation, but their ultimate implications are, of course, elusive. I need only point out that the seasonality-of-interment hypothesis is entirely dependent on the assumption that burial orientation is in reference to a solar position, an assumption that is quite unverifiable.

Farmstead and Local Center: The Scale of Defense and Aggregation

The presence of fortifications at Lubbub Creek provides additional important insights into the interaction between farmsteads and the local center. I have suggested that dispersed farmstead populations were under pressure to create defensive works in a central location to protect themselves and their harvest. Communal storage facilities at the local center would create conditions for the manipulation of surpluses and the delegation of authority. In this section, evidence that defensive works were constructed with the aid of farmstead populations is presented.

A total of six palisade lines and a circular ditch were built at Lubbub Creek. Bastioned palisades, some with both outer and inner lines, and ditches were all encountered as defensive works during the sixteenth-century Spanish *entradas* into the Southeast (Swanton 1979:433–439). There can be no doubt that the two bastioned palisades and the ditch at Lubbub Creek are defensive works (Cole and Albright 1983). The largest defensive feature, the Summerville I outer palisade, had six rectangular

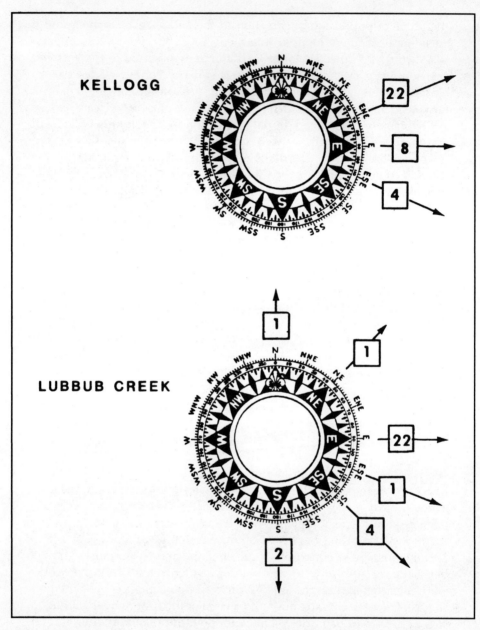

Figure 28 Summerville I Phase Burial Orientations at Kellogg and Lubbub Creek

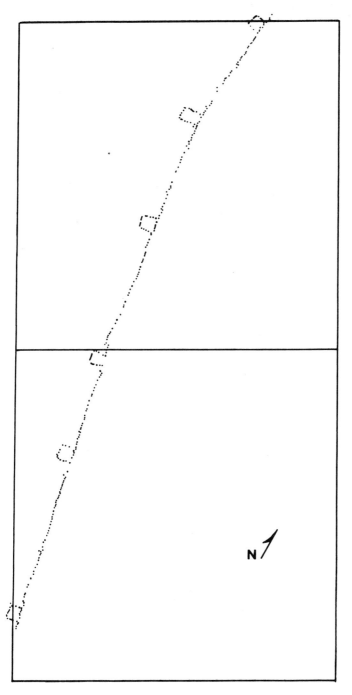

Figure 29 Outer Palisade with Bastions Crossing Two Hectares

bastions set apart at 30 m intervals along the excavated portion of the wall (Figure 29). These bastions are interpreted as having platforms for archers (see Lafferty 1973).

The outer palisade line was only partially excavated. A 240 m long segment was exposed. A 1942 aerial photograph of the bend shows crop lines that match the excavated portion. Based on the photo and the orientation of the excavated segment, the palisade made a southeasterly turn from the point where excavations terminated and continued across to the other side of the bend (Cole and Albright 1983:185), a straight-line distance of 360 m. It appears that less than one-half of the total length was uncovered. Therefore, if the palisade continued, closing the gap across the bend, it would have had to measure a minimum total of 600 m long.

Five inner palisade lines that represent sequential construction episodes tightly circumscribed the mound area (Figure 30). Since only one of the inner palisades had bastions, the other four may have been erected to demarcate the social space of the mound, rather than serving a strictly defensive function. Inner Palisades I and II are Summerville I phase features, Palisades IV and V are Summerville II–III phase constructions, and the bastioned Palisade III could not be assigned a phase association (Cole and Albright 1983:179–182). Because all five inner palisade lines were only partially excavated, their full extent and orientation could not be determined.

The Summerville IV ditch was a dry moat defensive work, perhaps originally backed by a palisade line set into a berm, but no evidence of this was found (Figure 31). A 1942 aerial shot clearly shows the ditch encircling the mound, and, together with the orientation of the exposed portions, it is estimated to have been about 230 m in diameter (Peebles 1983a:401). Summary dimensions of the outer palisade and ditch are presented in Table 7.

The most intriguing aspect of the fortifications is the incompatibility between the scale of the defensive works and the size of the resident population. Lubbub Creek was not a nucleated community in the sense of a densely packed settlement. Extensive horizontal excavation within the area enclosed by the outer palisade revealed large "empty" areas devoid of houses, features, and midden.

A rough population estimate was calculated for each phase (Peebles 1983a:399). For example, Peebles begins with the four excavated Summerville I phase structures and, on the basis of floor area, calculates that the mean density of structures was 1.21/ha ($sd = 2.47$/ha). He goes on to estimate the number of houses present: "Given 8.5 ha of village area, then there were as few as 10 houses and, taking one standard deviation as a guide, as many as 31 houses in the Summerville I community. If

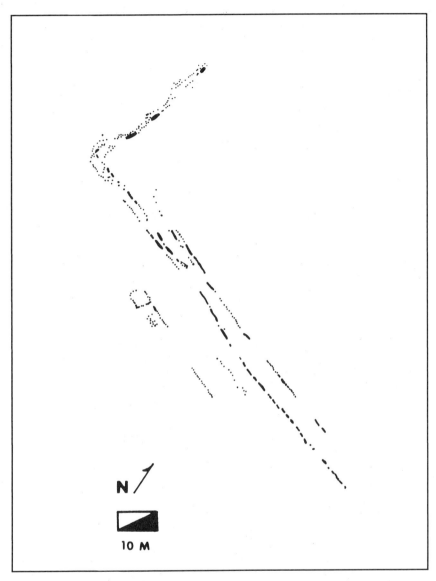

Figure 30   Inner Palisade Lines (Adapted from Cole and Albright 1983)

there were five persons/house, which is a reasonable estimate, then the community contained from 50 to 150 persons. If the span of the Summerville I period is set at 200 years, and if the site was continuously occupied during that period, and if useful lifespan of a house was 20 to 40 years, then there would have been only 1 to 6 houses occupied at one time" (Peebles 1983a:399).

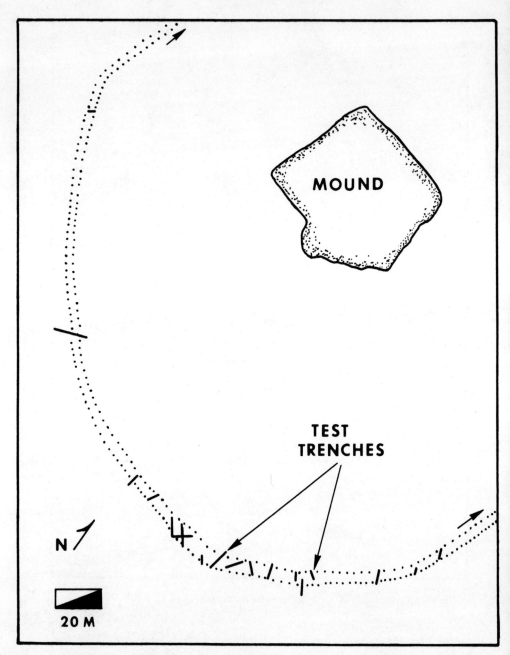

Figure 31   Summerville IV Ditch Defensive Work

Table 7 Outer Palisade and Ditch Dimensions

Outer Palisade		
Length of excavated segment	240	m
Total number of posts in excavated segment	293	
Total number of posts in excavated bastions	180	
Mean post diameter	25	cm
Mean posthole depth[a]	39.44	cm
Total estimated palisade length	600	m
Total estimated number of posts (includes 20 bastions)	1,332	
Ditch		
Mean width	4	m
Mean depth	1.30	m
Diameter	230	m
Projected length (circumference)	722.2	m

[a] Original posthole depth was greater prior to plow truncation.

Following these same procedures, Peebles (1983a:399–401) estimated the number of houses occupied at any one time for the Summerville II–III phase (five to 18 houses in an 11.5 ha community) and Summerville IV phase (two to seven houses in a 4.2 ha community). Using the five persons/house figure yields the following population estimate for persons occupying the community at any one time: Summerville I, 5 to 30 people; Summerville II–III, 25 to 90 people; and Summerville IV, 10 to 35 people. Even if these estimates are doubled (which is reasonable because testing revealed habitation locations at the apex of the bend beyond the intensively excavated areas), Lubbub Creek falls below the theoretical minimal size required for a viable endogamous human population (see Wobst 1974). Obviously, Lubbub Creek residents were connected to a larger population through a network of affinal kinship relations. In other words, the local center was a fortified cluster of households and midden in a landscape of farmsteads.

The estimated labor cost for construction of the outer palisade, a total of 333 person-days of labor, is shown in Table 8. If the Summerville I maximum estimate of 30 persons contained 15 adults, it would take this

Table 8   Estimated Labor Cost of Outer Palisade Construction

Unit Costs	
	Person-hour
Tree cutting (one 25 cm tree felled with stone axe)	0.34[a]
Post trimming	0.16
Yield: 16 posts cut and trimmed per person-day (8 hours)	
Post hauling and placement (per post)	0.67
Yield: 12 posts per person-day (8 hours)	

Unit Applications	
	Person-days
Tree cutting and post trimming	84
(1,332 posts at 16 posts/person-day)	
Post hauling and placement	111
(1,332 posts at 12 posts/person-day)	
Posthole excavation[b]	113
Additional bastion construction estimates	25
Total labor cost in person-days	333

[a] Measurement from Coles 1973:20.

[b] Does not include wall-trench excavation. Calculation: volume of cylinder using mean depth and mean radius times 1,332 posts equals 293.04 m^3.

work force 23 days to complete the outer palisade. In Table 9 the estimated labor cost is calculated for construction of the ditch, a total of 1,745 person-days of labor. If the Summerville IV maximum estimate of 35 residents were converted to a work force of 17 adults, it would take 103 days to complete the ditch (and longer if there were a palisade associated with this ditch). If the work force estimate is doubled, these figures are obtained: outer palisade, 11.1 days; and ditch, 51 days.

These estimates of population and labor cost imply that, under the threat of attack, fortification construction would take too long if undertaken by the resident population alone. Even if the estimated resident population were doubled, there would not be a sufficient number of people to defend the outer palisade unaided. The construction and defense of fortifications must have involved the dispersed farmstead populations.

Admittedly, calculations of residential population and labor cost are crude estimates. Because one-half of the site was not subject to intensive excavation, population estimates remain imprecise. Nevertheless, ex-

Table 9   Estimated Labor Cost of Ditch Construction

Unit Cost

2.6 m³ per person-day (5 hours) with digging stick[a]

Unit Application

Volume is calculated by converting the ditch to ideal geometric form:
  ½ of volume of cylinder, where *r* is ½ of ditch width, and total length of
  ditch is substituted for *h*. Thus, ditch volume equals
$$\frac{4535.416 \text{ m}^3}{2.6 \text{ m}^3}$$

Total labor cost in person-days   1,745

---

[a] Measurement from Erasmus 1965.

cavation was sufficient to reveal extensive "empty" areas throughout the
site, devoid of houses or midden, and this presents an additional
puzzle. Why was the outer palisade and the ditch constructed on such a
large scale? Certainly it had to be extensive enough to accept the surrounding population when they were threatened by attack, but even so
the outer palisade seems excessively large. The incompatibility between
the scale of the defensive works (at least the outer palisade) and the
extensive "empty" areas within the enclosed community raises the interesting possibility that the fortifications protected maize fields as well
as stored harvests and people.

Discussion and Summary

The examination of farmstead seasonality, residential mobility, and
subsistence activities in the previous sections provides insight not only
into the farmstead–local-center settlement system as an economic and
social unit, but also calls attention to factors that may have influenced the
origin and development of such a system. The dispersed farmstead–
local-center pattern is the product of various social and subsistence
requirements: access to dispersed wild resources; changes in the organization of labor that accompanied intensified maize cultivation; defense; and social integration.

The Late Woodland Miller III settlement pattern consisted of large
riverine base camps occupied for much of the year with seasonal or
regular dispersal to small transitory camps (Jenkins 1982). Possible limitations on the ability to amass or store sufficient quantities of food prior
to intensification of maize production, and the dispersed distribution of
wild foods, meant movement of people to resources for some portion of

the year. This oscillation of population dispersal and aggregation, an ancient pattern on the Gulf Coastal Plain, continued with the transition to intensified maize cultivation but with important alterations. Dispersed small sites became nuclear-family farmsteads, basic production units occupied for much of the year. The continuing reliance on wild food meant that settlement dispersal was still an efficient subsistence solution (Smith 1978), but problems arose that required new patterns of cooperation between domestic units.

The logistics of maize agriculture apparently affected hunting and gathering activities, as manifested in the Tombigbee faunal record: small game and aquatic resources taken in the vicinity of farmsteads in the warm season; and intensive late fall/early winter deer hunts. The greatest demands on labor and, therefore, the need for a large-group cooperative structure occurred in the fall: harvest and storage of maize; collection and storage of acorns and other nuts; and intensive deer/big-game hunts. The need for labor and the maximum availability of food coincided. Multiple-household cooperation and local-resource mobilization were facilitated through a ritualized cycle of population aggregation at the local center. There labor could be organized, food pooled and consumed to reaffirm social identity and integration, and risks minimized through a mutual security organization. These conditions helped promote formal leadership institutions.

While some degree of seasonality is implicated in the farmstead–local-center interactions, the timing and duration of such movements is far from certain. Alternatively, rather than impose too strict a seasonal boundary on aggregation and dispersal patterns, very short-term aggregations at the local center may have occurred throughout the year, such that faunal seasonal indicators signal only peak aggregation frequencies.

While this interpretation of the Summerville subsistence-and-settlement system emphasizes household flexibility, mobility, and cooperation to a greater degree than generally depicted for Mississippian populations, it shares some of the characteristic patterns described for the historical native peoples of Alabama and Mississippi (cf. Swanton 1911:67–79, 1931:46–56, 1979:262–265; Campbell 1959; Hudson 1976: 269–272; Caddell 1981:19–50; Blitz 1985:16–18). In the historical period it was common southeastern practice to produce two corn crops annually: a midsummer early corn picked green; and a fall late corn harvested dry. The early corn was typically grown in individual garden plots, and late corn worked communally in large fields (Hudson 1976:295–299). Such a pattern may be present at the prehistoric Tombigbee sites, since floral and faunal indicators suggest small garden plots at farmsteads and large fields at Lubbub Creek.

The Green Corn Ceremony was only the most important of the monthly calendrical ceremonies tied to the cycle of subsistence activities (Swanton 1979:260–261). These events, all of which involved feasts, meant regular assembly of some portion of the dispersed population at the local center. If the prehistoric Summerville pattern was similar to the widespread historical pattern, as appears to be the case, then movement back and forth from farmstead to local center was probably more frequent than we are able to detect in the archaeological record.

I have proposed that soon after A.D. 1000 the logistics of intensified maize cultivation and the need to protect dispersed households and their harvests from attack created conditions in which storage and food sharing at a local center were an attractive solution. Storage and defensive considerations created new opportunities for leadership. Mortuary evidence at Lubbub Creek suggests the existence of a formal office based upon leadership in war. War leadership may constitute a role separate from the office based on ritual and communal storage discussed in the previous chapter. If so, the civil chief/war chief duality so common in the historical period may have roots deep in prehistory.

Site seasonality and permanence, and subsistence activities were examined with data from four farmsteads. Summerville domestic units appear to have engaged in the same basic economic tasks regardless of location. There is no indication of subsistence specialization at farmsteads. Inventories of utilitarian artifacts at farmsteads and the Lubbub Creek center are comparable. Maize is ubiquitous at all farmsteads. A comparison of sizes of pottery vessels between farmsteads and Lubbub Creek reveals a smaller size range of farmstead jars, which is tentatively considered to reflect smaller group size, limited storage capacity, little variability in the social context of food consumption at farmsteads, and perhaps, transportation considerations.

Evidence was presented that farmstead populations participated in regular aggregations at local centers. Seasonal indicators suggest multiple-season farmstead occupation but with temporary abandonment in late fall/early winter. Complementarity in the proportions in deer skeletal parts between the Yarborough farmstead and the Lubbub center is evidence of intensive late fall/early winter deer hunts, and transportation of venison to the local center. This pattern is interpreted as group consumption of deer and stored foods by members of farmsteads during ceremonies held at the local center. Further evidence of farmstead–local-center integration is revealed in the incompatibility between the scale of fortifications at Lubbub Creek and the small residential population, and consequently, construction and defense involved farmstead populations.

CHAPTER 6

Ceramic Distributions at Lubbub Creek

IT HAS BEEN ARGUED that an important factor in the development of chiefdoms was the ability to manipulate or restrict access to valued resources (Service 1971, 1975; Peebles and Kus 1977; Wenke 1981; Wright 1984; Earle 1987). In previous chapters this issue was examined by focusing on food surpluses; but what about durable goods? Food surpluses may be used to support craft specialization, the products of which may enter into local and regional exchange networks. In such a system some high-cost items may be unevenly distributed and accrue to an "elite" segment of society (Peebles and Kus 1977:425–427).

Peebles's identification of social ranking at Moundville is based upon the assumption that differential distribution of artifact categories reflects some sort of institutionalized restricted or preferential access. Investigations in the Moundville area have documented differential distributions of nonlocal or high-cost materials and sought explanations in the non-egalitarian operation of chiefly political economy (Peebles 1987; Peebles and Kus 1977; Steponaitis 1989; Welch 1991). The Moundville political economy has been interpreted as a form of prestige-goods economy in which prestige goods and evidence for their production are expected to concentrate among an elite that resides at local and regional centers (Welch 1991).

Archaeological identification of presumed Mississippian prestige goods is largely restricted to copper, shell, stone, and ceramic artifacts. The differential distribution of certain valuables expected from theoretical models of Mississippian chiefly economy has received very limited testing and generally only at the largest regional polities such as Moundville. More investigations are necessary to determine whether patterns of dif-

ferential distributions and the hierarchical social order they imply operated within smaller Mississippian societies such as Lubbub Creek. Stated
another way, does the ranked social order and restricted access to resources so often assumed to be typical of Mississippian chiefdoms crosscut communities of various sizes, or is the degree of social ranking
dependent on the size of the polity?

In the prehistoric Southwest recent research has attempted to demonstrate that fineware ceramics may be a valued commodity with a differential distribution that connotes preferential access by an elite
(Upham et al. 1981; Upham 1982). In this view, "such distribution would
be evident in concentrations of particular classes of materials at administrative centers and their absence at secondary and tertiary sites. . . .
Even if less costly ceramics were to have been made locally and used by
most households, analysis and comparison of their distribution in relation to more costly vessels can provide insight into the sociopolitical
structure of communities and regions" (Upham et al. 1981:826).

It has been proposed that one area of craft specialization in chiefdoms is pottery production (Peebles and Kus 1977). Among Mississippian societies the social role of elaborate finewares is not entirely clear.
Because finewares are always a small portion of the total ceramic assemblage and often conspicuous only as grave goods, some investigators
suggest a sacred-and-secular dichotomy of use (Sears 1973). That finewares were restricted to the Mississippian elite is widely assumed (Anderson 1989:19), and the presence of finewares in burials is considered to
mark status (e.g., Hatch 1975).

The organization of fineware ceramic production among the Mississippian societies of western Alabama is difficult to assess. However,
the contention that fineware was a highly valued item is supported by
evidence that it represents a craft that was not produced within each
household (Steponaitis 1983; Welch 1991); the rarity of fineware (< 5% of
the Summerville ceramic complex); and the fact that fineware requires
greater energy expenditure in production, as measured in production
steps, than does mundane coarseware (see Appendix:Table 24).

The Summerville ceramic complex is part of the same ceramic tradition as that of Moundville (see Appendix). Technical and functional
characteristics of Moundville ceramics were studied by Steponaitis
(1983:33). He recognizes two basic groups: fine shell–tempered, burnished bowls and bottles used as eating and serving vessels (fineware);
and coarse shell–tempered, unburnished jars primarily used in cooking
(coarseware). The burnished finewares are commonly black-filmed: a
dark-to-black surface color that modern replicative experiments suggest
was produced by firing in a reducing atmosphere (Steponaitis 1983:26-27).

Additional evidence of elaboration in production occurred during the Moundville II and III phases when fineware vessel forms such as bottles were composed of joined hemispheres made from a "mold"—a bowl that served as a rest while the vessel was formed (Van der Leeuw 1981). Evidence of mold-assisted production of fineware vessels was also identified at Lubbub Creek (Mann 1983). Moundville Engraved, Carthage Incised, and Mound Place Incised are finewares that represent the greatest energy expenditure as measured in production steps. The most elaborate fineware, Moundville Engraved, and the mold-assisted technique appear at Lubbub Creek with the beginning of the Summerville II–III phase (A.D. 1200–1450/1500). This appearance correlates closely to the emergence of Moundville as an influential regional center. Summerville I and IV phase ceramics are technically and stylistically simpler, with less diversity of type-variety.

At Moundville, Peebles did not assign burials with ceramics to the superordinate segment of society: effigy vessels were found with adults of both sexes in cemeteries near mounds, while "water bottles," bowls, and jars were found with adults and subadults in cemeteries near mounds and village areas (Peebles and Kus 1977:439). Data for inferring socially determined fineware distributions at other Moundville sites are very limited. Differences in the ratios of serving to cooking wares at the White site, a local center, may indicate high-status and low-status locations within the site (Welch 1991:57–58). Apparently, locally made finewares "may have conveyed prestige as well as being objects of regular domestic use" (Welch 1991:177). Clearly, we need to examine more intrasite and intersite contexts to make the important distinction between fineware as a status item (restricted to a specific social status or rank) and fineware as a wealth item (a valued item that confers prestige but is not restricted to a specific social status or rank).

In this chapter intrasite ceramic distributions at Lubbub Creek are examined to explore the question of restricted access to specialized craft products. After the general pattern of use and disposal of pottery at the local center is evaluated, we will focus on the evidence of the production and consumption of finewares and other prestige goods throughout the settlement system, in Chapter 7.

Characteristics of the Ceramic Sample

The Lubbub Creek ceramic distributions are examined at three different scales of comparison: (1) large-scale intrasite distribution; (2) mound and village samples; and (3) sets of features referred to as household clusters. Each scale of comparison varies in the degree of social and behavioral specificity. Ceramic samples are compared to see whether inventories are disparate or comparable. Of course, it cannot be assumed that ceramic sample characteristics are determined only by social status or wealth. Temporal change must be controlled, and functional characteristics may reflect the nature of certain activities in specific contexts.

With these temporal and functional considerations in mind, the tentative assumption here is that a high degree of differential distribution of coeval ceramic types and attributes, together with a spatially restricted distribution pattern, implies restricted or preferential access to these materials by a subset of the community population and/or a specialized context of use within the community. A high degree of redundancy in the ceramic samples and a diffuse spatial distribution imply broad access to these items.

Inferences about the social implications of ceramic distributions involve assumptions about what factors shaped sample content. A wide assortment of factors may intercede in the transformation of the in-use assemblage (the artifact inventory originally in use at any one point in time) into the archaeological assemblage (those artifacts the archaeologist recovers). Different use-life spans of artifacts (Arnold 1988; Shott 1989; Mills 1989; DeBoer 1974, 1985), differential curation or retention (Binford 1973; Schiffer 1976), discard activities (Schiffer 1976; Deal 1985; Hayden and Cannon 1983), different time spans of deposits (Schiffer 1975), and other factors all militate against the probability that an archaeological assemblage approximates the in-use assemblage. In addition to this uncooperative human activity, archaeological deposits are under the constant probing, poking, and piling "perturbations" of the natural world.

Considerable effort has been expended by archaeologists to apply corrective formulas to separate useful information from the distortions. The fundamental problem with the various transformation-process formulas is that they are difficult to apply in any realistic manner. Inputs and values derived from modern observations are known, controlled, and measured. The archaeologist obviously cannot observe the prehistoric inputs, and they remain unknown. So it remains unclear what precision is gained by adding several more stages of inference whose validity is by no means secure. For these reasons I have limited comparisons of assemblage quantity and diversity to simple presence/absence and proportion measures. Conditions specific to each scale of comparison are discussed below.

The Mississippian occupation at Lubbub Creek was spread over a 23 ha area, which was sampled by auger holes and 1 m × 1 m test pits. However, most sherds discussed below represent an 18% sample of a 12 ha area of the site that was intensively excavated. Each of these hectares was randomly sampled by 10 m × 10 m units in which the plowzone was mechanically stripped away to expose in situ cultural features. Thus there are two types of sampling units at Lubbub: (1) the auger, 1 m × 1 m, and 10 m × 10 m arbitrary units; and (2) the cultural features. A 1 m³ plowzone sample from each 10 m × 10 m unit was water-screened through 1 mm mesh. Intact cultural features below the plowzone represent more-behavioral-specific units. The total ceramic sample (N = 56,144) is presented in Table 10.

Large-Scale Ceramic Distributions

The archaeological units at Lubbub Creek are partitioned into a three-phase sequence on the basis of associated diagnostic ceramic types. The diagnostic or marker types are Moundville Incised *var. Moundville* (Summerville I [S-I] phase), all varieties of Moundville Engraved (Summerville II–III [S-II–III] phase), and Alabama River Applique *var. Alabama River* (Summerville IV [S-IV] phase). Of these types, only Moundville Engraved can be considered a fineware.

The distribution of archaeological units with these types was used to demarcate the spatial extent of occupation, or a "community," for each phase (Peebles 1983a:397–402). The large-scale plot of units with each diagnostic type is presented in Figures 32–34. These distributions fail to exhibit a spatially restricted pattern expected if access to these types were limited to an elite segment of the community.

However, if high-status households were scattered throughout the community, it is possible that units with Moundville Engraved (see Figure 33) indicate their location within the community. Alternatively, the concentration of finewares in these units may merely reflect different degrees of length or intensity of occupation. An independent measure of occupation intensity is the density of daub and Mississippi Plain sherds per cubic meter of plowzone deposit. When the units with diagnostic types are plotted over the density of daub/Mississippi Plain, as in Figures 32–34, it is clear that they are highly correlated, although not isomorphic. In other words, fineware and coarseware occur together in various areas of the community where ceramics were used and discarded. The similar distribution pattern suggests that the concentration of finewares in these units is a function of intensity or duration of occupation. At the very least, the dispersed distribution of Moundville Engraved revealed in Figure 33 could be interpreted as the result of broad access and use of finewares within the Lubbub Creek community.

Table 10 Lubbub Creek Ceramic Sample: Count and Percentage

Type Variety	Total Count		Mound Count		Village Count	
	No.	%	No.	%	No.	%
Alabama River Applique						
var. Alabama River	67	0.119	22	0.367	45	0.090
Barton Incised						
Undetermined	12	0.021			12	0.024
var. Demopolis	3	0.005			3	0.006
Bell Plain						
var. Big Sandy	157	0.280	8	0.134	149	0.297
Carthage Incised						
Undetermined	106	0.189	14	0.234	92	0.183
var. Carthage	31	0.055	4	0.067	27	0.054
var. Foster	8	0.014			1	0.002
var. Moon Lake	51	0.091	13	0.217	38	0.076
var. Summerville	1	0.002			1	0.002
Mississippi Plain						
Undetermined	93	0.166	10	0.167	83	0.165
var. Warrior	49,367	87.918	5,297	88.401	44,070	87.861
var. Hull Lake	24	0.004	1	0.017	23	0.046
var. Hale	3,180	5.663	408	6.809	2,772	5.526
Mound Place Incised						
Undetermined	8	0.014			8	0.016
var. Akron	72	0.128	12	0.200	60	0.120
var. Havana	33	0.059	3	0.050	30	0.060
Moundville Engraved						
Undetermined	159	0.283	28	0.467	131	0.261
var. Hemphill	72	0.128	4	0.067	68	0.136
var. Maxwell Crossing	2	0.004			2	0.004
var. Taylorville	26	0.046			26	0.052
var. Tuscaloosa	25	0.045	3	0.050	22	0.044
var. Wiggins	64	0.114	9	0.150	55	0.110
Moundville Incised						
Undetermined	483	0.860	56	0.935	427	0.851
var. Moundville	102	0.182	19	0.317	83	0.165
var. Snow's Bend	108	0.192	24	0.401	84	0.167
var. Carrollton	1,855	3.304	57	0.951	1,798	3.585
Parkin Punctated						
Undetermined	42	0.074			42	0.074
Total	56,151	100	5,992	100	50,152	100

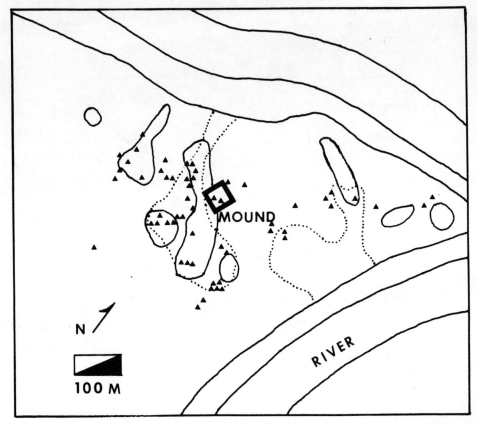

Figure 32   Plot of Units with Moundville Incised *var. Moundville,* Summerville I Phase.
Dotted lines mark the maximum concentrations of daub, and solid lines mark the
maximum concentrations of Mississippi Plain sherds. (Adapted from Peebles 1983a)

Mound and Village Ceramic Distributions

In the previous chapter functional characteristics of mound and village ceramic samples were examined as a measure of mound-related
activities. There are no significant differences in the proportions of vessel
shapes, nor are there important differences in the ratio of serving to
cooking wares, but significant vessel-size differences suggest a specialized social context, such as large-group feasts. An additional aspect of
ceramic variability—the social implications of fineware distributions—
remains to be considered.

Archaeologists have often stressed that artifact style may serve to
signify social boundaries (Wobst 1977). Highly visible, decorated pottery

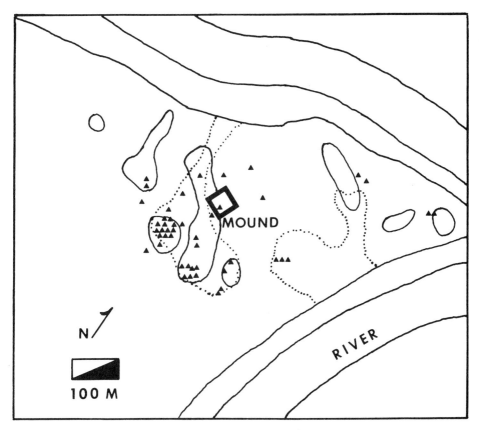

Figure 33   Plot of Units with Moundville Engraved, Summerville II–III Phase. Dotted lines mark the maximum concentrations of daub, and solid lines mark the maximum concentrations of Mississippi Plain sherds. (Adapted from Peebles 1983a)

might be expected in social contexts, such as ceremonial feasts, where status, wealth, or prestige "messages" are conveyed (Otto 1977; Kohler 1980; M. E. Smith 1987). In addition, at some point in its use the mound may have served as the location of a high-status residence. Either situation could result in greater use and discard of fineware ceramics at the mound location.

With these considerations in mind, the total ceramic sample from Lubbub Creek was subdivided into aggregate mound and village (off-mound) samples for comparative purposes (see Table 10). It is important to note the context of the samples. The village aggregate sample combines ceramics from all plowzone 10 m × 10 m samples plus all cultural features in the community and represents the entire Mississippian occupation.

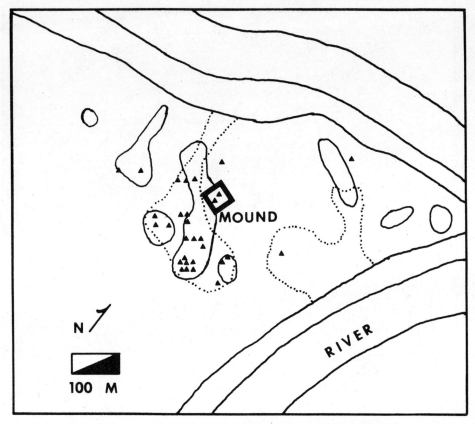

Figure 34 Plot of Units with Alabama River Applique *var. Alabama River,* Summerville IV Phase. Dotted lines mark the maximum concentrations of daub, and solid lines mark the maximum concentrations of Mississippi Plain sherds. (Adapted from Peebles 1983a)

The mound aggregate sample represents all ceramics from the mound. It includes those sherds recovered from 1 m³ plowzone samples from 10 m × 10 m units over the mound remnant; a volume sample from each of the major remnant mound construction stages; features on the premound zone; and the midden deposit at the mound edge that was formed by dumping debris from the mound summit.

Type-variety ceramic classification subdivides types into stylistic varieties. The presence or absence of decorated varieties in the two samples may serve as a simple diversity measure. Specifically, are there any type-varieties restricted solely to mound or village contexts? Inspection of Table 10 reveals that the composition of the two samples is very similar. Of the total 27 varieties, 19 are found in both mound and village contexts, but eight are found in the village sample only. Of these, Barton Incised and

Table 11   Frequency of Decorated Types in Mound and
Village Samples, S-I–S-II–III Phases

Decorated Types by Production-Step Measure[a]	Mound		Village	
	No.	%	No.	%
(5) Moundville Engraved	44	18	304	10
(4) Carthage Incised	31	13	166	6
(4) Mound Place Incised	15	6	98	3
(2) Moundville Incised	156	63	2,392	81
Total number	246		2,960	

[a] Production-step measures are after Feinman et al. 1981.

Parkin Punctated can be ignored because of comparative evidence that they may postdate mound use (see Appendix).

Moundville Engraved, Carthage Incised, and Mound Place Incised are the most "costly" finewares as measured by production steps. All three types are found in both mound and village samples. However, five stylistic varieties are present only in the village samples—in extremely small quantities. Contrary to expectations, the mound does not have the greatest diversity of stylistic varieties. Yet given the notorious positive correlation between assemblage diversity and sample size (Jones et al. 1983; Cowgill 1986), the one-sided distribution of these few rare types (38 out of a total 56,151 sherds) in the village sample is most likely due to the disproportionate sample sizes.

Mound and village aggregate ceramic samples can be subdivided into total decorated/undecorated sherds. The proportions of decorated sherds in the two samples were compared (mound = 0.04 and village = 0.06). While the proportion of decorated sherds is slightly higher in the village, the difference is minor. Relative frequencies of individual decorated types in mound and village samples are compared in Table 11, with the undecorated majority removed. There are higher relative frequencies of the three high-cost fineware types—Moundville Engraved, Carthage Incised, and Mound Place Incised—in the mound's decorated sample. Perhaps this could be interpreted as evidence of greater fineware use in mound contexts. This result would be consistent with the mound's proposed function as a focus of community rituals and feasts. However, in consideration of the tiny proportion of the total sample that these fineware types represent, proportion comparisons that include the undecorated majority probably provide a more standardized measure. On that basis the differences in the two samples must be considered minor.

Household Ceramic Samples

It is possible to examine ceramic distributions on a finer scale of context than the large-scale intrasite and mound-village patterns. If the mound were primarily a specialized communal or corporate-group facility, as seems to be the case, then perhaps a comparison of household ceramic samples would disclose differences in access or use of fineware ceramics within the community.

Ethnologists generally define households as the minimal economic and domestic unit in small prestate societies (Sahlins 1972). At Lubbub Creek functionally equivalent feature clusters were identified that represent the remains of domestic residences. These features are grouped into analytical units referred to as household clusters (see Flannery 1976; Drennan 1976). Each household cluster is composed of house floors, post molds, hearths, graves, pits, or small sheet middens that are spatially restricted and temporally associated. Some feature clusters that met these minimal requirements were, nevertheless, rejected because subsequent occupations had contributed to overlapping features from different phases. Only the most spatially distinct household clusters were used in the analysis.

While it is unlikely that all features grouped within a household cluster were in simultaneous use, all can be assigned to a single phase interval. Eleven household clusters are defined. Individual household clusters are illustrated in Figures 35–47. The floor area, number of features, and ceramic content of each household cluster are presented in Table 12.

To summarize, household clusters at Lubbub Creek are generally similar in terms of architecture, layout, and material remains. Oak and pine were the sources of poles used as a framework, and impressions on fired daub indicate that these structures were covered with a sheathing of cane. There is little direct evidence about the form of roof. The absence of interior post molds indicates that most structures were of flexible pole construction in which the pole framework was bent inward and lashed together at the top to form a dome-shaped structure. However, large interior post molds that may have supported a heavier roof were associated with the Household 1–2 (H 1-2), H 2-2, and H 4-4 structures. The H 3-2 structure appeared to be the only possible example of a circular dwelling with a sunken floor, a form possibly analogous to the traditional

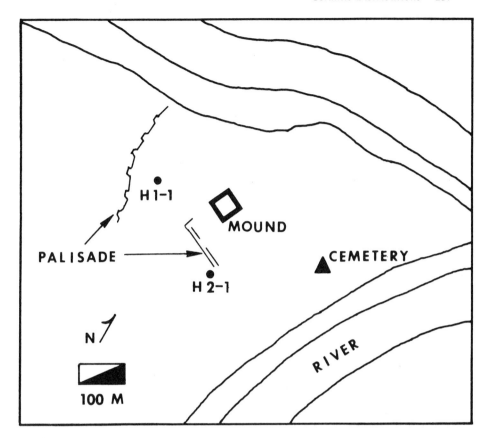

Figure 35 Household Clusters at Lubbub Creek, Summerville I Phase

winter house of the historical Southeast (Swanton 1979:386; Faulkner 1977).

All houses produced similar evidence of hunting and agricultural implements. Lithic tools and debitage were not abundant at Lubbub Creek. This is a frequently observed situation for late prehistoric sites on the Gulf Coastal Plain and apparently reflects reliance on cane, wood, bone, and other perishable materials. Several household clusters also produced chert microdrills of a form that has been linked to the manufacture of shell beads (the social implications of this activity are examined in Chapter 7).

The depositional characteristics of the household ceramic samples can be summarized as follows: small sherds incorporated into household floors, small internal pits, and post molds; sherds dispersed within a few meters of the household, some into thin sheet middens; sherds, together

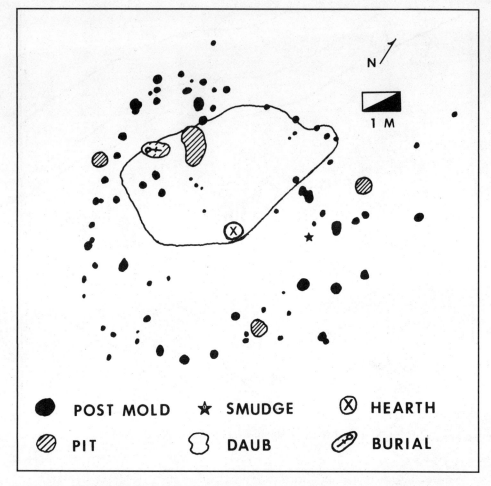

Figure 36   Household Cluster 1-1

with food debris, incorporated into abandoned storage pits or low places in the immediate household vicinity; and pottery interred either as intentional offerings or unintentional fill in graves in the immediate household vicinity. All evidence indicates sherds were deposited in the vicinity of their use.

Three measures of household ceramic variability are examined: (1) the abundance of finewares; (2) the ratio of decorated to undecorated ceramics; and (3) the ratio of serving to cooking wares. Did all households have access to or use finewares? The decorated potsherds found in each household cluster are tabulated in Table 13. In all three phases household clusters contain the basic decorated types, including finewares. During

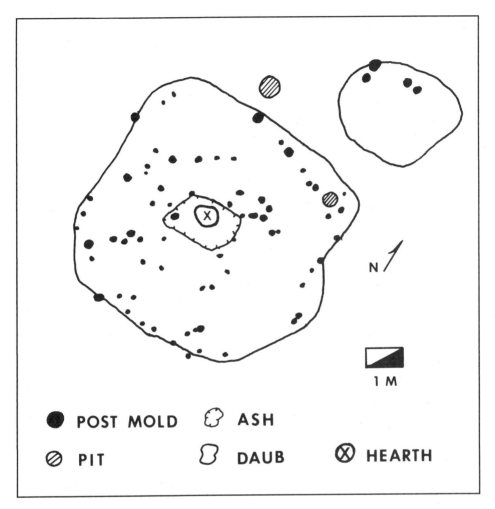

Figure 37 Household Cluster 2-1

the Summerville II–III phase, the highest-cost fineware—Moundville Engraved—is present in each household cluster. While the ceramic content of the households is not uniform, it is clear that there was broad access to or use of finewares in household contexts.

When household-cluster samples are grouped by phase assemblages found in household contexts can be compared to the aggregate mound and village samples. The important distinction between burnished and unburnished pottery and the strong relationship these categories have to serving and cooking functions have been discussed. The expectation is that a higher ratio of serving to cooking wares should indicate food

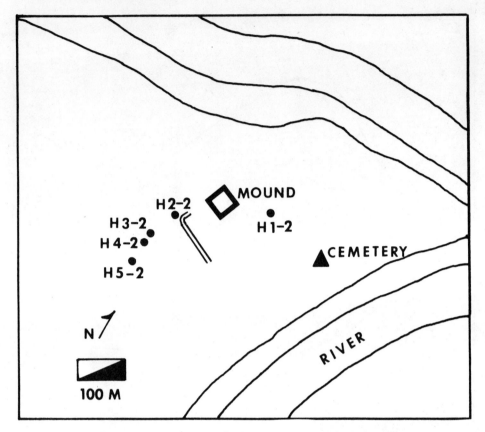

Figure 38   Household Clusters at Lubbub Creek, Summerville II–III Phase

consumption contexts that emphasize displays of status or wealth. A comparison of the mean proportion of burnished sherds from households in each phase (Summerville I: $\bar{x} = 0.06$; Summerville II–III: $\bar{x} = 0.08$; Summerville IV: $\bar{x} = 0.07$) are not very different from those observed for the aggregate village (0.06) and mound (0.08) samples. The slightly higher proportion of burnished sherds in Summerville II–III households is probably a direct reflection of the increase in the number of burnished types in use during this phase.

Similarly, ratios of decorated to undecorated sherds may indicate status or wealth differences. The mean proportion of decorated sherds found in total households of each phase is remarkably constant (Summerville I: $\bar{x} = 0.02$; Summerville II–III: $\bar{x} = 0.03$; Summerville IV: $\bar{x} = 0.02$). Again, these values appear to be influenced primarily by the increase or decrease of total decorated types present in each phase. Thus the Summerville II–III value may be higher simply because a greater diversity of

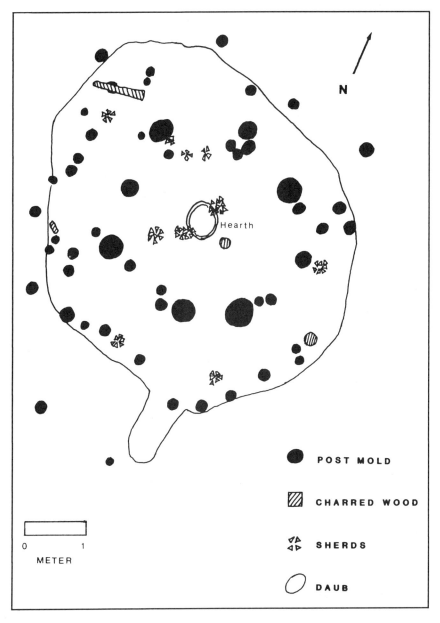

N

Hearth

● POST MOLD

▨ CHARRED WOOD

SHERDS

◯ DAUB

0   1
METER

Figure 39   Household Cluster 1-2 (From Jenkins and Ensor 1981:Figure 64)

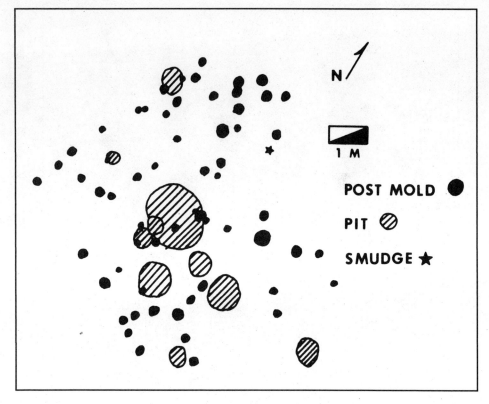

Figure 40   Household Cluster 2-2 (From Blitz and Peebles 1983:Figure 2)

decorated types were in use during that interval. It is less clear why the mean proportions are lower than the aggregate village (0.06) and mound (0.04). Possibly this reflects variation in household depositional processes.

Several attempts to compare ceramic quantity and diversity in individual household clusters were abandoned as unproductive. A subtle scale of wealth based on quantity and diversity of sherds is not possible because there is no way to separate or determine confidently which factors—transformational conditions, social access, or length of occupation—contributed to the content of individual household assemblages. No convincing methodology is available to solve the equifinality problem.

Summary

It has been argued by some that ranked social order and restricted access to certain resources, such as specialized craft products, are typical

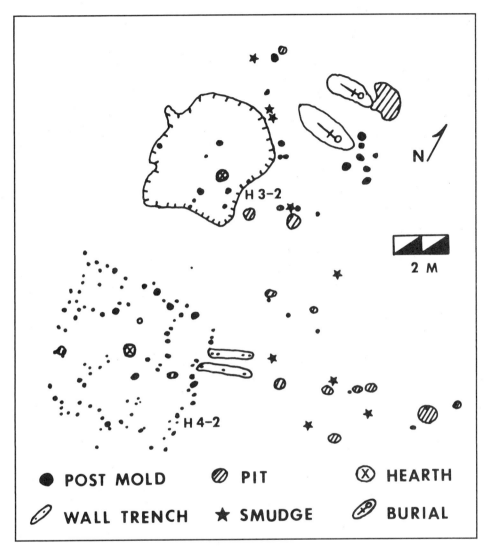

Figure 41 Household Clusters 3-2 and 4-2 (From Blitz and Peebles 1983:Figure 11)

of Mississippian chiefdoms. Because Mississippian fineware ceramics in western Alabama are presumably valued items that some investigators believe to be specialized craft products, ceramic distributions may provide the basis for social inferences about access or use. The question of differential access to ceramics at Lubbub Creek was examined on three different scales: (1) large-scale intrasite distribution; (2) comparison of mound and village samples; and (3) comparison of ceramic samples

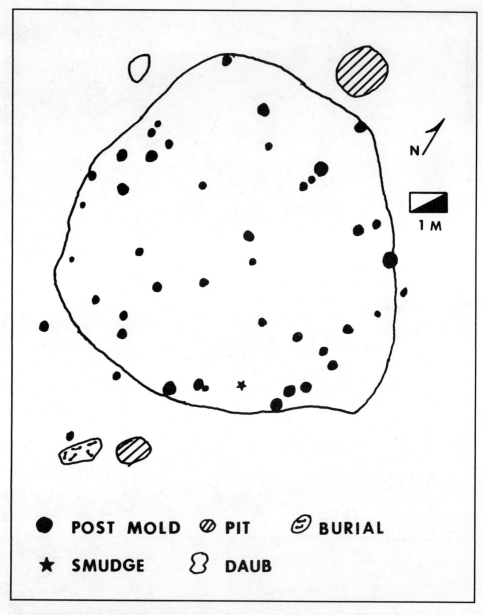

Figure 42   Household Cluster 5-2 (From Blitz and Peebles 1983:Figure 9)

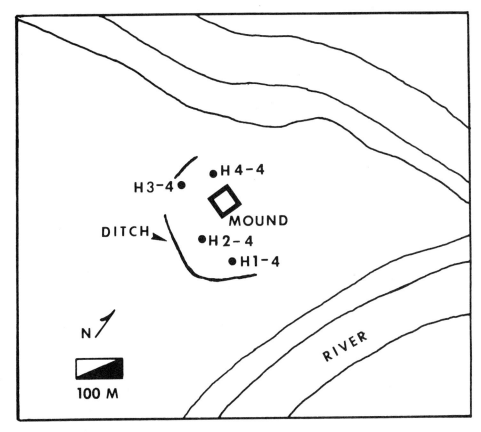

Figure 43   Household Clusters at Lubbub Creek, Summerville IV Phase

between individual household clusters. Large-scale intrasite distributions failed to reveal the highly concentrated pattern of finewares expected if access were restricted to an elite. Instead, fineware and coarseware were deposited together in community middens. Measured as a proportion of the total decorated sample (undecorated majority removed), there are slightly higher frequencies of finewares in the mound sample. However, ratios of decorated to undecorated sherds, and burnished to unburnished sherds, vary little in mound and village samples. All household-cluster samples contain low frequencies of finewares. Mean proportions of decorated and burnished sherds in household assemblages vary little from aggregate mound and village samples.

The ubiquitous presence of finewares in all community contexts suggests that fineware ceramics at Lubbub Creek were broadly accessible

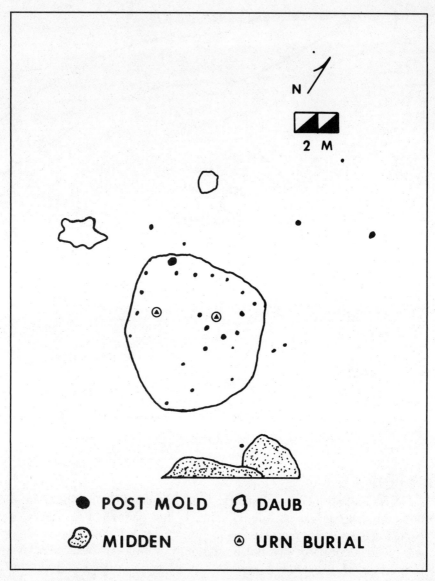

N

2 M

● POST MOLD   ⏵ DAUB

⬯ MIDDEN   ⊚ URN BURIAL

Figure 44   Household Cluster 1-4 (From Albright 1983:Figure 15)

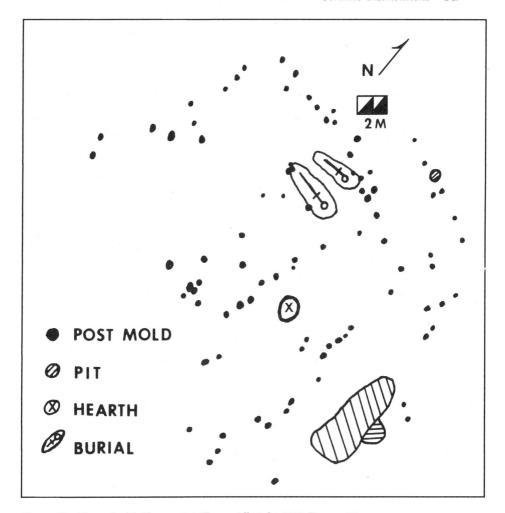

Figure 45   Household Cluster 2-4 (From Albright 1983:Figure 25)

wealth items and were not restricted to an "elite." Possible evidence of greater fineware use in mound contexts, if valid, is consistent with the mound's proposed function as the focus of community rituals and feasts.

Up to this point, we have considered the intrasite distribution of only one highly valued artifact category, fineware ceramic vessels. If there was a positive correlation among access to valued items, degree of social ranking, and size of polity, then two-tiered and three-tiered settlement systems might have different patterns of access. If prestige goods

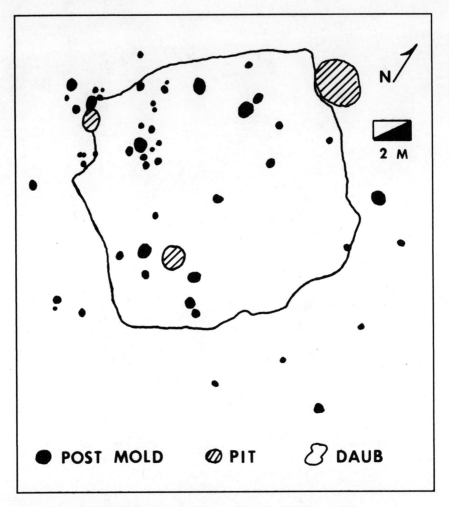

● POST MOLD   ⊘ PIT   ∂ DAUB

Figure 46   Household Cluster 3-4 (From Albright 1983:Figure 30)

and evidence of their manufacture were largely restricted to local centers, as current interpretations of the Moundville political economy suggest (e.g., Welch 1991), was this the case at Lubbub Creek as well? This
question can be answered by a comparison of prestige-goods production
and consumption distributions, including artifacts other than fineware
ceramics, at both farmsteads and the local center.

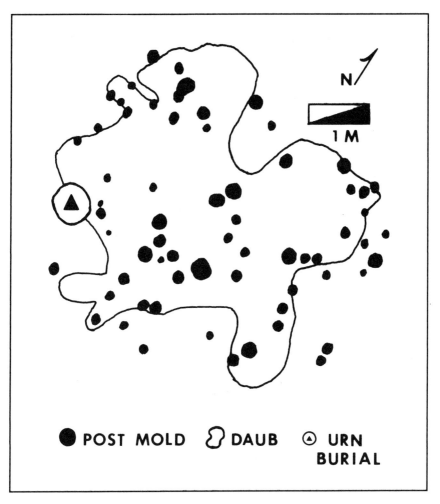

Figure 47   Household Cluster 4-4 (From Albright 1983:Figure 35)

Table 12 Summary of Household Cluster Floor Size, Number of Features, and Ceramic Content

	Summerville I		Summerville II–III					Summerville IV			
	H 1-1	H 2-1	H 1-2	H 2-2	H 3-2	H 4-2	H 5-2	H 1-4	H 2-4	H 3-4	H 4-4
Floor (m^2)	35	35	24	56	42	52	42	38	36	48	22
No. of burnished sherds	17	46	123	177	142	84	61	42	96	30	55
No. of unburnished sherds	469	477	2,058	1,314	2,395	705	727	1,023	1,190	750	439
No. of decorated sherds	14	6	43	65	74	33	12	25	36	15	10
No. of undecorated sherds	472	517	2,138	1,426	2,463	756	776	1,040	1,250	765	484
Total No. of ceramics	486	523	2,181	1,491	2,537	789	778	1,065	1,286	779	494
No. by type-variety	5	5	11	11	14	12	11	7	11	6	8
No. of features	64	50	55	62	35	85	56	25	80	55	64

Table 13 Decorated Potsherds from Household Clusters

	Summerville I Phase				
	H 1-1	H 2-1			
Moundville Incised					
var. Carrollton	2	0			
var. Moundville	3	2			
Undetermined	9	0			
Carthage Incised					
var. Moon Lake	0	1			
Undetermined	0	1			

	Summerville II–III Phase				
	H 1-2	H 2-2	H 3-2	H 4-2	H 5-2
Carthage Incised					
var. Carthage	1	0	1	0	0
var. Moon Lake	0	2	2	1	1
Undetermined	5	2	1	0	2
Mound Place Incised					
var. Akron	0	0	1	1	1
var. Havana	0	0	2	1	2
Undetermined	1	1	1	1	0
Moundville Engraved					
var. Hemphill	1	1	3	3	0
var. Tuscaloosa	0	0	2	0	0
var. Wiggins	0	0	13	5	0
Undetermined	0	0	15	7	2
Moundville Incised					
var. Carrollton	8	8	18	3	1
var. Snow's Bend	4	4	4	0	2
Undetermined	23	23	44	5	4

	Summerville IV Phase			
	H 1-4	H 2-4	H 3-4	H 4-4
Alabama River Applique				
var. Alabama River	1	24	6	1
Barton Incised				
Undetermined	6	0	0	0
Carthage Incised				
var. Carthage	0	5	1	0
Undetermined	3	2	0	0

Table 13 (continued)

	Summerville IV Phase			
	H 1-4	H 2-4	H 3-4	H 4-4
Moundville Incised				
var. Carrollton	2	2	0	2
Undetermined	12	5	3	3
Parkin Punctated				
Undetermined	0	3	0	2

CHAPTER 7

Prestige Goods at
Lubbub Creek and Beyond

I N CHAPTER 2, models of Mississippian sociopolitical organization
and political economy, developed from research at Moundville, were
examined. A question was posed: what form will social ranking and
resource control take in a smaller two-tiered settlement system—a local
center and farmsteads—when compared to a three-tiered system such
as Moundville?

The Moundville models (Peebles and Kus 1977; Peebles 1978, 1983b;
Welch 1991) can be briefly summarized. Differential distribution of certain artifact categories are assumed to reflect the prerogatives of an
ascribed status, which in turn becomes the basis for definition of super-
ordinate/subordinate social rank at Moundville. Political administration,
and specifically craft production and distribution, is considered to be
under the centralized control of the superordinate rank at Moundville.
Prestige goods of nonlocal raw materials were either imported whole or
made only at Moundville. Distribution of prestige goods is expected to
be largely restricted to Moundville except for a few prestige goods
passed down the settlement hierarchy to local centers, where possession
is restricted to a "nobility." High-ranking individuals at local centers
will not have access to those symbols that mark paramount status at
Moundville.

In the Moundville models social hierarchy is assumed to map directly onto settlement hierarchy, with a strict dichotomy between "commoners" on farmsteads and "nobility" at local centers. Subsistence
products from farmsteads provision elites at the local center. Since prestige goods of nonlocal materials are said to be restricted to the local
center, it is difficult to see what benefit farmstead occupants gained from

such actions or what factors would bind them to such an arrangement. Perhaps they obtained greenstone celts and finewares, which are found at farmsteads but presumably produced only at Moundville (Welch 1991).

The degree to which Summerville patterns are similar or different from the Moundville models should be very informative about organizational variability in Mississippian societies. If Tombigbee sites were organized as a part of the Moundville polity, or in a similar manner, then artifacts that mark Peebles's superordinate rank would be expected to occur only at local centers such as Lubbub Creek. Supralocal artifacts that identify a rank or formal office should not be equivalent to those that mark the highest-status positions at Moundville. Production of prestige goods from nonlocal raw materials would not be expected at the local center, since such activities are thought to be restricted to Moundville. Consumption of craft items of nonlocal materials would be restricted to a subset of the local-center population. Prestige goods of nonlocal raw materials would not occur at farmsteads.

The purpose of this chapter is to examine evidence for production and consumption of prestige goods, in light of expectations from the Moundville models, within a two-tiered settlement system on the Moundville periphery. These questions are addressed:

1. Were prestige goods produced at the local center?
2. Were prestige goods produced at farmsteads?
3. Were prestige goods consumed at farmsteads?
4. Do the context and distribution of prestige goods suggest the presence of craft specialization or control of access by an elite?
5. To what degree did the Summerville peoples participate in regional exchange/alliance networks?

Craft Specialization

Assumptions about the ability of a Mississippian elite to control access to resources or wealth are closely tied to the development of specialized craft production (Peebles and Kus 1977). In this view, craft specialists produced goods for an elite and those items accrued to an elite. Theoretically, support of craft specialists permits elites to convert subsistence surpluses into scarce durable goods and then control, restrict, or manipulate access to them in order to further political ambitions. For this reason investigation of craft specialization must play an important role in understanding Mississippian societies.

Unfortunately, there is little agreement among southeastern archaeologists about what constitutes craft specialization or how to recognize the evidence in archaeological remains. A further complication is that the degree of social ranking, polity size, availability of raw materials, and a host of other factors will no doubt result in considerable organizational variability in craft production among Mississippian societies. Nor can it be expected that all classes of craft items were produced, distributed, or consumed in the same manner.

Interpretations of Mississippian political economy will be most secure when the production and consumption of prestige goods are examined at all levels of the settlement system. Given the interpretive ambiguities so common to archaeological remains, criteria for identifying archaeological evidence of craft specialization should permit comparison to investigations at other Mississippian sites. Of the criteria suggested by Yerkes (1989; following Evans 1978), the most important evidence for the present study would be workshops or specialized areas for craft production; specialized tool kits; hoards or caches for storing finished craft products; and differential distributions of finished products and evidence of craft production, both within sites and within settlement systems.

In the following sections production and consumption evidence for prestige goods is examined within the two-tiered Summerville settlement system. Provenance and context data for selected artifact classes are summarized in Table 14.

Pottery Manufacture and Consumption

Evidence of ceramic production at Lubbub Creek consisted of fired coils, tempered clay lumps, and pottery "trowels" (Mann 1983:106). Fired coils are tempered coils of paste for forming the vessel, and clay lumps are masses of prepared, tempered paste. These materials were presumably fired as an accidental by-product of pottery making. Pottery trowels apparently functioned as an anvillike support held against the interior of the pot as the vessel walls were shaped with a paddle (Steponaitis 1983:22, Figure 3).

Provenance and context data for these materials (Table 15) reveal no concentrated pattern and no single provenance in which all three categories are associated together. Trowels, lumps, and coils are all found in household clusters, suggesting manufacture within the domestic unit. Inspection of the size of coil temper indicates that both coarseware and fineware were manufactured at Lubbub Creek.

No evidence of pottery manufacture—coils, lumps, or trowels—was recorded for any of the farmstead sites. Excavation units sometimes

Table 14 Distribution of Production Evidence for Selected Artifacts

Artifact	Raw Material	Source	Location of Production		Comments
			Farmstead	Lubbub	
Celt (axe)	greenstone	nonlocal	no	?	no preforms; fragments present
Discoidal	greenstone	nonlocal	no	no	no local evidence
Beads, gorgets, pendants	marine shell	nonlocal	yes	yes	inferred from microliths
Earspools, symbol badges	copper	nonlocal	no	no	no local evidence
Beads, hoe	freshwater shell	local	yes	yes	microliths, cut shell by-product
Points, flake tools	chert	local	yes	yes	hammerstones, preforms, primary debitage
Groundstone tools, discoidal	sandstone, hematite, limestone, quartzite	local	yes	yes	fragments; primary debitage(?); discoidal preforms
Incised disk	sandstone	?	no	no	
Fineware ceramics	clay	local	no	yes	fired coils, prepared paste lumps, trowels
Coarseware ceramics	clay	local	no	yes	fired coils, prepared paste lumps, trowels

Table 15 Provenance and Context of Pottery Production Evidence at Lubbub Creek

Hectare	Unit	Context	Evidence	Temper
600N/-400E	5212/115	plowzone	lumps	coarse shell
600N/-400E	5048/478	plowzone	lumps	fine shell
600N/-300E	7187/10	?	coils	fine shell
500N/-400E	3612/387	Household Cluster 1-1	lumps	coarse shell
500N/-400E	4300/11	?	trowel	—
500N/-400E	4123/501	?	coil	coarse shell
500N/-300E	4712	?	coils	coarse shell
500N/-300E	8407/48	Household Cluster 4-4	coils	fine shell
500N/-300E	6479	plowzone	coils	coarse shell
500N/-300E	8530/2	Mound Structure 5A	coil	coarse shell
500N/-300E	4588/723	Mound midden dump	coil	coarse shell
500N/-300E	4775/206	plowzone	coil	coarse shell
500N/-300E	6408/23	?	coil	coarse shell
500N/-300E	6478	plowzone	coil	coarse shell
500N/-200E	8510	plowzone	lump	fine shell
400N/-400E	2317/91	Household Cluster 4-2	trowel	coarse shell
400N/-300E	3454	Household Cluster 2-4	coils	coarse shell
400N/-300E	2562/3,4	plowzone	coils	coarse shell
400N/-300E	4859/539	Structure 6	coils	coarse shell
400N/-300E	8164	Household Cluster 2-2	coil	coarse shell
400N/-300E	6311	?	coil	fine shell
400N/-300E	8174	Household Cluster 2-2	coil	fine shell

included "fired clay" pieces but it is unlikely that tempered lumps, coils, or trowels were overlooked in analysis. Assuming this negative result is not due to sampling error, pottery production seems to have been restricted to the local centers. The lack of evidence for pottery production at farmsteads lends additional support to the possibility, mentioned in Chapter 5, that the smaller size of farmstead jars may have resulted from transportation considerations.

Nevertheless, Moundville Engraved and other finewares were found at farmsteads (Jenkins 1981:Tables 8–15), mirroring the broad access evident at the local center. It is interesting to note, however, that diversity of fineware type-varieties at the one excavated Summerville II–III phase farmstead, 1Gr2, is considerably less than that of Lubbub Creek assemblages. Because of small surface collections, available samples are inadequate to evaluate fineware diversity at other Summerville farmsteads. But, given that fineware sherds are repeatedly encountered at farmsteads (Rucker 1974:84–85; Blakeman 1975:Plate 16; Jenkins et al.

1975:122), fineware diversity most likely reflects site function or duration rather than status-based restrictions to access.

Celts and Discoidals

Low-density tool production debris, composed almost entirely of local stone, is common to all domestic unit contexts. The most valued nonlocal stone was probably greenstone (greenschist), for which the closest raw source is in the eastern Alabama Piedmont. Whole or broken greenstone celts (axes) were present both at Lubbub Creek (N = 16) and at farmstead sites (N = 4). Greenstone "fragments" (N = 35) were dispersed throughout the Lubbub Creek site in contexts dated to the latter part of the Mississippian occupation (Allan 1983:188). I have not examined these pieces to determine whether they represent production debris or merely use-wear chips. So the question of whether unfinished blanks or finished celts were imported into the central Tombigbee area cannot be answered at this time. No greenstone fragments occur at farmsteads in Mississippian contexts. The scarcity of recovered greenstone presumably reflects very low-volume importation and careful curation.

Discoidals, or "chunkey stones," are gaming pieces found at both Lubbub Creek (N = 11) and farmsteads (N = 3). All were made of local hematite, sandstone, limestone, or quartzite except for one finished greenstone example from Lubbub Creek. Discoidal preforms at both Lubbub Creek and Tibbee Creek imply that these were items produced within the household. See Table 14 for provenance and production evidence for selected lithic artifacts.

Microliths and Shell Beads

Marine shell was cut, drilled, and ground for various ornaments— especially disk and cylindrical beads—in the Late Woodland Miller III phase and subsequent Summerville phases. Ensor (1981, 1991) has defined a distinctive microlithic technology used principally for shell-bead manufacture. According to Ensor (1991), the production of microliths from chert flakes that appeared in Miller III was replaced, in the transition to Summerville I, with a more complex microlithic core-blade technology that emphasized microdrills (mean length 21 mm).He subjected a large sample of microdrills from Lubbub Creek to microscopic use-wear analysis and concluded that a majority were used to drill shell beads. He even discovered that some samples still retained shell residue (Ensor 1991:30). Ensor notes that similar microlithic industries appear during the Emergent or Early Mississippi period in the American Bottom,

Central Mississippi Valley, and northwestern Florida, as well as the Moundville area itself (cf. Steponaitis 1986). (I would add that a possible adjunct to the adoption of the bow in these regions ca. A.D. 700—the bow drill—may have played an important role in the amplification of these industries by permitting greater efficiency in bead production.)

Ensor examined the context of microlith and shell-bead production for indicators of craft specialization at Lubbub Creek. He adopts a definition of craft specialization as "the relatively regular and standardized production of a craft product at levels clearly higher than those necessary for household consumption, by persons having restricted access to specific technology, skills, and raw materials characterized by a full-blown or emergent division of labor" (Michaels 1987:61, cited in Ensor 1991:33).

Ensor's sample of 195 microcores, microblades, and microdrills was obtained during excavations in the 1Pi33 area of the community about 150 m southeast of the platform mound. Of 195 microliths, 89 (74 microdrills) were found in a single pit, Feature 51. The rest of the 1Pi33 sample was recovered from various surface, feature, burial, and structure locations. Extensive excavations elsewhere at the site, despite the increase in area and volume, recovered less than half the number of microdrills found in the 1Pi33 area and no concentrations as in Feature 51 (Allan 1983). From this distribution, Ensor (1991:36) infers "the presence of one or more specialized areas of craft production or workshops." The overall distributional concentration, together with a technological "standardization" in the microlith assemblage, suggests "that reasonable evidence for a part-time lithic craft specialization exists at Lubbub Creek" (Ensor 1991:36).

Much of Ensor's argument depends on interpretation of the unusual Feature 51 context. Feature 51 is not a workshop. Microliths had been "systematically collected from a restricted area and redeposited there" (Ensor 1991:36), mixed together with typical domestic refuse (Jenkins and Ensor 1981:Table 9). Nor does it appear to be a hoard, in the usual meaning of the term as a cache of finished tools, because all stages of microlith reduction were deposited there. But if it was not a hoard, one wonders why so many complete tools were thrown away. Because these tools exhibit use-wear, perhaps they were worn, judged unfit for further use, and discarded.

The general form of Feature 51 suggests an unused open storage pit that served as a convenient receptacle for trash generated close by, perhaps even by several households. Distinct layers visible within the feature (Jenkins and Ensor 1981:Figure 68) clearly indicate that microliths and garbage entered the deep pit in multiple dumping episodes. Cer-

tainly concentrated production activities occurred in the immediate locale, but the vicinity of Feature 51 is not a workshop in the sense of a
community area for specialized activities separate from domestic contexts, as interpreted by Ensor (1991:34). It is part of an extensive area of
Miller III and Summerville I occupation with burials, numerous post
molds, daub, and abundant domestic debris.

Ensor assigns the microlith assemblage in Feature 51 to the Summerville I phase, although he notes there is difficulty with this assessment.
Two radiocarbon samples from Feature 51 both date to A.D. 1030 ± 55.
These samples fall within the eleventh-century interval in which several
Miller III and Summerville I phase absolute dates overlap. However, the
vast majority of ceramics recovered from Feature 51 are Miller III, mixed
with minor amounts of Summerville I sherds (Jenkins 1982:Table 24). On
this basis, Feature 51 was assigned to the Miller III Gainesville subphase
in the original report (Jenkins and Ensor 1981:Table 9). This seems to be
the most plausible assignment. In other words, this feature is a typical
Miller III food-storage pit into which an unusually large number of microdrills and associated debitage were dumped. The intensification of
microdrill production that Ensor identifies begins at the Late Woodland–
Mississippian transition, and not in spatially discrete, specialized workshops but domestic contexts.

Interestingly, there is no marine-shell debris such as blanks, preforms, or scraps associated with Feature 51, or anywhere else on the site
(Curren 1981:Table 4; Woodrick 1983b:Table 9). Instead, Feature 51 contains only local freshwater-shell artifacts: seven finished *Goniobasis*
beads, 16 cut shell by-products, and 13 mussel-shell hoes. The shell hoes
exhibit use-wear (Curren 1981:185). This suggests that they were not a
hoard for future use, but discards. Utilized shell hoes were occasionally
found in domestic debris elsewhere at Lubbub Creek (Woodrick 1983b:
Table 9), as they were at farmsteads (Atkinson et al. 1980:144).

Microdrills were discovered throughout the community in the
plowzone, in domestic refuse, on structure floors, and in burial contexts
(Table 16). Cut shell by-products of freshwater mussel and isolated
marine- or freshwater-shell beads are dispersed in very low numbers in
contexts similar to those of microliths. It must be concluded that microlith production and use, and presumably the making of beads and other
shell artifacts, was an activity carried out in a number of households.

There is a somewhat different situation at farmsteads. With the absence of microliths at Tibbee Creek and Kellogg, it seems likely that
microtool manufacture or shell-bead production was not a part of farmstead activities during Summerville I. These circumstances changed in
the Summerville II–III and IV phases. Ensor reports that at the 1Gr2

Table 16 Microdrill Provenance

Phase	Location	Quantity	References
S-I	Household Cluster 2-1, Structure 2	3	Blitz 1983c:261; Allan 1983:182
S-II–III	Household Cluster 2-2, Structure 7	1	Allan 1983:182
Mississippian	mound fill	1	Allan 1983:182
Mississippian?	plowzone	7	Allan 1983:182
1Pi33 Area			
S-I, Mississippian	Features, burials	30	Ensor 1991:Table 1
Miller III?	Feature 51	74	Ensor 1991:Table 1
Mississippian	test units	33	Ensor 1991:Table 1
Mississippian?	plowzone	15	Ensor 1991:Table 1
S-II–III	Household Cluster 1-2, Structure 1, Feature 6	1	Ensor 1991:Table 69
Farmsteads			
S-II–III	1Gr2; Burial 2	3	Ensor 1981:Table 31
S-II–III	1Gr2; Burial 17	1	Ensor 1981:Table 31
Mississippian?	1Gr2; units, features	15	Ensor 1981:Tables 27, 28
Mississippian?	Yarborough; units	9	Solis and Walling 1982:Tables 24, 28
Mississippian?	Yarborough, Feature 19B	1	Solis and Walling 1982:Table 19
Mississippian	Yarborough, Feature 3B	1	Solis and Walling 1982:Table 19

Note: Microcores and microblades also occur but are not included in these counts because these categories were not tabulated or classified in a standardized manner for all sites.

farmstead an adult male was buried with three microdrills and a tool kit that consisted of an abrader and possible bone flakers. Another adult burial in the 1Pi33 area of Lubbub Creek had a similar tool kit but with arrow points rather than microdrills. Ensor (1991:34) suggests these may be individuals involved in "specialization of labor." Several microliths at the Yarborough farmstead are from potentially mixed deposits, but one microdrill is in a Mississippian context—Feature 3B. At farmsteads, as at Lubbub Creek, no marine-shell debris or bead blanks were recovered.

Where Did the Beads Go and Who Got Them?

Within the Summerville settlement system marine-shell beads are found almost exclusively as direct burial associations at both farmsteads and Lubbub Creek. The quantity of marine shell beads, together with age and sex of the recipient, is presented in Table 17, for all burials with marine-shell beads at Lubbub Creek, Tibbee Creek, Kellogg, and 1Gr2. While the total sample is quite small, an age-sex pattern for the individual recipients of these beads seems to be evident. At the farmsteads only subadults (including infants) receive marine-shell beads, while at Lubbub Creek both sexes and all ages receive beads, but the single adult male burial with beads contains the greatest quantity. However, in the total sample, subadults receive the greatest number of beads. Three of the four freshwater-shell-bead accompaniments are also associated with subadults.

Only a few other marine-shell ornaments were discovered. A total of five engraved shell gorgets, all associated with adult men and women, were present at farmsteads, but not at Lubbub Creek. Three marine-shell "dippers" were recovered: two with an adult male at Kellogg; and one with a subadult at Lubbub Creek. Large conch/whelk-shell "dippers" are known to have been used by historical southeastern peoples to ladle hot "black drink" *(Ilex vomitoria)* from large pots, and marine-shell "dippers" have considerable antiquity in the archaeological record of the Gulf Coastal Plain (Milanich and Fairbanks 1980:87, 124).

"Superordinate" Prestige Goods at Summerville Sites

Peebles's identification of a superordinate social dimension of ascribed social status at Moundville was based upon the differential distribution of certain rare artifacts in burial associations. Several of these Moundville "superordinate" artifacts are present at Summerville sites but in contexts not always consistent with the Moundville model of status hierarchy. The Tombigbee materials are found in both burial and nonburial contexts (Tables 18–19). Copper symbols and galena cubes are found only at Lubbub Creek. Incised stone disk "palette" fragments, mineral pigments, marine-shell beads, and pendants of black bear teeth are found at both farmsteads and Lubbub Creek.

Black bear teeth and raw minerals for pigments are probably the only categories that were locally available. Raw minerals for pigments are so common in all contexts that it is improbable that access was in any way socially restricted. The black bear tooth pendants are found only with subadult burials. Copper-covered earspools and other copper ar-

Table 17 Age and Sex Association of Marine-Shell Cylindrical
and Disk Beads in Burial Contexts

	No. of beads	*Material*	*Age and Sex*
	Lubbub Creek (S-I phase)[a]		
Burial 20	165	whelk/conch	adult male (35 yrs.)
Burial 30	67	whelk/conch	adult female (21–23 yrs.)
Burial 31	24	whelk/conch	infant (1.5–2.5 yrs.)
Burial 25	14	whelk/conch	subadult (12 yrs.)
	Tibbee Creek (S-I phase)[b]		
Burial 15	183	*Marginella*	infant (2 yrs.)
Burial 9	4	whelk/conch	infant (2 yrs.)
	Kellogg (S-I phase)[c]		
Burial 2	467	whelk/conch	subadult (10 yrs.)
Burial 3	327	whelk/conch	subadult (4–6 yrs.)
	Lubbub Creek (S-II–III phase)[d]		
Burial 24	202	whelk/conch	subadult (9–11 yrs.)
Burial 2	19	*Marginella*	subadult (15 yrs.)
	1Gr2 (S-II–III phase)[e]		
Burial 2	51	whelk/conch	subadult (4.5–5.5 yrs.)

[a] From Cole et al. 1982:Table 2.
[b] From O'Hear et al. 1981:202–203.
[c] From Atkinson et al. 1980:Table 10.
[d] From Cole et al. 1982:Table 2.
[e] From Jenkins 1975:81, 263.

tifacts are found only with adult male burials at Lubbub Creek. Also at Lubbub Creek, single galena cubes were found with two adult male burials, and two other cubes were recovered from the plowzone. Incised stone disk palette fragments occur in nonburial contexts: one fragment from premound compound Structure 5B; and 32 fragments (perhaps all from one disk) in a single Summerville II–III phase house, Structure 7 (Household Cluster 2-2). In addition, four stone palette fragments were recovered from the Yarborough farmstead (Solis and Walling 1982: Tables 26, 29).

Before we leave the subject of superordinate artifacts and the Sum-

Table 18   Distribution of Prestige Items in Burial Contexts

Artifact	Farmstead	Lubbub Creek	References
Copper plate, symbol badge		X	Jenkins 1982:130–133
Copper earspool*		X	Allan 1983:189; Blitz and Peebles 1983:301; Cole et al. 1982:Table 9
Copper fragment		X	Cole et al. 1982:Table 9
Mineral pigments* (raw/modified)	X	X	Blitz and Peebles 1983:301; Cole et al. 1982:Table 9; Ensor 1981:Table 29
Galena cube*		X	Cole et al. 1982:Table 9
Black bear tooth pendant*	X	X	Cole et al. 1982:Table 2; O'Hear et al. 1981:201; Curren 1981:Table 9
Greenstone celt (axe)	X	X	Atkinson et al. 1980:Table 10; Cole et al. 1982:Table 2
Engraved marine-shell gorget	X		Atkinson et al. 1980:Table 10; O'Hear et al. 1981:202
Marine-shell beads*	X	X	Atkinson et al. 1980:Table 10; Cole et al. 1982:Table 2; O'Hear et al. 1981:202; Jenkins 1975:81
Miscellaneous marine-shell ornaments	X	X	Atkinson et al. 1980:Table 10; Cole et al. 1982:Table 2
Marine-shell dipper	X	X	Atkinson et al. 1980:Table 10; Cole et al. 1982:Table 2
Freshwater-shell beads/ornaments	X	X	Atkinson et al. 1980:Table 10; Cole et al. 1982:Table 2; O'Hear et al. 1981:202–203
Cougar humerus artifact		X	Cole et al. 1982:Table 2

Note: Asterisks denote artifacts used to define superordinate rank at Moundville (Peebles and Kus 1977).

merville sites, an important observation first made by the Kellogg excavators should be expanded. Excavations at Kellogg revealed that the grave with the most diverse burial offerings (Burial 36: an adult male with one marine-shell gorget, two marine-shell "dippers," and five antler tines) also included infant bones (designated Burial 42) as an accompaniment (Atkinson et al. 1980: Table 10). Phillips and Atkinson note that the

Table 19 Distribution of Prestige Items in Nonburial Contexts

Artifact	Farmstead	Lubbub Mound	Lubbub Village	References
Incised stone disk (palette)*	X	X	X	Allan 1983:188; Blitz 1983b:252; Solis and Walling 1982: Tables 26, 29
Mineral pigments* (raw/modified)	X	X	X	Allan 1983:140–141; Atkinson et al. 1980:103; Blitz 1983b:252; Ensor 1981:Table 22
Galena cube*			X	Allan 1983:142
Marine shell*	X		X	Curren 1981:Tables 4, 5; Woodrick 1983b:Table 9
Black bear tooth pendant*			X	Woodrick 1983a:Table 1
Mica		X		Blitz 1983b:252
Red slate pendant	X			Rucker 1974:Plate 4
Discoidal (chunkey stone)	X		X	Allan 1983:188; O'Hear et al. 1981:195; Solis and Walling 1982:124
Greenstone celt (axe)	X	X	X	Allan 1983:185–188; Atkinson et al. 1980:102
Greenstone gorget			X	Allan 1983:188
Terraced rectangular vessel (sherds)		X	X	Mann 1983:89; Peebles 1983a:Appendix C
Bobcat ulna artifact		X		Woodrick 1983a:385

Note: Asterisks denote artifacts used to define superordinate rank at Moundville (Peebles and Kus 1977).

highest superordinate positions at Moundville (Peebles's Cluster Ia) are adult males buried in mounds with copper emblems, pearl beads, and "ritual" accompaniments of skulls or infant bones. They comment further that, "although it is unlikely that Burial 36 at Kellogg held nearly as high a status as those found with infant bones in the mounds at Moundville, the possibility exists that a similar ceremonialism was practiced in regard to the highest[-]ranking members of village populations" (Atkinson et al. 1980:171).

Subsequent analysis of burials at Lubbub Creek and 1Gr2 lend support to this contention. At 1Gr2, as was the case at Kellogg, the adult male with the most diverse grave goods (Burial 20: three microdrills; two pointed bone tools; and a sandstone abrader) also included infant bones as a burial offering (Hill 1981:267). And at the Lubbub Creek center, again, the most diverse grave offerings were found with an adult male (Burial 20) and once again this grave had human-bone accompaniments, in this case "trophies" rather than infants.

High-status men at farmsteads, local center, and regional center apparently participated in a shared ceremonialism that was elaborated in material quantity and diversity at each level of site hierarchy. While the important men at the Kellogg and 1Gr2 farmsteads did not possess copper symbols of formal leadership, they did share the symbolism of human-bone offerings. The symbolic linkage extends further. The more complex Burial 20 at Lubbub Creek exhibits a similar set of symbolic elements as those that compose the top-ranking superordinate position (Cluster Ia) at Moundville: copper emblems; pearl beads; and human-bone accompaniments. The shared symbolism differs, however, in certain specifics. Some of the superordinate males at Moundville have types of copper emblems absent at Lubbub Creek (copper axes, copper gorgets), and mound burial for top-ranking individuals has yet to be documented at Summerville sites.

There is some basis to conclude, then, that influential men at the most humble of settlements had pretentions to symbols wielded by the most exalted at Moundville. This discovery serves to remind us that status is but one dimension of mortuary ritual and that status-striving behavior was embedded in a pervasive belief system that archaeologists have yet to decode.

Regional Exchange/Alliance

Interpretation of regional exchange/alliance processes in Mississippian societies is exceedingly difficult. First among these difficulties in the Southeast are limitations on the ability to determine the source of prestige goods, which hinders the possibility of charting the flow of items between regions. Despite this problem, ceramics offer one of the more promising materials with which to measure regional interaction.

Whole vessels and sherds that represent ceramic traditions located in the Lower Mississippi Valley, Cumberland Plateau, and Alabama Gulf Coast have been identified at Moundville (Steponaitis 1983). Exotic pottery has not yet been found at local centers in Moundville's hinterland, perhaps because only the regional center engaged in long-distance interactions (Welch 1991:171–172). At Lubbub Creek only a handful of sherds have paste or decoration that diverge from the local ceramic tradition (Mann 1983:99, 101). Probably nonlocal, these sherds are so fragmented that little else can be determined from stylistic clues alone. If vessels from distant ceramic traditions were brought to Lubbub Creek or surrounding farmsteads, it was in such low quantities as to be virtually undetectable.

The possibility remains that some fineware vessels at Lubbub Creek originated at Moundville. Hardin (1981), working with whole vessels at Moundville, has had some success in isolating distinctive variation in decorative execution that may mark the work of individual potters, or microstyles. The feasibility of extending this analysis to Lubbub Creek has been discussed, but the analysis has not been attempted (Mann 1983; Hardin 1983). One problem is the difficulty of working with sherds rather than whole vessels. At any rate, the presence of fine shell–tempered coils and paste lumps at Lubbub, probably used for finewares, makes an exclusive Moundville source for elaborate pottery unlikely.

A number of the Tombigbee prestige goods represent distinctive artifacts of panregional symbolic significance. The copper repoussé falcon plate and copper arrow-shaped cutouts, interpreted as the insignia of rank or leadership for the adult man buried at Lubbub Creek, have widespread stylistic equivalents (see Larson 1959; Waring 1968:Figure 13; Schnell et al. 1981:218–226), as do the copper-covered earspools.

An incised rectangular terraced vessel found with an adult male (Burial 6, Summerville II–III phase Household Cluster 3-2) is a possible import. Five sherds of this vessel form were also found—one at the mound and four in the village. These vessels are quite rare in the Southeast and have been found most frequently at Moundville, the probable source (Steponaitis 1983:69, Figure 63). The copper-covered earspools with Burial 6 reveal that this man had access to nonlocal items, perhaps the vessel among them.

Incised stone disk "palettes" are another possible import. Both the sandstone source and location of manufacture are unknown for these artifacts. Because of frequency of occurrence, Moundville has long been considered the point of origin for incised stone disks (Webb and DeJarnette 1942:287-291).

Another distinctive artifact, a fragment of a red slate pendant, was recovered from the surface of a Mississippian farmstead (22Lo558) near the Coleman local center north of Lubbub Creek (Rucker 1974:Plate 4). Pendants of this style are known from Moundville and the contemporary Seven Mile Island local center on the Tennessee River in northwestern Alabama (Webb and DeJarnette 1942:Plate 58, 2). These pendants are cut and ground to a triangular shape and incised with cross-in-circle and hand-eye motifs.

It is possible to examine chronological patterns in regional exchange in the study area. Nonlocal prestige goods from burial contexts at Lubbub Creek (Table 20) and the Tombigbee farmsteads (Table 21) can be tabulated by phase interval, plotted on graphs, and the relative abundance of nonlocal goods compared through time. At Lubbub Creek nonlocal prestige goods increase slightly from Summerville I to Summerville II–III, then decline to zero in Summerville IV (Figure 48). As can be seen on the farmstead graph (Figure 49), marine shell is even more common at Summerville I phase farmsteads (Tibbee Creek and Kellogg) than at Lubbub Creek, but declines dramatically in the Summerville II–III phase (1Gr2). Nonlocal stone artifacts are found with Summerville I farmstead burials but are absent in the Summerville II–III burials at 1Gr2. No copper is found with farmstead burials.

As symbols to express and validate rank, status, or wealth, prestige goods were in constant demand to fuel the growth of social ranking. In various interpretations of the prestige-goods economy the inability to assure a steady flow of prestige goods is said to promote political instability and, ultimately, govern the rise-and-decline cycle of social hierarchies and polity size (Peebles and Kus 1977; Welch 1991; Steponaitis 1989; Anderson 1989). If, as has been suggested, success in the regional competition for prestige goods was dependent on the size of the polity, then the proximity of a more powerful neighbor was likely to influence the availability of goods locally. For the people of Lubbub Creek and other small centers in the central Tombigbee River area, the powerful neighbor was, of course, Moundville.

Chronological changes in the relative abundance of artifacts of nonlocal materials in dated burials at Moundville have been documented by Steponaitis (1989). He found that the maximum availability of nonlocal materials peaked around A.D. 1250, when Moundville emerged as a large regional polity, and then gradually declined (Figure 50). Steponaitis gathered similar data on the availability of nonlocal artifacts in the Pocahontas region along the lower Big Black River valley in Mississippi. In this area Mississippian polities are represented by a sequence of small local centers, and a three-tiered settlement hierarchy dominated by a powerful regional center like Moundville never developed. He discovered that nonlocal artifacts in the Pocahontas region were most abundant from A.D. 1000 to 1200, then steadily declined during the time when availability peaked at Moundville.

Steponaitis concluded that these patterns were not unrelated but reflect panregional political competition for nonlocal goods. With the

Table 20   Chronological Distribution of Nonlocal Artifacts in
Dated Burials at Lubbub Creek

	Phase	
	S-I	S-II–III
Copper		
Earspools	1	2
Symbol badge cutouts[a]	1	0
Ornaments (misc.)	2	0
Total	4	2
Marine shell		
Beads[a]	4	2
Gorget	0	0
Dipper/cup	1	0
Ornaments (misc.)	1	1
Total	6	3
Nonlocal stone		
Greenstone celt	0	1
Galena	2	0
Total	2	1
Total artifacts	12	6
Total burials	33	14

Note: This table includes all burials dated to a specific phase by association with diagnostic ceramics. It includes burials listed in Cole et al. 1982:Table 2 and Powell 1983:Appendix A. This table follows the same method of compilation as Steponaitis's (1989) data for Moundville in order to facilitate comparison.

[a] Multiple items found within the same burial are regarded as a set and counted as a single occurrence.

rise of a few large polities such as Moundville and Lake George (the regional center closest to the Pocahontas area) after A.D. 1200, small local polities could no longer compete as equals for access to prestige goods. The result would be a decline in the relative abundance of nonlocal goods through time within the small polities. If that were the case, the rise of a powerful center in one river valley might effectively curtail a similar development in an adjacent area (Steponaitis 1989).

The compilation and plotting of the Tombigbee nonlocal artifacts in Figures 48 and 49 follow Steponaitis's procedure for Moundville, but it is difficult to directly compare the graphs. These data are combined in

Table 21 Chronological Distribution of Nonlocal Artifacts in Dated Burials at Farmsteads

	Site and Phase		
	Tibbee Creek S-I	Kellogg S-I	1Gr2 S-II–III
Marine shell			
Beads[a]	2	2	1
Gorgets	1	4	0
Dippers/cups	0	2	0
Ornaments (misc.)	0	0	0
Total	3	8	1
Nonlocal stone			
Greenstone celts	0	2	0
Galena	0	0	0
Total	0	2	0
Total artifacts	3	10	1
Total burials	11	33	24

Note: This table includes all burials dated to a specific phase by diagnostic ceramics. It includes burials listed in O'Hear et al. 1981:149–152; Atkinson et al. 1980:Table 10; and Hill 1981:Table 8. This table follows the same method of compilation as Steponaitis's (1989) data for Moundville in order to facilitate comparison. No copper was found.

[a] Multiple items found within the same burial are regarded as a set and counted as a single occurrence.

Figure 51 to chart chronological trends in relative abundance of copper, marine shell, and nonlocal stone in Summerville and Moundville burials. The Summerville data consist of all burials in Tables 20 and 21. The Moundville data consist of all burials in Steponaitis's Table 1 (1989), except sample I/II. Sample I/II is composed of both Moundville I phase and Moundville II phase burials (Steponaitis 1989:Table 1, b). Burials from these two sequential phases cannot be combined to create a chronological interval between Moundville I and Moundville II, and so this composite sample is omitted.

On the horizontal axis for each graph in Figure 51, A, B, and C represent approximate points along a chronological scale: A = ca. A.D. 1100; B = ca. A.D. 1350; and C = ca. A.D. 1550. To the left of the heavy vertical bar, interval A–B represents the period when Moundville rose to prominence among competing local centers. To the right of the heavy vertical bar, interval B–C represents the period when Moundville ex-

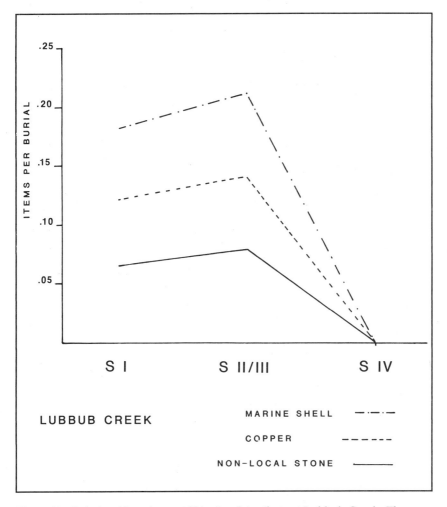

Figure 48 Relative Abundance of Nonlocal Artifacts at Lubbub Creek. The vertical axis represents the ratio between the number of nonlocal items and the number of burials that date to each phase, based on Table 20.

erted maximum influence as a regional center. After point C, no non-local artifacts are found in the Moundville IV (Alabama River phase) burial sample at Moundville or in the Summerville IV phase burials at Lubbub Creek.

Chronological trends in the relative abundance of copper in the region are depicted by the upper graph in Figure 51. At the beginning of interval A–B the relative abundance of copper in the Moundville and Summerville samples is the same, but at B, when Moundville had be-

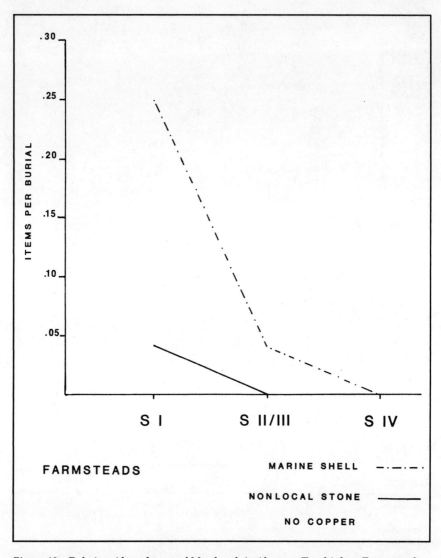

Figure 49   Relative Abundance of Nonlocal Artifacts at Tombigbee Farmsteads. The vertical axis represents the ratio between the number of nonlocal items and the number of burials that date to each phase, based on Table 21.

come established as the regional power, copper reached maximum relative abundance in the Moundville sample. The relative abundance of copper remained unchanged in the Summerville sample. In interval B–C the relative frequency of copper declined in both samples.

On the middle graph in Figure 51 marine shell was initially more common in Summerville burials than in Moundville burials, but at the

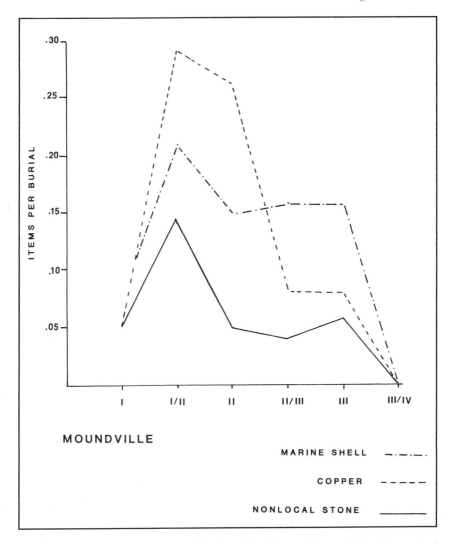

Figure 50   Relative Abundance of Nonlocal Artifacts at Moundville. The vertical axis represents the ratio between the number of nonlocal items and the number of burials that date to that phase. The horizontal axis represents phase intervals. (From Steponaitis 1989:Figure 30)

end of interval A–B marine shell declined dramatically in Summerville as it increased in Moundville. In interval B–C the relative abundance of marine shell decreased in both samples.

On the bottom graph in Figure 51 the relative frequency of nonlocal stone remains unchanged in the Moundville sample while it declined slightly in Summerville. As was the case for copper and shell, the rela-

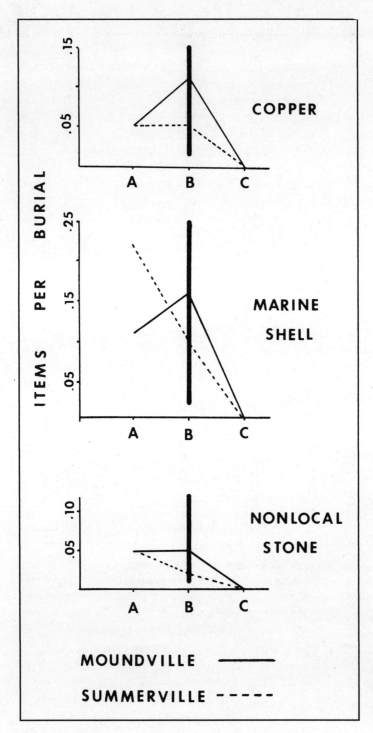

Figure 51 Regional Chronological Trends in the Relative Abundance of Nonlocal Artifacts

tive abundance of nonlocal stone declined in both samples in interval B–C.

Steponaitis proposes that nonlocal goods were critical to the political strategies that enabled regional centers to arise from competing local centers. Once the size and power of Moundville expanded beyond the capabilities of its rivals, the regional competition for nonlocal materials would proceed on an unequal basis. If so, one would expect the relative abundance of nonlocal artifacts in the Moundville sample to increase while they decreased in the Summerville sample.

The chronological trend in marine-shell abundance follows this expectation in interval A–B and presumably reflects specific interpolity influences. However, copper and nonlocal stone do not exhibit the expected pattern. Either the rise of Moundville had no effect on the availability of copper in Summerville or it prevented any increase in relative frequency. The relative abundance of nonlocal stone at Moundville was unaffected in interval A–B while it declined only slightly in the Summerville sample.

All three categories of nonlocal items in both samples decrease in relative abundance during interval B–C. Therefore, the graphs apparently reflect the overall pace of regional production and distribution through time during Moundville's reign of regional power, and specific interpolity influences remain obscure. Perhaps after the rise of Moundville, chronological trends in the availability of nonlocal items in the two samples follow a parallel course because Summerville populations entered into the political alliance/exchange structure of Moundville's domain. One trend is clear: the absolute quantity of nonlocal material items dropped sharply in the Summerville II–III phase (see Tables 20–21).

The vagaries of archaeological sampling being what they are, a certain degree of healthy skepticism about the ultimate meaning of the chronological distributions in Figure 51 is in order, but, certainly, if a series of such comparisons can be constructed for Mississippian polities, we will be in a better position to understand cycles of chiefdom development and organizational variability. It would seem that the political fortunes of Tombigbee local centers such as Lubbub Creek were intertwined with those of Moundville. When the occupation span of the other Tombigbee local centers can be dated, then responses to the rise of Moundville might be detected. For instance, it is likely that the Coleman center was abandoned around this time, perhaps reflecting new alliances and buffer zones. Possibly other related events were the appearance of Moundville Engraved pottery at central Tombigbee sites and the suspension of fortification construction at Lubbub Creek. As always, our interpretations of such regional processes, now only intimated, require much further investigation and evaluation.

Summary

Models of Mississippian sociopolitical organization stress the use of prestige goods as a means to legitimate and expand social ranking. Identification of social ranking at Moundville is based upon the assumption that differential distribution of artifact categories reflects institutionalized restricted access. The Moundville models also assume that prestige-goods production and consumption will be largely restricted to a hereditary elite at local centers. When expectations derived from the Moundville models are examined with evidence from a smaller, two-tiered settlement system, a somewhat different pattern of prestige-goods production and consumption emerges.

To begin with, there was the expectation that high-status leaders at local centers would not have access to those symbols that mark paramount positions at Moundville. These positions are identified as adults (presumed male) interred in mounds with copper axes, pearl beads, and infant/crania accompaniments (Peebles and Kus 1977:441). Because the upper stages of the Summerville Mound were destroyed, a context equivalent to the Moundville discoveries cannot be examined at Lubbub Creek. Elsewhere in the community, however, the copper emblems, pearl bead, and human-bone offerings of Burial 20 represent a less diverse, yet similar set of symbolic elements as those that mark the highest-status positions at Moundville. Important males at farmsteads also had human-bone burial offerings. Beyond male formal leadership positions marked by copper insignia at Lubbub Creek, there is no evidence that prestige goods, including "superordinate" categories, are status items that are the prerogative of an elite.

Male formal leadership positions aside, there is no evidence of economically based superordinate/subordinate rank at Lubbub Creek, insofar as the distribution of prestige goods can be assumed to adequately measure such status. Age, sex, and achievement are the only perceptible qualities that shaped access. With the exception of marine-shell beads, the greatest quantity and diversity of nonlocal items were found with adult men (Table 22).

The distribution of prestige goods, notably marine shell, is more consistent with a function as wealth items, access to which was potentially open to all. Most likely, this wealth was disposed of at funerals in a display of conspicuous consumption that conferred prestige in the competition for social influence. In addition, there may have been a cultural tradition, independent of rank, that directed subadults to be interred with shell beads.

Contrary to the Moundville model of chiefdom political economy,

Table 22 Age and Sex Association of Prestige Items in Burial Contexts

Artifact	Number of Burials	Age and Sex
Copper plate, symbol badges	1	adult male
Copper earspool*	2	adult male
Copper fragment	1	adult male
Galena cube*	2	adult male
Greenstone celt (axe)	2	adult male
Mineral pigments*	undetermined[a]	all ages, both sexes
Black bear tooth pendant*	3	subadult
Engraved marine-shell gorget	5	adult males (3); adult females (2)
Marine-shell beads*	11	subadults/infants (9); adult male; adult female
Miscellaneous marine-shell ornaments	2	subadult; adult male
Marine-shell "dippers"	3	adult males (2); subadult
Freshwater beads, ornaments	4	subadults (3); adult male
Cougar humerus artifact	1	adult male

Note: Asterisks denote artifacts used to define superordinate rank at Moundville (Peebles and Kus 1977).

[a] Unmodified raw source material occurs locally and is ubiquitous in all contexts. Quantitative data on modified/prepared pigment is unavailable because of lack of standardized recording for this category, but "ocher" and "lumps" are mentioned in field notes for various burials.

prestige items—utilitarian and nonutilitarian, of local materials and nonlocal materials—are found in small quantities throughout the Summerville system in burial and nonburial contexts. Production evidence has not been identified for some prestige goods: copper artifacts; stone disk palettes; and greenstone axes. It seems likely these items were imported as finished products. Evidence of coarseware and fineware ceramic production was limited to the local center. Production of microdrills for shell-bead manufacture, limited to the local center in Summerville I, occurred at both Lubbub Creek and farmsteads in later phases.

All evidence indicates that fineware ceramics, microdrills, marine-shell beads, and discoidals were produced within the household. It is unlikely that all of these prestige items, in contrast to many utilitarian artifacts of local materials, were produced in every household. Thus there was some "specialization" or variability in production of prestige items at the household level. However, part-time, low-level production of these artifacts was probably a widespread domestic activity. This household variability and the intensity of production are within the magnitude attributable to individual ability, skill, and episodic opportunities. There is no unequivocal evidence of specialized areas for craft production segregated from household contexts, nor is there evidence of restricted access to specific technology, knowledge, or raw materials. If this level of production is to be considered craft specialization, it clearly fails to meet the criteria of most accepted definitions (e.g., Evans 1978; Michaels 1987, in Ensor 1991).

Household production of prestige goods at farmsteads, the presence at farmsteads of fineware ceramics, abundant marine-shell beads and ornaments, and the occasional fragments of stone disk palettes and other rare prestige goods are contrary to expectations about access derived from the Moundville models. Instead of centralization of production and restriction of access to an elite, the widespread distribution of these wealth items and the materials to make them reveals that the ability of would-be elites to monopolize durable wealth was minimal. This does not mean that ambitious individuals did not have opportunities to benefit from unequal disbursement of nonlocal materials or finished goods. Rather, these opportunities were severely limited at the modest social scale of two-tiered settlement systems and subject to regional social dynamics beyond local control.

Interpretations and Conclusion

I HAVE ATTEMPTED to document changing social and economic conditions in a prehistoric native southeastern population over a 600 year interval. Several general issues have been addressed: the process of local chiefdom formation; the basis of formal leadership in simple chiefdoms such as Lubbub Creek; and the sociopolitical variation and developmental relationships between simple and complex chiefdoms in the region. Important factors believed to account for the observed changes have been identified and every effort has been made to be explicit about the material evidence that forms the basis for interpretations offered. These interpretations of cultural processes can be summarized as follows.

Around A.D. 1000, Tombigbee populations, stimulated by various technological, social, and demographic factors, began to intensify their production of maize beyond low-level gardening. This intensification created logistical problems in a subsistence economy that continued to rely heavily on wild foods. Dispersed farmsteads provided optimal access to natural resources but left families and their maize harvest vulnerable to attack. New cooperative labor patterns were initiated to address these problems. Communal storage of food surpluses at a fortified center was one solution. Formal leadership roles emerged to oversee a cooperative economic and mutual defense organization—the local-center–farmstead polity.

Two potential spheres of influence were created: (1) management of pooled food surpluses; and (2) leadership in war. Delegation of authority, maintenance of consensus, and the allaying of dissent required ideological legitimization, which was most effectively accomplished by amplification of ritual. Local resource mobilization was facilitated through a ritualized cycle of population aggregation at the local center. Platform mounds, established as a location for social integration in a ceremonial format, reflect this developmental relationship among formal leadership institutions, group ritual, and disbursement of food surpluses.

In short, the move toward chiefdom formation and social ranking in the central Tombigbee River valley began as a pragmatic attempt to resolve problems simultaneously posed by defensive and subsistence-oriented considerations. Some archaeologists argue that management of centralized storage to minimize risk to households was not central to chiefdom formation and, instead, represents the chief's co-option of a preexisting arrangement in order to further expand his power (Earle 1987:293). In contrast, the Summerville data are more consistent with the interpretation that a formal office or "chief" evolved in conjunction with management needs, aided by appeals to the sacred. It is difficult to conceive how permanent delegation of authority could be accomplished within small kin-based communities unless families initially considered such actions to be in their own best interest.

Once formal authority roles were institutionalized, however, opportunities were created for individuals and kin groups to manipulate and disburse surpluses unequally to perpetuate their influence. Further expansion of power and social ranking, beyond the ideologically based roles for security maintenance, depended on extending control over the economy (Earle 1987:294; Wolf 1982:72–100). Although it is difficult to substantiate this, the local subsistence economy probably had a low potential for resource control. Reliance on wild foods and readily abundant soils would have made it difficult to restrict access effectively to the means of subsistence production.

Participation in the alliance/exchange networks of the prestige-goods economy held greater promise as a strategy for resource control. At least potentially, access to nonlocal materials entering the polity could be restricted, and production, distribution, and consumption of nonlocal items could be monopolized by an elite. In addition, alliance/exchange networks provided new panregional symbols and ideologies that could be deployed to further sanctify growing authority.

In the case of the Summerville phases both production evidence and wealth items were found to be widespread in various contexts within the settlement system and failed to follow the restricted pattern expected for economically based social ranking. Would-be elites at Lubbub Creek were apparently unsuccessful in expanding economic control. Perhaps one reason for this failure was the inability to compete on an equal basis with larger polities in the regional struggle for nonlocal goods. If so, then low-volume or sporadic importation of goods would inhibit the establishment of fixed control hierarchies. It would appear that the sanctified, security maintenance roles of food-storage management and leadership in war were a sufficient basis for formal chiefly authority in small-scale Mississippian societies such as Summerville, but insufficient to sustain economic social stratification.

Although archaeologists have identified regional mosaics of two-tiered and three-tiered Mississippian settlement systems as evidence of variation in sociopolitical complexity, our ability to identify political boundaries or interrelationships is very limited. This difficulty inhibits the evaluation of certain theoretical models. For example, Carneiro (1981) has proposed that one of the most important processes in social evolution was the forced incorporation of a number of formerly autonomous villages under the centralized control of a single political structure—a minimal chiefdom. Throughout this study I have referred to each Tombigbee local-center–farmstead unit as a polity, in the sense of an independent political entity. I have assumed that the lack of a three-tiered settlement system in the central Tombigbee River valley indicates the absence of a larger unit. Although Lubbub Creek displays evidence of institutionalized offices of authority or "chiefs," Lubbub Creek was not, by Carneiro's criterion, a chiefdom.

The nature and extent of polity relationships in the region remains obscure. For instance, did Lubbub Creek and other Tombigbee local centers participate in a loose alliance/exchange structure with Moundville while remaining politically autonomous? Alternatively, were they effectively incorporated directly into the Moundville polity as "tribute-paying" subordinate centers? Were there degrees of political integration and control exercised upon subordinate centers, perhaps affected by distance from Moundville? The problem is that we still do not have adequate information on how local centers articulate with the regional center.

The spatial distribution of local mound centers may reflect the scale of Mississippian polity interrelationships (Steponaitis 1978; Bozeman 1982). In the Black Warrior River valley the most extensive settlement occurred during the Moundville III phase, where the straight-line distance between the northernmost (1Tu3) and southernmost (1Ha7, 8) local mound centers thought to be contemporary is approximately 33 km.

A 30–40 km distance may demarcate the effective maximum size of the Moundville polity. Hally (1987) measured distances between a large number of Mississippian centers in Georgia and discovered that mound sites were "spaced either less than 17 km apart or more than 31 km apart" (Hally 1987:8). The average distance between clusters was 44 km. Hally concluded that the maximum diameter of Mississippian chiefdoms was approximately 40 km. Noting that a similar spatial pattern characterizes other middle-range societies worldwide, Hally (1987:5) suggests that distances beyond one day's travel by foot from chiefdom center to border (20 km) "represented the practical limit to which effective administrative control could be extended."

Although it is not yet possible to determine which central Tombigbee centers were occupied simultaneously, there are spatial regularities in mound locations. At the upper end of the study area the Butler, Chowder Springs, and Coleman centers cluster together (< 17 km apart). The next center, Lubbub Creek, lies more than 30 km south of the northern cluster. Farther south, undated platform mounds (Hilman, Brasfield) are similarly widely spaced (see Figure 1).

Presumably, the spatial regularities identified by Hally and manifest in the central Tombigbee and Black Warrior River regions identify autonomous territorial units of varying sizes. If 40 km is the effective limit for political integration, then we should not be surprised that Lubbub Creek (53 km from Moundville) produced no evidence of direct Moundville political control. Not even the formidable site of Cahokia was capable of extending political control beyond approximately 80 km along the Mississippi River (Milner 1990:7–8). In light of these discoveries, the roughly 400 km × 100 km boundary reconstructed for the sixteenth-century Coosa chiefdom (Hudson et al. 1985), if valid, probably demarcates the extent of mere military threat and expedient alliance, not centralized political control.

Small-scale and large-scale polities such as Lubbub Creek and Moundville, respectively, are best interpreted as products of regional competition for resources. Within the mode of production available to Mississippian societies, demographic success translated into competitive success and the need for new political arrangements. Viewed from the perspective of regional social dynamics, if the objective of Mississippian political strategies was regional dominance over resources (especially prestige goods), then the successful polity was the one that could muster the largest number of people into production or warfare. Given the apparent correlation between size of polity and degree of social ranking, within Moundville's 40 km unit we can perceive a greater degree or range of social ranking and a greater concentration of nonlocal prestige items. Beyond the 40 km Moundville boundary, small polities such as Lubbub Creek may have been dealt out of the arrangement and placed at a disadvantage in regional competition for nonlocal items.

The current Moundville models of social organization and political economy reflect a widely held perception of Mississippian societies as fixed hierarchies of centralized political integration and economic control (Peebles and Kus 1977; Peebles 1983b; Welch 1991). Yet it is also obvious that, whether large or small, powerful or weak, Mississippian territorial arrangements were composed of the same basic modular unit—a local center and associated households or farmsteads. All evidence suggests that local-center modules were economically self-sufficient, and therefore, political interests and loyalties were probably quite localized. In other words, local-center–farmstead units may have been organized on a similar social and economic basis throughout the region.

An alternative interpretation of Mississippian political arrangements must be considered. Instead of a politically centralized and economically controlled administrative hierarchy, territorial units may have been composed of a network of interacting modules in which political "administration" was ritualistic, competitive, segmented, and unstable—in short, a confederation or league of semiautonomous participating modules (see Johnson 1984; Milner 1990).

As we have seen, no evidence was found that production of highly valued items was under the centralized control of a superordinate rank or that access was restricted to an elite at Summerville phase sites. While Moundville's size and concentrated wealth place it at the apex of regional social complexity, it remains to be demonstrated how or whether access to and control of resources at Moundville phase sites differ from those of Summerville phase sites. The Summerville discoveries make it imperative that investigators be sensitive to the possibility that specific artifact classes may exhibit different patterns of distribution and association according to status, wealth, or functional distinctions. Patterns of distribution cannot be narrowly interpreted solely in terms of status. Teleological reasoning that automatically transforms any "superordinate" artifact's provenance into an "elite" context (by definition) must be avoided.

Because of the lack of excavation data, we really know very little about interrelationships between farmsteads and local centers in the Black Warrior River valley, Moundville's immediate hinterland. Production and consumption of craft products may be more dispersed and less centralized than current models suggest. For example, in the only published excavation of a Moundville farmstead, Mistovich (1987:167) found evidence for tool manufacture from nonlocal stone, contrary to expectations that production would be limited to the Moundville site (e.g., Welch 1991:152, 176).

Similarly, seasonal and logistical aspects of Moundville phase local resource mobilization remain poorly understood. If these characteristics should parallel Summerville phase patterns, then the social dichotomies and consumption patterns of Moundville phase farmstead–local centers may be more intertwined than we now perceive. The provisioning of "noble" elites with subsistence products by farmstead "commoners" may be embedded in a ritualized cycle of population aggregation at the local center in such a way as to complicate current assumptions about what constitutes elite and nonelite middens or contexts. The person tending a farmstead maize field in June may be the same individual who consumes "choice cuts" of venison with kin in a ceremonial building atop a mound in December.

One of the advantages of turning our attention to local-center–farmstead comparisons is that Mississippian societies such as Moundville may take on a very different character when viewed from the bottom up. In this study I have attempted to illustrate how small-scale Mississippian societies such as Summerville are critical in furthering our knowledge about Mississippian organizational variability. Careful comparison of small-scale and large-scale Mississippian societies helps place both systems in dynamic perspective. Awareness of this variability, in turn, provides insights into cycles of chiefdom formation and fragmentation.

Mississippian Ceramic Type and Variety Descriptions

RIEF DESCRIPTIONS of the Mississippian pottery recovered during the Lubbub Creek excavations are provided here so that the reader may identify those type and variety names discussed in the text. This appendix is not intended to replace the detailed type-variety analysis in the original report (Mann 1983), and researchers should consult Mann for serious comparative study, illustrations, and bibliographic references.

Presented below is a glossary that lists ceramic type names in alphabetical order. Each type description is followed by associated variety names (in italics). All types and varieties are shell-tempered unless otherwise noted. Associated vessel shapes identified in the Lubbub Creek sample are listed when known. A summary chronology of ceramic types, varieties, vessel shapes, and other attributes can be found in Table 23, while production steps for selected types as a relative measure of pottery production "costs" are seen in Table 24. Vessel-shape counts and percentages in Lubbub Creek village and mound samples are summarized in Table 25. Finally, basic vessel-shape classes are illustrated in Figure 52.

Glossary of Ceramic Type and Variety Descriptions

Alabama River Applique

The principle diagnostic marker for the Summerville IV phase, Alabama River Applique exhibits multiple appliqued strips or residual (false) handles placed vertically around the vessel neck. This type is essentially a rim mode added to Mississippi Plain. Functional triangular

Table 23 Summary Chronology of Ceramic Types and Varieties, Vessel Shapes, and Other Attributes

	Summerville Phase		
	I	*II–III*	*IV*
Type and Variety			
Alabama River Applique			
var. *Alabama River*		(late?)	X
Alabama River Incised			
Unspecified			X
Bell Plain			
var. *Big Sandy*	X	X	X
Carthage Incised			
var. *Carthage*		X	X
var. *Foster*		X	
var. *Moon Lake*	X	X	?
Chickachae Combed			
Unspecified			X (historic)
Mississippi Plain			
var. *Hale*	X	X	X
var. *Hull Lake*		X	X
var. *Warrior*	X	X	X
Mound Place Incised			
var. *Akron*	?	X	?
var. *Havana*	?	X	
Moundville Engraved			
var. *Hemphill*		X (late?)	
var. *Taylorville*		X	
var. *Tuscaloosa*	X (late)	X	
var. *Wiggins*		X	
Moundville Incised			
var. *Carrollton*	X	X	X
var. *Snow's Bend*		X	
var. *Moundville*	X		
Parkin Punctated			
Unspecified			(late?)
Vessel Shape			
Jar (miscellaneous)	X	X	X
Standard jar	X	X	X
Neckless jar	?		
Bowl (miscellaneous)		X	X

Table 23 (continued)

	Summerville Phase		
	I	*II–III*	*IV*
Vessel Shape			
Cylindrical bowl		X	
Flaring-rim bowl	X	X	X
Outslanting bowl	?	X	
Restricted bowl		X	
Short-neck bowl		X	?
Simple bowl	X	X	X
Terraced rectangular bowl		X (early)	
Bottle	X	X	X
Secondary Shape Attributes			
Nodes (not on handles)		X	X
Beaded rim		X	?
Beaded shoulder	X	X	
Folded rim		X	?
Folded flattened rim		X	
Horizontal lug		X (late?)	X
Notched rim		X	
Scalloped rim	?	?	
Pedestaled base		?	
Indentations	X	X (early?)	
Notched lip		X	
Jar with 2 handles	X	X	
Jar with 10 handles		?	X
Handle Attributes			
Single node at top	?	X	
Two nodes at top		X	
Three nodes at top		X	
Single node in middle		X	
Two nodes in middle	X	X (early)	
Vertical bar in middle	?	X (early)	
Single node at bottom		X	

Source: Peebles and Mann 1983:73–75.

Table 24   Ceramic Production-Step Measures

Type		Production Steps
Moundville Engraved	(5 steps)	fine paste smoothed burnished engraving complex design
Carthage Incised	(4 steps)	fine paste smoothed burnished incised
Mound Place Incised	(4 steps)	fine paste smoothed burnished incised
Mississippi Plain *var. Hale;* Bell Plain	(3 steps)	fine paste smoothed burnished
Alabama River Applique	(2 steps)	appliqued smoothed
Moundville Incised	(2 steps)	smoothed incised

Note: Methodology based on Feinman et al. 1981.

luted handles may co-occur with appliqued strips or residual handles. Vessel shapes: jars predominant; short-neck bowls.

   Alabama River: as above.

Alabama River Incised

Alabama River Incised was used to describe repeated sets of four to eight concentric circles or stylized hand-and-triangle motifs placed from rim to shoulder on interior surfaces of shallow flaring-rim bowls used as covers for burial urns. Criteria will have to be established to refine this catch-all category, which overlaps with Carthage Incised *var. Foster.* Summerville IV phase.

Barton Incised

Barton Incised has rectilinear incised motifs, usually placed on the vessel's exterior neck and shoulder.

   Demopolis: a series of parallel lines incised vertically from the lip. This design mode, executed on various pastes, extends into the early

Table 25 Lubbub Creek Vessel Shapes: Village and Mound Samples (Identified from Sherds)

	Village		*Mound*	
	No.	*%*	*No.*	*%*
Bottle	34	5	16	7
Cylindrical bowl	19	3	4	2
Flaring-rim bowl	108	16	46	21
Miscellaneous bowl	98	15	23	11
Outslanting bowl	52	8	19	9
Restricted bowl	18	3	6	3
Short-neck bowl	30	5	9	4
Simple bowl	125	19	32	14
Terraced rectangular bowl	5	–	1	–
Standard jar	173	26	65	29
Neckless jar	1	–	–	–
Total number	663		221	

historical period in eastern Mississippi (Atkinson 1987:Figure 14; Blitz 1985:Figure 7). The small quantity recovered at Lubbub Creek suggests that this variety was very late in the sequence or even postdated the major occupation episode.

Bell Plain

Bell Plain is a fine mixed-shell-and-grog-tempered ware. Burnished surfaces predominate but burnishing was not a criterion for inclusion in this type.

Big Sandy: as above. All vessel shapes represented but serving forms are predominant.

Carthage Incised

Carthage Incised is a type with a burnished surface and broad-trailed incision, U-shape in cross section.

Carthage: two-to-five-line running scroll on exterior surface of bottles and bowls or interior rim surfaces of flaring-rim bowls

Foster: free-standing motifs—hands, skulls, long bones on interior rim surfaces of flaring-rim bowls

Moon Lake: zones of parallel oblique lines on interior rim surfaces of flaring-rim bowls and exterior surfaces of bottles

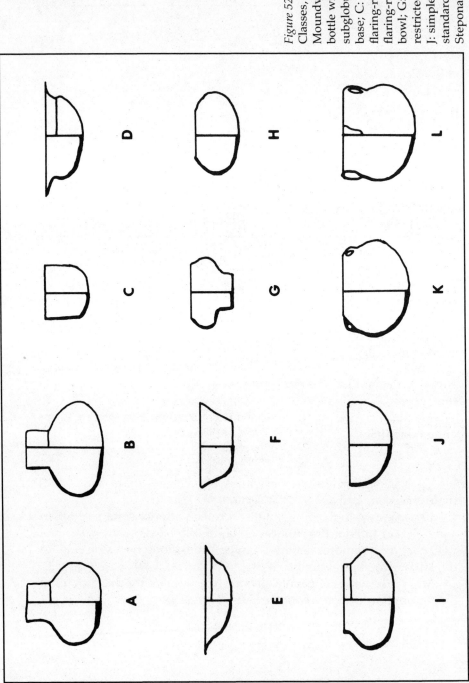

Figure 52 Basic Vessel-Shape Classes, Summerville and Moundville Phases. A: subglobular bottle with slab base; B: subglobular bottle with simple base; C: cylindrical bowl; D: deep flaring-rim bowl; E: shallow flaring-rim bowl; F: outslanting bowl; G: pedestaled bowl; H: restricted bowl; I: short-neck bowl; J: simple bowl; K: neckless jar; L: standard jar. (Adapted from Steponaitis 1983:Figure 67)

Summerville: incised lines that form arches on exterior bottle shoulders or restricted bowls

Mississippi Plain

The type name Mississippi Plain encompasses all undecorated shell-tempered ceramics at Lubbub Creek, whether burnished or unburnished surfaces occur.

Warrior: coarse-shell temper with particles 2 mm or larger. All vessel shapes occur but unburnished cooking forms are predominant.

Hale: fine-shell temper with particles less than 2 mm. All vessel shapes occur but burnished serving forms are predominant.

Hull Lake: originally defined as coarse shell with shell-tempered clay inclusions, but the ceramic analyst concluded that the inclusions were accidental (Mann 1983:67). Thus this variety is of no analytical utility.

Mound Place Incised

Mound Place Incised is defined as two or more parallel lines incised horizontally on the exterior rim, sometimes with lines dipping down as concentric festoons.

Akron: line width 1 mm or larger. Vessel shapes: bowl forms

Havana: line width less than 1 mm. Vessel shapes: bowl forms

Moundville Engraved

Moundville Engraved is the principle diagnostic marker for the Summerville II–III phase. The type has engraved lines executed on bone-dry or fired paste. Surfaces are burnished and usually black-filmed.

Hemphill: freestanding motifs—death's head, long bones, etc. Vessel shapes: bottles

Maxwell Crossing: vertical crosshatched bands

Taylorville: running scroll of three or four lines superimposed on a crosshatched background

Tuscaloosa: curvilinear scroll of 15–40 closely spaced lines

Wiggins: two-to-five-line scroll. Vessel shapes: bottles, bowl

Moundville Incised

Moundville Incised has an incised arch motif placed end to end around the upper portion of the vessel. Unburnished surfaces predominate.

Moundville: diagnostic marker of the Summerville I phase. A series of short incisions radiates upward from arch. Vessel shapes: jars predominate but short neck bowls also occur.

Carrollton: arch unembellished with any secondary design elements. Vessel shapes: jars predominate but short-neck bowls and restricted bowls also occur.

Snow's Bend: arches of punctations placed above incised arch. Vessel shapes: jars and simple bowls

Parkin Punctated

Parkin Punctated is a coarse-shell-tempered type with punctations applied to the vessel surface and unburished surfaces. Chronological placement of this type at Lubbub Creek was uncertain but probably very late in the sequence.

Bibliography

Adair, James
1968   *A History of the American Indians.* Reprinted. Johnson Reprint, New York. Originally published 1775, London.

Albright, Caroline H.
1983   The Summerville IV Community. In *Prehistoric Agriculture Communities in West Central Alabama: Excavations in the Lubbub Creek Archaeological Locality,* vol. 1, ed. Christopher S. Peebles, pp. 309–390. University of Michigan. Submitted to the U.S. Army Corps of Engineers, Mobile District. National Technical Information Services, Springfield, Va.

Allan, Aljean W.
1983   An Analysis of Lithic Materials from the Lubbub Creek Archaeological Locality. In *Prehistoric Agricultural Communities in West Central Alabama: Studies of Material Remains from the Lubbub Creek Archaeological Locality,* vol. 2, ed. Christopher S. Peebles, pp. 138–193. University of Michigan. Submitted to the U.S. Army Corps of Engineers, Mobile District. National Technical Information Services, Springfield, Va.

Anderson, David G.
1989   Factional Competition and the Political Evolution of Mississippian Chiefdoms in the Southeastern United States. MS in possession of the author.
1990   Stability and Change in Chiefdom Level Societies: An Examination of Mississippian Political Evolution on the South Atlantic Slope. In *Lamar Archaeology: Mississippian Chiefdoms in the Deep South,* ed. Mark Williams and Gary Shapiro, pp. 187–213. University of Alabama Press, Tuscaloosa and London.

Arnold, Phillip J., III
1988   Household Ceramic Assemblage Attributes in the Sierra de los Tuxtlas, Veracruz, Mexico. *Journal of Anthropological Research* 44:357–383.

Atkinson, James R.
1987   Historic Chickasaw Cultural Material: A More Comprehensive Identi-
          fication. *Mississippi Archaeology* 22(2):32–62.

Atkinson, James R., John C. Phillips, and Richard Walling
1980   *The Kellogg Village Site Investigations, Clay County, Mississippi.* Depart-
          ment of Anthropology, Mississippi State University. Submitted to the
          U.S. Army Corps of Engineers, Mobile District.

Bartram, William
1958   *The Travels of William Bartram.* Yale University Press, New Haven,
          Conn.

Belmont, John S.
1983   Appendix D: Faunal Remains. In *Excavations at Lake George, Yazoo
          County, Mississippi, 1958–1960,* Stephen Williams and Jeffrey P. Brain,
          pp. 451–474. Papers of the Peabody Museum of Archaeology and
          Ethnology 74. Cambridge, Mass.

Bender, Barbara
1979   Gatherer-Hunter to Farmer: A Social Perspective. *World Archaeology*
          10:204–222.
1985   Emergent Tribal Formations in the American Midcontinent. *American
          Antiquity* 50(1):52–62.

Benson, Charlotte L.
1983   Anasazi Social Organization and Social Structure: Evolution of the
          Evidence. Paper presented at the Sixteenth Chacmool Conference,
          Calgary, Alberta.

Binford, Louis R.
1973   Interassemblage Variability: The Mousterian and the Functional Argu-
          ment. In *The Explanation of Culture Change: Models in Prehistory,* ed.
          Colin Renfrew, pp. 227–253. G. Duckworth, London.

Blakeman, Crawford H., Jr.
1975   *Archaeological Investigations in the Upper Central Tombigbee Valley: 1974
          Season.* Department of Anthropology, Mississippi State University.
          Submitted to the U.S. National Park Service.

Blalock, Hurbert M., Jr.
1972   *Social Statistics.* 2d ed. McGraw-Hill, New York.

Blitz, John H.
1983a   Pre-Mississippian Communities. In *Prehistoric Agricultural Commu-
          nities in West-Central Alabama: Excavations in the Lubbub Creek Archae-
          ological Locality,* vol. 1, ed. Christopher S. Peebles, pp. 128–139.
          University of Michigan. Submitted to the U.S. Army Corps of Engi-
          neers, Mobile District. National Technical Information Services,
          Springfield, Va.
1983b   The Summerville Mound. In *Prehistoric Agricultural Communities in*

West-Central Alabama: Excavations in the Lubbub Creek Archaeological Locality, vol. 1, ed. Christopher S. Peebles, pp. 198–253. University of Michigan. Submitted to the U.S. Army Corps of Engineers, Mobile District. National Technical Information Services, Springfield, Va.

1983c   The Summerville I Community. In *Prehistoric Agricultural Communities in West-Central Alabama: Excavations in the Lubbub Creek Archaeological Locality,* vol. 1, ed. Christopher S. Peebles, pp. 254–278. University of Michigan. Submitted to the U.S. Army Corps of Engineers, Mobile District. National Technical Information Services, Springfield, Va.

1984   *A Cultural Resources Survey in the Tombigbee National Forest, Mississippi.* USDA Forest Service, Jackson, Miss.

1985   *An Archaeological Study of the Mississippi Choctaw Indians.* Mississippi Department of Archives and History, Archaeological Report 16. Jackson.

1988   Adoption of the Bow in Prehistoric North America. *North American Archaeologist* 9(2):123–145.

Blitz, John H., and Christopher S. Peebles
1983   The Summerville II and III Community. In *Prehistoric Agricultural Communities in West-Central Alabama: Excavations in the Lubbub Creek Archaeological Locality,* vol. 1, ed. Christopher S. Peebles, pp. 279–308. University of Michigan. Submitted to the U.S. Army Corps of Engineers, Mobile District. National Technical Information Services, Springfield, Va.

Bogan, A. E.
1980   *A Comparison of Late Prehistoric Dallas and Overhill Cherokee Subsistence Strategies in the Little Tennessee River Valley.* Ph.D. dissertation, University of Tennessee. University Microfilms, Ann Arbor, Mich.

Bourne, Edward Gaylord (editor)
1973   *Narratives of the Career of Hernando de Soto in the Conquest of Florida.* 2 vol. Reprinted AMS Press, New York. Originally published 1922, Allerton, New York.

Bozeman, Tandy K.
1982   *Moundville Phase Communities in the Black Warrior River Valley, Alabama.* Ph.D. dissertation, University of California, Santa Barbara.

Bridges, Patricia S.
1989   Changes in Activities with the Shift to Agriculture in the Southeastern United States. *Current Anthropology* 30:385–394.

Brose, David S., Ned J. Jenkins, and Russell Weisman
1982   *Cultural Resources Reconnaissance Study of the Black Warrior–Tombigbee System Corridor, Alabama: Archaeology,* vol. 1 (draft report). University of South Alabama. Submitted to the U.S. Army Corps of Engineers, Mobile District.

Brown, James A.
1985   The Mississippian Period. *In Ancient Art of the American Woodland Indi-
            ans*, pp. 92–145. Harry N. Abrams, New York.

Byington, Cyrus
1915   *A Dictionary of the Choctaw Language*, ed. H. S. Halbert and J. R. Swan-
            ton. Smithsonian Institution, Bureau of American Ethnology, Bulletin
            46.

Caddell, Gloria M.
1981   Plant Resources, Archaeological Plant Remains, and Prehistoric Plant-
            Use Patterns in the Central Tombigbee River Valley. *In Archaeological
            Investigations in the Gainesville Lake Area of the Tennessee-Tombigbee Water-
            way*, vol. 4. Office of Archaeological Research, Report of Investigations
            14. The University of Alabama.
1982   Plant Remains from the Yarborough Site. *In Archaeological Investiga-
            tions at the Yarborough Site (22Cl1814) Clay County, Mississippi*, Carlos
            Solis and Richard Walling, pp. 134–140. Office of Archaeological Re-
            search, Report of Investigations 30. The University of Alabama.
1983   Floral Remains from the Lubbub Creek Archaeological Locality. *In
            Prehistoric Agricultural Communities in West-Central Alabama: Studies of
            Material Remains from the Lubbub Creek Archaeological Locality*, vol. 2, ed.
            Christopher S. Peebles, pp. 194–271. University of Michigan. Submit-
            ted to the U.S. Army Corps of Engineers, Mobile District. National
            Technical Information Services, Springfield, Va.

Campbell, T. N.
1959   Choctaw Subsistence: Ethnographic Notes from the Lincecum Manu-
            script. *Florida Anthropologist* 12:9–24.

Carneiro, Robert L.
1967   On the Relationship Between Size of Population and Complexity of
            Social Organization. *Southwestern Journal of Anthropology* 23:234–243.
1981   The Chiefdom: Precursor of the State. *In The Transition to Statehood in
            the New World*, ed. Grant D. Jones and Robert R. Kantz, pp. 37–79.
            Cambridge University Press, New York.

Cleland, Charles E., Jr.
1965   Appendix 2: Analysis of the Faunal Remains of the Fatherland Site. *In
            Archaeology of the Fatherland Site: The Grand Village of the Natchez*, Robert
            S. Neitzel, pp. 96–101. Anthropological Papers of the American
            Museum of Natural History 51(1). New York.

Cole, Gloria G.
1983   Environmental Background. *In Prehistoric Agricultural Communities in
            West-Central Alabama: Excavations in the Lubbub Creek Archaeological Lo-
            cality*, vol. 1, ed. Christopher S. Peebles, pp. 10–63. University of
            Michigan. Submitted to the U.S. Army Corps of Engineers, Mobile
            District. National Technical Information Services, Springfield, Va.

Cole, Gloria G., and Caroline H. Albright
1983   Summerville I–II Fortifications. In *Prehistoric Agricultural Communities of West-Central Alabama: Excavations in the Lubbub Creek Archaeological Locality,* vol. 1, ed. Christopher S. Peebles, pp. 140–196. University of Michigan. Submitted to the U.S. Army Corps of Engineers, Mobile District. National Technical Information Services, Springfield, Va.

Cole, Gloria, G., Mary C. Hill, and H. Blaine Ensor
1982   Appendix 3: Bioarchaeological Comparisons of the Late Miller III and Summerville I Phases in the Gainesville Lake Area. In *Archaeological Investigations in the Gainesville Lake Area of the Tennessee-Tombigbee Waterway,* vol. 5, Ned J. Jenkins, pp. 187–258. Office of Archaeological Research, Report of Investigations 12. The University of Alabama.

Coles, John
1973   *Archaeology by Experiment.* Charles Scribner's Sons, New York.

Cowgill, George L.
1975   On Causes and Consequences of Ancient and Modern Population Changes. *American Anthropologist* 77(3):505–525.
1986   Archaeological Applications of Mathematical and Formal Methods. In *American Archaeology Past and Future,* ed. David J. Meltzer, Don D. Fowler, and Jeremy A. Sabloff, pp. 369–393. Smithsonian Institution Press, Washington, D.C.

Crane, Cathy J.
1980   Kellogg Floral Analysis. In *The Kellogg Village Site Investigations, Clay County, Mississippi,* James R. Atkinson, John C. Phillips, and Richard Walling, pp. 331–337. Department of Anthropology, Mississippi State University. Submitted to the U.S. Army Corps of Engineers, Mobile District.

Crook, Morgan R., Jr.
1986   *Mississippi Period Archaeology of the Georgia Coastal Zone.* Georgia Archaeological Research Design Papers 1. Laboratory of Archaeology, University of Georgia, Athens.

Cross, Ralph D. (editor)
1974   *Atlas of Mississippi.* University Press of Mississippi, Jackson.

Curren, Cailup B., Jr.
1981   Appendix: A Zooarchaeological Analysis of 4,991 Bone and Shell Artifacts from the Gainesville Lake Area. In *Archaeological Investigations in the Gainesville Lake Area of Tennessee-Tombigbee Waterway,* vol. 4, Gloria M. Caddell, Anne Woodrick, and Mary C. Hill. Office of Archaeological Research, Report of Investigations 14. The University of Alabama.
1984   *The Protohistoric Period in Central Alabama.* Alabama Tombigbee Regional Commission, Camden.

Deal, Michael
1985   Household Pottery Disposal in the Maya Highlands: An Ethno-archaeological Interpretation. *Journal of Anthropological Archaeology* 4:243–291.

DeBoer, Warren R.
1974   Ceramic Longevity and Archaeological Interpretation: An Example from the Upper Ucayali, Peru. *American Antiquity* 39:335–343.
1981   Buffer Zones in the Cultural Ecology of Aboriginal Amazonia: An Ethnohistorical Approach. *American Antiquity* 46:364–377.
1985   Pots and Pans Do Not Speak, Nor Do They Lie: The Case for Occasional Reductionism. In *Decoding Prehistoric Ceramics*, ed. B. A. Nelson, pp. 347–357. Southern Illinois University Press, Carbondale.
1988   Subterranean Storage and the Organization of Surplus: The View from Eastern North America. *Southeastern Archaeology* 7:1–20.

DeBoer, Warren R., and Donald Lathrap
1979   The Making and Breaking of Shipibo-Conibo Ceramics. In *Ethnoarchaeology: Implications of Ethnography for Archaeology*, ed. Carol Kramer, pp. 102–138. Columbia University Press, New York.

Dickens, Roy S.
1978   Mississippian Settlement Patterns in the Appalachian Summit Area: The Pisgah and Qualla Phases. In *Mississippian Settlement Patterns*, ed. Bruce D. Smith, pp. 115–139. Academic Press, New York.

Dobyns, Henry F.
1983   *Their Number Become Thinned: Native American Population Dynamics in Eastern North America*. University of Tennessee Press, Knoxville.
1990   Links Between Demographic and Cultural Changes. Paper presented to the Fifty-fifth Annual Meeting, Society for American Archaeology, Las Vegas, Nev.

Drennan, Richard
1976   *Fábrica San José and the Middle Formative Society in the Valley of Oaxaca, Mexico*. Memoirs of the University of Michigan Museum of Anthropology 8. University of Michigan, Ann Arbor.
1983   Ritual and Ceremonial Development at the Early Village Level. In *The Cloud People: The Divergent Evolution of the Zapotec and Mixtec Civilizations*, ed. Kent V. Flannery and Joyce Marcus, pp. 46–50. Academic Press, New York.

Earle, Timothy K.
1977   A Reappraisal of Redistribution: Complex Hawaiian Chiefdoms. In *Exchange Systems in Prehistory*, ed. T. Earle and J. Ericson, pp. 213–229. Academic Press, New York.
1987   Chiefdoms in Archaeological and Ethnohistorical Perspective. *Annual Review of Anthropology* 16:279–308.
1989   The Evolution of Chiefdoms. *Current Anthropology* 30(1):84–88

Eliade, Mircea
1959   *The Sacred and the Profane.* Harcourt and Brace, New York.

Emerson, T. E., and D. K. Jackson
1984   *The BBB Motor Site: An Early Mississippian Occupation.* Department of Anthropology, University of Illinois at Urbana-Champaign, FAI-270 Report 38.

Ensor, H. Blaine
1981   Gainesville Lake Area Lithics: Chronology, Technology and Use. In *Archaeological Investigations in the Gainesville Lake Area of the Tennessee-Tombigbee Waterway,* vol. 3. Office of Archaeological Research, Report of Investigations 13. The University of Alabama.
1991   The Lubbub Creek Microlith Industry. *Southeastern Archaeology* 10(1):18–39.

Erasmus, Charles J.
1965   Monument Building: Some Field Experiments. *Southwestern Journal of Anthropology* 21(4):277–301.

Evans, Robert K.
1978   Early Craft Specialization: An Example from the Balkan Chalcolithic. In *Social Archaeology: Beyond Subsistence and Dating,* ed. C. L. Redman, M. J. Berman, E. V. Curtin, W. T. Langhorne, N. M. Versaggi, and J. C. Wanser, pp. 113–129. Academic Press, New York.

Faulkner, Charles H.
1977   The Winter House: An Early Southeast Tradition. *Mid-Continental Journal of Archaeology* 2(2):141–160.

Feinman, Gary M., and Jill Neitzel
1984   Too Many Types: An Overview of Sedentary Prestate Societies in the Americas. In *Advances in Archaeological Method and Theory,* vol. 7, ed. Michael B. Schiffer, pp. 39–102. Academic Press. New York.

Feinman, Gary M., Steadman Upham, and Kent G. Lightfoot
1981   The Production Step Measure: An Ordinal Index for Labor Input in Ceramic Manufacture. *American Antiquity* 46:871–884.

Fish, Suzanne K.
1980   Pollen from the Kellogg Site (22Cl527). In *The Kellogg Village Site Investigations, Clay County, Mississippi,* James R. Atkinson, John C. Phillips, and Richard Walling, pp. 338–341. Department of Anthropology, Mississippi State University. Submitted to the U.S. Army Corps of Engineers, Mobile District.

Flannery, Kent V.
1972   The Cultural Evolution of Civilizations. *Annual Review of Ecology and Systematics* 3:399–426.

1976   Contextual Analysis of Ritual Paraphernalia from Formative Oaxaca.

In *The Early Mesoamerican Village*, ed. K. V. Flannery, pp. 329–345. Academic Press, New York.

Ford, Richard I.
1974   Northeastern Archaeology: Past and Future Directions. *Annual Review of Anthropology* 4:385–414.

Frankenstein, Susan, and Michael J. Rowlands
1978   The Internal Structure and Regional Context of Early Iron Age Society in Southwestern Germany. *University of London Institute of Archaeological Bulletin* 15:73–112.

Fried, Morton H.
1967   *The Evolution of Political Society: An Essay in Political Anthropology.* Random House, New York.

Friedman, J.
1975   Tribes, States and Transformations. In *Marxist Analysis and Social Anthropology,* ed. M. Bloch, pp. 161–202. Wiley, New York.

Futato, Eugene M.
1987   *Archaeological Investigations at Shell Bluff and White Springs, Two Late Woodland Sites in the Tombigbee River Multi-Resource District.* Office of Archaeological Research, Report of Investigations 50. The University of Alabama.

Gatschet, Albert S.
1969   *A Migration Legend of the Creek Indians,* vol. 1. Reprinted. AMS Press, New York. Originally published 1884, Brinton's Library of Aboriginal American Literature, Philadelphia.

Gernet, Alexander von, and Peter Timmins
1987   Pipes and Parakeets: Constructing Meaning in an Early Iroquoian Context. In *Archaeology as Long-Term History,* ed. Ian Hodder, pp. 31–42. Cambridge University Press, New York.

Gibson, Jon L., and J. Richard Shenkel
1988   Louisiana Earthworks: Middle Woodland and Predecessors. In *Middle Woodland Settlement and Ceremonialism in the Mid-South and Lower Mississippi Valley,* ed. Robert C. Mainfort, Jr., pp. 7–18. Mississippi Department of Archives and History, Archaeological Report 22. Jackson.

Gilbert, Robert I., Jr.
1980   Appendix A: The Human Skeletal Remains. In *The Kellogg Village Site Investigations, Clay County, Mississippi,* James R. Atkinson, John C. Phillips, and Richard Walling, pp. 300–330. Department of Anthropology, Mississippi State University. Submitted to the U.S. Army Corps of Engineers, Mobile District.

Goldstein, Lynne G.
1980   *Mississippian Mortuary Practices: A Case Study of Two Cemeteries in the Lower Illinois Valley.* Northwestern University Archaeological Program, Scientific Papers 4, Evanston, Ill.

Griffin, James B.
1985   Changing Concepts of the Prehistoric Mississippian Cultures of the Eastern United States. In *Alabama and the Boarderlands: From Prehistory to Statehood,* ed. R. Reid Badger and Lawrence A. Clayton, pp. 40–63. University of Alabama Press, University.

Gyllenhal-Davis, Charlotte
1982   Ecotones, Transition Zones, and the Yarborough Site. In *Archaeological Investigations at the Yarborough Site (22 Cl 814), Clay County, Mississippi,* Carlos Solis and Richard Walling, pp. 157–167. Office of Archaeological Research, Report of Investigations 30. The University of Alabama.

Halbert, Henry S.
1900   *Funeral Customs of the Mississippi Choctaws.* Publications of the Mississippi Historical Society, vol. 3, pp. 353–366.

Hally, David J.
1986   The Identification of Vessel Function: A Case Study from Northwest Georgia. *American Antiquity* 51:267–295.
1987   Platform Mounds and the Nature of Mississippian Chiefdoms. Paper presented at the Southeastern Archaeological Conference, Charleston, S.C.

Hardin, Margaret
1981   The Identification of Style on Moundville Engraved Vessels: A Preliminary Note. *Southeastern Archaeological Conference Bulletin* 24:108–110.
1983   Recommendations for a Comparative Stylistic Analysis of Lubbub and Moundville Ceramics. In *Prehistoric Agricultural Communities in West-Central Alabama: Studies of Material Remains from the Lubbub Creek Archaeological Locality,* vol. 2, ed. Christopher S. Peebles, pp. 132–137. University of Michigan. Submitted to the U.S. Army Corps of Engineers, Mobile District. National Technical Information Service, Springfield, Va.

Hatch, James W.
1975   Social Dimensions of Dallas Burials. *Southeastern Archaeological Conference Bulletin* 18:132–138.

Hayden, Brian
1990   Nimrods, Piscators, Pluckers, and Planters: The Emergence of Food Production. *Journal of Anthropological Archaeology* 9:31–69.

Hayden, Brian, and Aubrey Cannon
1983   Where the Garbage Goes: Refuse Disposal in the Maya Highlands. *Journal of Anthropological Archaeology* 2:117–163.

Helms, Mary W.
1979   *Ancient Panama: Chiefs in Search of Power.* University of Texas Press, Austin.

Hertz, Robert
1960   *Death and the Right Hand.* Trans. Rodney and Claudia Needham. Free Press, Glencoe, Ill. Originally published 1928.

Hickerson, Harold
1965   The Virginia Deer and Inter-Tribal Buffer Zones in the Upper Mississippi Valley. In *Man, Culture, and Animals,* ed. A. Leeds and A. P. Vayda, pp. 43–65. American Association for the Advancement of Science, Washington, D.C.

Hill, Mary C.
1981   Analysis, Synthesis, and Interpretation of the Skeletal Material Excavated for the Gainesville Section of the Tennessee-Tombigbee Waterway. In *Archaeological Investigations in the Gainesville Lake Area of the Tennessee-Tombigbee Waterway,* vol. 4. Office of Archaeological Research, Report of Investigations 14. The University of Alabama.

Howard, James H.
1968   *The Southeastern Ceremonial Complex and Its Interpretation.* Memoir of the Missouri Archaeological Society 6. Columbia.

Hudson, Charles
1976   *The Southeastern Indians.* University of Tennessee Press, Knoxville.

Hudson, Charles, Marvin Smith, David Hally, Richard Polhemus, and Chester DePratter
1985   Coosa: A Chiefdom in the Sixteenth-Century Southeastern United States. *American Antiquity* 50:723–737.

Huss-Ashmore, Rebecca, Alan H. Goodman, and George J. Armelagos
1982   Nutritional Inference from Paleopathology. In *Advances in Archaeological Method and Theory,* vol. 5, ed. Michael B. Schiffer, pp. 241–295. Academic Press, New York.

Jenkins, Ned J.
1975   *Archaeological Investigations in the Gainesville Lock and Dam Reservoir: 1974.* Department of Anthropology, University of Alabama. Submitted to the National Park Service. National Technical Information Services, Springfield, Va.
1981   Gainesville Lake Area Ceramic Description and Chronology. In *Archaeological Investigations in the Gainesville Lake Area of the Tennessee-Tombigbee Waterway,* vol. 2. Office of Archaeological Research, Report of Investigations 12. The University of Alabama.
1982   Archaeology of the Gainesville Lake Area: Synthesis. In *Archaeological Investigations in the Gainesville Lake Area of the Tennessee-Tombigbee Waterway,* vol. 5. Office of Archaeological Research, Report of Investigations 12. The University of Alabama.

Jenkins, Ned J., Cailup B. Curren, Jr., and Mark F. DeLeon
1975   *Archaeological Site Survey of the Demopolis and Gainesville Lake Navigation*

Channels and Additional Construction Areas. University of Alabama. Submitted to the National Park Service, National Technical Information Services, Springfield, Va.

Jenkins, Ned J., and H. Blaine Ensor
1981   The Gainesville Lake Area Excavations. In *Archaeological Investigations in the Gainesville Lake Area of the Tennessee-Tombigbee Waterway,* vol. 1. Office of Archaeological Research, Report of Investigations 11. The University of Alabama.

Jenkins, Ned J., and Richard A. Krause
1986   *The Tombigbee Watershed in Southeastern Prehistory.* The University of Alabama Press, University.

Jennings, Jesse D.
1941   Chickasaw and Earlier Indian Cultures of Northeast Mississippi. *The Journal of Mississippi History* 3(3):155–226.

Johnson, Gregory A.
1982   Organizational Structure and Scalar Stress. In *Theory and Explanation in Archaeology,* ed. Colin Renfrew, Michael J. Rowlands, and Barbara A. Seagraves, pp. 389–421. Academic Press, New York.
1984   Dynamics of Southwestern Prehistory: Far Outside—Looking In. In *Dynamics of Southwestern Prehistory,* ed. Linda Cordell and George Gummerman. Smithsonian Institution Press, Washington, D.C.

Johnson, Jay K., and John T. Sparks
1986   Protohistoric Settlement Patterns in Northeastern Mississippi. In *The Protohistoric Period in the Mid-South: 1500–1700,* ed. David H. Dye and Ronald C. Brister, pp. 64–82. Mississippi Department of Archives and History, Archaeological Report 18. Jackson.

Jones, George T., Donald K. Grayson, and Charlotte Beck
1983   Sample Size and Functional Diversity in Archaeological Assemblages. In *Lulu Linear Punctated: Essays in Honor of George Irving Quimby,* ed. R. C. Dunnell and D. K. Grayson, pp. 55–73. University of Michigan Museum of Anthropology, Anthropological Papers 72.

Josselin de Jong, J.P.B. de
1928   The Natchez Social System. In *Proceedings of the Twenty-third International Congress of Americanists,* pp. 553–562. New York.

Kelly, John E., Steven J. Azuk, Douglas K. Jackson, Dale L. McElrath, Fred A. Finney, and Duane Esarey
1984   Emergent Mississippian Period. In *American Bottom Archaeology,* ed. C. Bareis and J. Porter, pp. 128–157. University of Illinois Press, Urbana.

Kirchhoff, Paul
1959   The Principles of Clanship in Human Society. In *Readings in Anthro-*

pology, vol. 2, ed. Morton H. Fried, pp. 260–270. Thomas Y. Crowell, New York.

Knight, Vernon James, Jr.
1986   The Institutional Organization of Mississippian Religion. *American Antiquity* 51(4):675–687.
1989   Certain Aboriginal Mounds at Moundville: 1937 Excavations in Mounds H, I, J, K, and L. Paper presented at the 1989 Southeastern Archaeological Conference, Tampa, Fla.
1990   Social Organization and the Evolution of Hierarchy in Southeastern Chiefdoms. *Journal of Anthropological Research* 46(1):1–23.

Kohler, Timothy A.
1980   The Social Dimension of Village Occupation at the McKeithen Site, North Florida. *Southeastern Archaeological Conference Bulletin* 22:5–11.

Krause, Richard A.
1987   *The Snodgrass Small Mound and Middle Tennessee Valley Prehistory.* Tennessee Valley Authority Publications in Anthropology 52. Chattanooga.

Lafferty, Robert H.
1973   *An Analysis of Prehistoric Southeastern Fortifications.* Unpublished M.A. thesis, Department of Anthropology, Southern Illinois University, Carbondale.

Lankford, George E.
1981   *A Documentary Study of Native American Life in the Lower Tombigbee Valley.* Submitted to U.S. Army Corps of Engineers, Mobile District.

Larson, Lewis H., Jr.
1959   A Mississippian Headdress from Etowah, Georgia. *American Antiquity* 25(1):109–112.
1971   Archaeological Implications of Social Stratification at the Etowah Site, Georgia. In *Approaches to the Social Dimensions of Mortuary Practices*, ed. J. A. Brown. Society for American Archaeology Memoirs 25, pp. 58–67.

Lewis, Thomas M. N., and Madeline Kneberg
1946   *Hiwassee Island.* University of Tennessee Press, Knoxville.

Lineback, Neal G. (editor)
1973   *Atlas of Alabama.* The University of Alabama Press, University.

Lorenz, Karl G.
1988   A Comparative Ethnohistorical Reanalysis of Natchez Sociopolitical Organization. Paper presented at the American Society for Ethnohistory, Williamsburg, Va.

Mainfort, Robert C., Jr.
1986   *Pinson Mounds: A Middle Woodland Ceremonial Center.* Tennessee Department of Conservation, Division of Archaeology, Research Series 7. Nashville.

Malinowski, Bronislaw
1935   *Coral Gardens and Their Magic.* Allen and Unwin, London.

Mann, Cyril B., Jr.
1983   Classification of Ceramics from the Lubbub Creek Archaeological Lo-
        cality. In *Prehistoric Agricultural Communities in West-Central Alabama:
        Studies of Material Remains from the Lubbub Creek Archaeological Locality,*
        vol. 2, ed. Christopher S. Peebles, pp. 2–137. University of Michigan.
        Submitted to the U.S. Army Corps of Engineers, Mobile District. Na-
        tional Technical Information Services, Springfield, Va.

Marshall, Richard A.
1977   Lyon's Bluff Site (22OK1) Radiocarbon Dated. *Journal of Alabama Ar-
        chaeology* 23(1):53–57.

Meggitt, Mervin J.
1973   The Pattern of Leadership Among the Mae-Enga of New Guinea. In
        Politics in New Guinea, ed. R. M. Berndt and P. Lawrence, pp. 191–206.
        University of Washington Press, Seattle.

Mensforth, Robert P., C. Owen Lovejoy, John W. Lallo, and George J. Armelagos
1978   The Role of Constitutional Factors, Diet, and Infectious Disease in the
        Etiology of Porotic Hyperstosis and Periosteal Reactions in Prehistoric
        Infants and Children. *Medical Anthropology* 2(1):1–57.

Michaels, George H.
1987   *A Description and Analysis of Early Postclassic Lithic Technology at Colha,
        Belize.* Master's thesis, Department of Anthropology, Texas A&M Uni-
        versity, College Station.

Milanich, Jerald T., and Charles H. Fairbanks
1980   *Florida Archaeology.* Academic Press, New York.

Mills, Barbara J.
1989   Integrating Functional Analyses of Vessels and Sherds through Mod-
        els of Ceramic Assemblage Formation. *World Archaeology* 21(1):
        133–147.

Milner, George R.
1984   *The Julien Site (11–S–63): An Early Bluff and Mississippian Multicompo-
        nent Site.* FAI-270 Report 37, Department of Anthropology, University
        of Illinois, Urbana-Champaign.
1990   The Late Prehistoric Cahokia Cultural System of the Mississippi River
        Valley: Foundations, Flourescence, and Fragmentation. *Journal of
        World Prehistory* 4(1):1–43.

Mistovich, Tim S.
1987   *The Mill Creek Site, 1Tu265, Black Warrior River, Alabama.* Report of
        Investigations 54, Office of Archaeological Research. The University of
        Alabama.
1988   Early Mississippian in the Black Warrior Valley: The Pace of Transition.
        Southeastern Archaeology 7(1):21–38.

Moore, Clarence B.
1901   Certain Aboriginal Remains of the Tombigbee River. *Journal of the Academy of Natural Sciences of Philadelphia* 11:504–505.

Muller, Jon
1983   The Southeast. In *Ancient Native Americans*, ed. Jesse D. Jennings, pp. 280–325. Freeman, San Francisco.
1986   *Archaeology of the Lower Ohio River Valley.* Academic Press, Orlando, Fla.

Nassaney, Michael S.
1987   On the Causes and Consequences of Subsistence Intensification in the Mississippi Alluvial Valley. In *Emergent Horticultural Economies of the Eastern Woodlands*, ed. William F. Keegan, pp. 129–151. Center for Archaeological Investigations, Occasional Paper 7. Southern Illinois University at Carbondale.

Nelson, Ben A.
1981   Ethnoarchaeology and Paleodemography: A Test of Turner and Lofgren's Hypothesis. *Journal of Anthropological Research* 37:107–129.
1985   Ceramic Frequency and Use Life: A Highland Mayan Case in Cross-Cultural Perspective. Paper presented to the advanced seminar "Social and Behavioral Sources of Ceramic Variability on Ethnohistorical Perspective." School of American Research, Santa Fe, N.M.

O'Hear, John W., Clark Larsen, Margaret M. Scarry, John Phillips, and Erica Simons
1981   *Archaeological Salvage Excavations at the Tibbee Creek Site (22Lo600), Lowndes County, Mississippi.* Department of Anthropology, Mississippi State University. Submitted to the U.S. Army Corps of Engineers, Mobile District.

Otto, John Solomon
1977   Artifacts and Status Differences: A Comparison of Ceramics from Planter, Overseer and Slave Sites on an Antebellum Plantation. In *Research Strategies in Historical Archaeology*, ed. Stanley South, pp. 91–118. Academic Press, New York.

Peebles, Christopher S.
1971   Moundville and Surrounding Sites: Some Structural Considerations of Mortuary Practices. In *Approaches to the Social Dimensions of Mortuary Practices*, ed. J. A. Brown. Society for American Archaeology Memoirs 25, pp. 68–91.
1978   Determinants of Settlement Size and Location in the Moundville Phase. In *Mississippian Settlement Patterns*, ed. B. Smith, pp. 369–416. Academic Press, New York.
1983a   Summary and Conclusions: Continuity and Change in a Small Mississippian Community. In *Prehistoric Agricultural Communities in West-Central Alabama: Excavations in the Lubbub Creek Archaeological Locality,*

vol. 1, ed. Christopher S. Peebles, pp. 394–407. University of Michigan. Submitted to the U.S. Army Corps of Engineers, Mobile District. National Technical Information Services, Springfield, Va.

1983b   Moundville: Late Prehistoric Sociopolitical Organization in the Southeastern United States. In *The Development of Political Organization in Native North America*, ed. Elizabeth Tooker, pp. 183–198. The American Ethnological Society, Washington, D.C.

1986   Paradise Lost, Strayed and Stolen: Prehistoric Social Devolution in the Southeast. In *The Burden of Being Civilized: An Anthropological Perspective on the Discontents of Civilization*, ed. Miles Richardson and Malcolm Webb, pp. 24–40. Southern Anthropological Society Proceedings 18. University of Georgia Press, Athens.

1987   The Rise and Fall of the Mississippian in Western Alabama: The Moundville and Summerville Phases, A.D. 1000 to 1600. *Mississippi Archaeology* 22(1):1–31.

Peebles, Christopher S. (editor)
1983c   *Prehistoric Agricultural Communities in West-Central Alabama.* 3 vols. University of Michigan. Submitted to the U.S. Army Corps of Engineers, Mobile District. National Technical Information Services, Springfield, Va.

Peebles, Christopher S., and Susan Kus
1977   Some Archaeological Correlates of Ranked Societies. *American Antiquity* 42:421–448.

Peebles, Christopher S., and Cyril B. Mann, Jr.
1983   Culture and Chronology in the Lubbub Creek Archaeological Locality. In *Prehistoric Agricultural Communities in West-Central Alabama: Excavations in the Lubbub Creek Archaeological Locality*, vol. 1, ed. Christopher S. Peebles, pp. 64–78. University of Michigan. Submitted to the U.S. Army Corps of Engineers, Mobile District. National Technical Information Services, Springfield, Va.

Penman, John T.
1983   Appendix 3: Faunal Remains. In *The Grand Village of the Natchez Revisited*, Robert S. Neitzel, pp. 146–165. Mississippi Department of Archives and History Archaeological Report 12. Jackson.

Polhemus, Richard R.
1987   *The Toqua Site-40MR6: A Late Mississippian, Dallas Phase Town.* Publications in Anthropology 44, Tennessee Valley Authority.

Powell, Mary Lucas
1983   Biocultural Analysis of Human Skeletal Remains from the Lubbub Creek Archaeological Locality. In *Prehistoric Agricultural Communities in West-Central Alabama: Studies of Material Remains from the Lubbub Creek Archaeological Locality*, vol. 2, ed. Christopher S. Peebles, pp. 430–477. University of Michigan. Submitted to the U.S. Army Corps of Engi-

neers, Mobile District. National Technical Information Services, Springfield, Va.

1988   *Status and Health in Prehistory: A Case Study of the Moundville Chiefdom.* Smithsonian Institution Press, Washington and London.

Prentice, Guy
1986   An Analysis of the Symbolism Expressed by the Birger Figurine. *American Antiquity* 51(2):239–266.
1987   Marine Shells as Wealth Items in Mississippian Societies. *Midcontinental Journal of Archaeology* 12:193–223.

Rafferty, Janet
1986   A Critique of the Type-Variety System as Used in Ceramic Analysis. *Mississippi Archaeology* 21(2):40–50.

Rafferty, Janet, and Mary Evelyn Starr
1986   *Test Excavations at Two Woodland Sites, Lowndes County, Mississippi.* Cobb Institute of Archaeology , Report of Investigations 3. Mississippi State University, Mississippi State.

Rappaport, Roy A.
1971   Ritual, Sanctity, and Cybernetics. *American Anthropologist* 73:59–76.

Rice, Prudence M.
1987   *Pottery Analysis: A Source Book.* University of Chicago Press, Chicago.

Rose, Jerome C., Murray K. Marks, and Larry L. Tieszen
1991   Bioarchaeology and Subsistence in the Central and Lower Mississippi Valley. In *What Mean These Bones? Studies in Southeastern Bioarchaeology,* ed. M. L. Powell, P. S. Bridges, and A.M.W. Mires, pp. 7–21. The University of Alabama Press, Tuscaloosa and London.

Rucker, Mark D.
1974   *Archaeological Survey and Test Excavations in the Upper Central Tombigbee River Valley: Aliceville-Columbus Lock and Dam Impoundment Areas, Alabama and Mississippi.* Mississippi State University. Submitted to the National Park Service. Report on file, Department of Anthropology, Mississippi State University.

Rudolph, James L.
1984   Earth Lodges, and Platform Mounds: Changing Public Architecture in the Southeastern United States. *Southeastern Archaeology* 3(1):33–45.

Sahlins, Marshall D.
1958   *Social Stratification in Polynesia.* University of Washington Press, Seattle.
1972   *Stone Age Economics.* Aldine, Chicago.

Scarry, C. Margaret
1986   *Change in Plant Procurement and Production during the Emergence of the Moundville Chiefdom.* Ph.D. dissertation, University of Michigan. University Microfilms, Ann Arbor, Mich.

1988   Variability in Mississippian Crop Production Strategies. Paper presented at the Forty-fifth Annual Meeting of the Southeastern Archaeological Conference, New Orleans.

Scarry, Margaret M.
1981   Floral Remains. In *Archaeological Salvage Excavations at the Tibbee Creek Site (22LO600) Lowndes County, Mississippi*, John W. O'Hear, Clark Larsen, Margaret M. Scarry, John Phillips, and Erica Simons, pp. 207–217. Department of Anthropology, Mississippi State University. Submitted to the U.S. Army Corps of Engineers, Mobile District.

Schiffer, Michael B.
1975   The Effects of Occupation Span on Site Content. In *The Cache River Project*, ed. M. B. Schiffer and J. House, pp. 265–269. Arkansas Archaeological Survey, Fayetteville.
1976   *Behavioral Archaeology.* Academic Press, New York.

Schnell, Frank T., Vernon J. Knight, Jr., and Gail S. Schnell
1981   *Cemochechobee: Archaeology of a Mississippian Ceremonial Center on the Chattahoochee River.* University Presses of Florida, Gainesville.

Scott, Susan
1982   Yarborough Site Faunal Remains. In *Archaeological Investigations at the Yarborough Site (22Cl814), Clay County, Mississippi,* Carlos Solis and Richard Walling, pp. 140–152. Office of Archaeological Research, Report of Investigations 30. The University of Alabama.
1983   Analysis, Synthesis and Interpretation of Faunal Remains from the Lubbub Creek Archaeological Locality. In *Prehistoric Agricultural Communities in West-Central Alabama: Studies of Material Remains from the Lubbub Creek Archaeological Locality,* vol. 2, ed. Christopher S. Peebles, pp. 272–379. University of Michigan. Submitted to the U.S. Army Corps of Engineers, Mobile District. National Technical Information Services, Springfield, Va.

Sears, William H.
1973   The Sacred and the Secular in Prehistoric Ceramics. In *Variation in Anthropology: Essays in Honor of J. C. McGregor,* ed. Donald W. Lathrap, pp. 31–42. Illinois Archaeological Survey Publications, Urbana, Ill.

Seeman, Mark F.
1979   Feasting with the Dead: Ohio Hopewell Charnel House Ritual as a Context for Redistribution. In *Hopewell Archaeology: The Chillicothe Conference,* ed. David S. Brose and N'omi Greber, pp. 39–46. The Kent State University Press, Kent, Oh.

Service, Elman R.
1971   *Primitive Social Organization: An Evolutionary Perspective.* 2d ed. Random House, New York.
1975   *Origins of the State and Civilization.* Norton, Chicago.

Shapiro, Gary
1984   Ceramic Vessels, Site Permanence, and Group Size: A Mississippian
          Example. *American Antiquity* 49(4):696–712.

Sheldon, Craig T., Jr.
1974   *The Mississippian-Historic Transition in Central Alabama.* Unpublished
          Ph.D. dissertation, Department of Anthropology, University of
          Oregon, Eugene.

Sheldon, Craig T., Jr., David W. Case, Teresa L. Paglione, Gregory A. Waselkov,
and Elisabeth S. Sheldon
1982   *Cultural Resources Survey of Demopolis Lake, Alabama, Fee Owned Lands.*
          Auburn University, Archaeological Monograph 6. Auburn, Ala.

Sheldon, Craig T., and Ned J. Jenkins
1986   Protohistoric Development in Central Alabama. In *Protohistoric Period
          in the Mid-South: 1500–1700,* ed. David H. Dye and Ronald C. Brister,
          pp. 95–102. Mississippi Department of Archives and History, Archae-
          ological Report 18. Jackson.

Shott, Michael J.
1989   On Tool-Class Use Lives and the Formation of Archaeological As-
          semblages. *American Antiquity* 54:9–30.

Smith, Bruce D.
1978   Variation in Mississippian Settlement Pattern. In *Mississippian Settle-
          ment Patterns,* ed. Bruce D. Smith, pp. 479–503. Academic Press, New
          York.
1986   The Archaeology of the Southeastern United States, from Dalton to
          DeSoto (10,500 B.P.–500 B.P.). In *Advances in World Archaeology,* vol. 5,
          ed. Fred Wendorf and Angela E. Close, pp. 1–92. Academic Press,
          Orlando.
1989   Origins of Agriculture in Eastern North America. *Science* 246:1566–
          1571.

Smith, Marvin T.
1987   *Archaeology of Aboriginal Culture Change in the Interior Southeast: De-
          population during the Early Historic Period.* Ripley P. Bullen Monographs
          in Anthropology and History 6. University of Florida Press and The
          Florida State Museum, Gainesville.

Smith, Michael E.
1987   Household Possessions and Wealth in Agrarian States: Implications
          for Archaeology. *Journal of Anthropological Archaeology* 6(4):297–335.

Snow, Frankie
1990   Pine Barrens Lamar. In *Lamar Archaeology: Mississippian Chiefdoms in the
          Deep South,* ed. Mark Williams and Gary Shapiro, pp. 82–93. The
          University of Alabama Press, Tuscaloosa and London.

Solis, Carlos, and Richard Walling
1982   *Archaeological Investigations at the Yarborough Site (22Cl814), Clay County,*

Mississippi. Office of Archaeological Research, Report of Investigations 30. The University of Alabama.

Spencer, Charles S.
1982   *The Cuicatlan Canada and Monte Alban: A Study in Primary State Formation*. Academic Press, New York.

Steponaitis, Vincas P.
1978   Locational Theory and Complex Chiefdoms: A Mississippian Example. In *Mississippian Settlement Patterns*, ed. Bruce D. Smith, pp. 417–453. Academic Press, New York.
1983   *Ceramics, Chronology, and Community Patterns: An Archaeological Study at Moundville*. Academic Press, New York.
1986   Prehistoric Archaeology in the Southeastern United States, 1970–1985. *Annual Reviews of Anthropology* 15:363–404.
1989   Contrasting Patterns of Mississippian Development. Paper presented at the seminar "Chiefdoms: Their Evolutionary Significance," School of American Research, Santa Fe, N.M.

Stowe, Neal R.
1974   A Preliminary Report on Four Dugout Canoes from the Gulf Coast. *Journal of Alabama Archaeology* 20(2):194–203.

Swanton, John R.
1911   *Indian Tribes of the Lower Mississippi Valley and Adjacent Coast of the Gulf of Mexico*. Smithsonian Institution, Bureau of American Ethnology, Bulletin 43. U.S. Government Printing Office, Washington, D.C.
1928   Social Organization and Social Usages of the Indians of the Creek Confederacy. In *Forty-fourth Annual Report of the Bureau of American Ethnology for the Years 1924–1925*, pp. 25–472. Washington, D.C.
1931   *Source Material for the Social and Ceremonial Life of the Choctaw Indians*. Smithsonian Institution, Bureau of American Ethnology, Bulletin 103. U.S. Government Printing Office, Washington, D.C.
1979   *The Indians of the Southeastern United States*. Reprinted. Smithsonian Institution Press, Washington, D.C. Originally published 1946, Bureau of American Ethnology Bulletin 137, Smithsonian Institution, U.S. Government Printing Office, Washington, D.C.

Titiev, Mischa
1960   A Fresh Approach to the Problem of Magic and Religion. *Southwestern Journal of Anthropology* 16:292–298.

Trigger, Bruce G.
1982   Archaeological Analysis and Concepts of Causality. *Culture* 2(2):31–42.

Turner, Christy G., and Laurel Lofgren
1966   Household Size of Prehistoric Western Pueblo Indians. *Southwestern Journal of Anthropology* 22:117–132.

Upham, Steadman
1982   *Polities and Power: An Economic and Political History of the Western Pueblo*. Academic Press, New York.

Upham, Steadman, Kent G. Lightfoot, and Gary Feinman
1981   Explaining Socially Determined Ceramic Distributions in the Pre-
         historic Plateau Southwest. *American Antiquity* 46:822–833.

Van der Leeuw, Sander E.
1981   Preliminary Report on the Analysis of Moundville Phase Ceramic
         Technology. *Southeastern Archaeological Conference Bulletin* 24:105–108.

Walthall, John A.
1980   *Prehistoric Indians of the Southeast: Archaeology of Alabama and the Middle
         South.* The University of Alabama Press, University.

Ward, Trawick
1965   Correlation of Mississippian Soil Types. *Southeastern Archaeological
         Conference Bulletin* 3:42–48.

Waring, Antonio
1968   The Southern Cult and Muskhogean Ceremonial. In *The Waring Pa-
         pers,* ed. Stephen Williams, pp. 30–69. Papers of the Peabody Museum
         of Archaeology and Ethnology, Harvard University, vol. 58. Cam-
         bridge, Mass.

Webb, William S., and David L. DeJarnette
1942   *An Archaeological Survey of Pickwick Basin in the Adjacent Portions of the
         States of Alabama, Mississippi, and Tennessee.* Bureau of American Eth-
         nology, Bulletin 129. U.S. Government Printing Office, Washington,
         D.C.

Welch, Paul D.
1990   Mississippian Emergence in West-Central Alabama. In *The Mississip-
         pian Emergence,* ed. Bruce D. Smith, pp. 197–225. Smithsonian Institu-
         tion Press, Washington and London.
1991   *Moundville's Economy.* The University of Alabama Press, Tuscaloosa
         and London.

Wenke, Robert J.
1981   Explaining the Evolution of Cultural Complexity: A Review. In *Ad-
         vances in Archaeological Method and Theory,* vol. 6, ed. Michael B.
         Schiffer, pp. 79–127. Academic Press, New York.

Wheatley, Paul
1971   *The Pivot of the Four Quarters.* Aldine, Chicago.

Whitehouse, Ruth, and John Wilkins
1986   *The Making of Civilization: History Discovered Through Archaeology.* Alfred
         A. Knopf, New York.

Williams, Stephen, and Jeffrey P. Brain
1983   *Excavations at Lake George, Yazoo County, Mississippi, 1958–1960.* Papers
         of the Peabody Museum of Archaeology and Ethnology 74. Cam-
         bridge, Mass.

Wobst, H. Martin
1974   Boundary Conditions for Paleolithic Social Systems: A Simulation Approach. *American Antiquity* 39:147–178.
1977   Stylistic Behavior and Information Exchange. In *For the Director: Research Essays in Honor of James B. Griffin,* ed. Charles E. Cleland, pp. 317–342. Museum of Anthropology, University of Michigan Anthropological Papers 61. Ann Arbor.

Woodrick, Anne
1981   An Analysis of the Faunal Remains from the Gainesville Lake Area. In *Archaeological Investigations in the Gainesville Lake Area of the Tennessee-Tombigbee Waterway,* vol. 4. Office of Archaeological Research, Report of Investigations 14. The University of Alabama.
1983a   Appendix D: Bone Artifacts. In *Prehistoric Agricultural Communities in West-Central Alabama: Studies of Material Remains from the Lubbub Creek Archaeological Locality,* vol. 2, ed. Christopher S. Peebles, pp. 380–390. University of Michigan. Submitted to the U.S. Army Corps of Engineers, Mobile District. National Technical Information Services, Springfield, Va.
1983b   Molluscan Remains and Shell Artifacts. In *Prehistoric Agricultural Communities in West-Central Alabama: Studies of Material Remains from the Lubbub Creek Archaeological Locality,* vol. 2, ed. Christopher S. Peebles, pp. 391–429. University of Michigan. Submitted to the U.S. Army Corps of Engineers, Mobile District. National Technical Information Services, Springfield, Va.

Wolf, Eric R.
1982   *Europe and the People without History.* University of California Press, Berkeley and Los Angeles.

Wright, Henry T.
1977   Recent Research on the Origin of the State. *Annual Review of Anthropology* 6:367–397.
1984   Prestate Political Formations. In *On the Evolution of Complex Societies,* ed. Timothy Earle, pp. 41–77. Undena Publications, Malibu, Calif.

Wynn, Jack T.
1990   *Mississippi Period Archaeology of the Georgia Blue Ridge Mountains.* Georgia Archaeological Research Design Paper 5. Laboratory of Archaeology, University of Georgia, Athens.

Yerkes, Richard W.
1987   *Prehistoric Life on the Mississippi Floodplain.* The University of Chicago Press, Chicago and London.
1989   Mississippian Craft Specialization on the American Bottom. *Southeastern Archaeology* 8:93–106.

Index

ABOUT THE AUTHOR

John H. Blitz is Visiting Assistant Professor at Bowdoin College, Maine. He received his first field training in archaeology as an undergraduate at The University of Alabama and later participated in archaeological field-work in Mexico and Ecuador. He earned his doctorate degree from the City University of New York.